D0076420

To Secure These Rights

The Report of Harry S Truman's Committee on Civil Rights

Edited with an Introduction by

Steven F. Lawson

Rutgers University

BEDFORD/ST. MARTIN'S   Boston   ◆   New York

For Bedford/St. Martin's

Publisher for History: Patricia A. Rossi
Director of Development for History: Jane Knetzger
Developmental Editor: Sara Wise
Editorial Assistant: Carina Schoenberger
Assistant Editor, Publishing Services: Maria Burwell
Production Supervisor: Nancy Myers
Marketing Manager: Jenna Bookin Barry
Project Management: Books By Design, Inc.
Text Design: Claire Seng-Niemoeller
Indexer: Books By Design, Inc.
Cover Design: Billy Boardman
*Cover Photo: Members of the National Association of Colored Women Picket the White House
    in Protest of a Quadruple Lynching in Georgia.* © Bettmann/CORBIS
Composition: Stratford Publishing Services, Inc.
Printing and Binding: Haddon Craftsmen, an RR Donnelley & Sons Company

President: Joan E. Feinberg
Editorial Director: Denise B. Wydra
Director of Marketing: Karen R. Melton
Director of Editing, Design, and Production: Marcia Cohen
Manager, Publishing Services: Emily Berleth

Library of Congress Control Number: 2003100449

Copyright © 2004 by Bedford/St. Martin's

Manufactured in the United States of America.

9 8 7 6 5 4
f e d c b a

For information, write: Bedford/St. Martin's, 75 Arlington Street, Boston, MA 02116
(617-399-4000)

ISBN: 0-312-40214-7

Foreword

The Bedford Series in History and Culture is designed so that readers can study the past as historians do.

The historian's first task is finding the evidence. Documents, letters, memoirs, interviews, pictures, movies, novels, or poems can provide facts and clues. Then the historian questions and compares the sources. There is more to do than in a courtroom, for hearsay evidence is welcome, and the historian is usually looking for answers beyond act and motive. Different views of an event may be as important as a single verdict. How a story is told may yield as much information as what it says.

Along the way the historian seeks help from other historians and perhaps from specialists in other disciplines. Finally, it is time to write, to decide on an interpretation and how to arrange the evidence for readers.

Each book in this series contains an important historical document or group of documents, each document a witness from the past and open to interpretation in different ways. The documents are combined with some element of historical narrative — an introduction or a biographical essay, for example — that provides students with an analysis of the primary source material and important background information about the world in which it was produced.

Each book in the series focuses on a specific topic within a specific historical period. Each provides a basis for lively thought and discussion about several aspects of the topic and the historian's role. Each is short enough (and inexpensive enough) to be a reasonable one-week assignment in a college course. Whether as classroom or personal reading, each book in the series provides firsthand experience of the challenge — and fun — of discovering, recreating, and interpreting the past.

Natalie Zemon Davis
Ernest R. May
Lynn Hunt
David W. Blight

iii

Preface

To Secure These Rights, the report written by President Harry S Truman's Committee on Civil Rights, is one of the most important documents in the history of the modern civil rights movement. When the committee released its report in October 1947 after nearly a year of work, it issued a clarion call to wipe out racial injustice and made recommendations about how to close the gap between America's democratic promises of equality and the reality of discrimination. It also provided a comprehensive blueprint for achieving first-class citizenship and legal equality for all, thus setting the federal government's agenda on civil rights.

In resurrecting the largely forgotten document, this volume makes it clear that the civil rights movement did not begin in the mid-1950s as is popularly believed, but at least a decade earlier when African American activists pressured the federal government—through electoral politics and protest—to join the struggle against Jim Crow. In 1946, following the war against Hitler and his doctrines of racial supremacy, domestic turmoil in the form of widespread discrimination, violent racial attacks, and lynchings galvanized the Truman administration to combat white supremacy at home. To reduce racial conflict, Truman established the President's Committee on Civil Rights to assess the racial situation nationwide and to propose solutions to a broad range of civil rights problems.

To Secure These Rights was hailed by civil rights advocates and white liberals as a pathbreaking document and denounced by white southern segregationists as an assault against their way of life. Both views were correct, because in calling for "the elimination of segregation based on race, color, creed, or national origin, from American life," Truman's committee passed on a legacy for the next generation of civil rights activists to build upon in overthrowing Jim Crow. Civil rights groups embraced the basic tenets of the report, and groups such as the National Association for the Advancement of Colored

People (NAACP) forged a judicial and legislative strategy to put them into law. In later years, more activist groups such as the Southern Christian Leadership Conference (SCLC), Student Nonviolent Coordinating Committee (SNCC), and Congress of Racial Equality (CORE) adopted different tactics from those of the NAACP, but they all pursued the goals first outlined by the President's Committee. Only with the emergence of the Black Power movement in the late 1960s would the racial agenda change significantly. The Black Power movement brought a shift away from the desegregation, integration, and nonviolence recommended by the report toward separatism, self-reliance, and self-defense.

Part one of this book is an introduction that chronicles these early efforts and details the political and social climate of the era to help students better understand the report that follows. It begins by exploring the impact of Franklin D. Roosevelt's New Deal Coalition and World War II on the early civil rights movement and then documents the chilling climate of postwar violence that prompted President Truman to appoint the Committee on Civil Rights. The introduction examines Truman's motivation in establishing the committee and the political constraints he faced in addressing racial issues. It also describes the committee's members and its workings in detail, offering perspective on how it reached its recommendations. The introduction concludes with reactions to the report and Truman's civil rights legacy, further underscoring the close relationship between national and local efforts in shaping the black freedom struggle.

Part two, "The Document," presents the complete text of the committee's report, including much of the original artwork. The graphs and diagrams are instructive both for the data they present and as historical artifacts. Many reveal stereotypical characterizations of minorities that might surprise today's students. Overall, in reading the report students will gain an understanding of the political, economic, diplomatic, and moral considerations that promoted the civil rights movement.

In addition to the introduction and the full report, this volume includes a chronology of events to help students place the document in historical context, a list of questions for classroom discussion, and a selected bibliography for further reading.

In reading *To Secure These Rights* today, students will have a better understanding of how difficult it was to achieve civil rights in the United States. Recommendations that will no doubt look mild and obvious from a contemporary standpoint appeared radical back in

1947. And to a considerable extent they were. To achieve these civil rights goals required a mighty effort, one that demanded protest, the spilling of blood, and perseverance to convince the federal government to put into law the principles articulated in *To Secure These Rights.*

ACKNOWLEDGMENTS

I had the idea of doing this book for a long time, but it was not until I met Patricia Rossi that I saw the possibility that it could get done. I greatly appreciate her efforts as well as those of Joan Feinberg of Bedford/St. Martin's. Sara Wise made my life easier in supervising the project through its final stages of publication. Thanks also to Emily Berleth, Nancy Benjamin, and Alison Fields for producing a book that looks and reads much better than the manuscript. At Rutgers, I was lucky to have Abigail Lewis as a research assistant and relied on her wizardry in tracking down material on the Internet. Conversations with Peter Lau confirmed for me that this book was a good idea. The reviewers that Bedford/St.Martin's obtained to read the manuscript— Darlene Clark Hine of Northwestern University, David Colburn of the University of Florida, Edward Crowther of Adams State College, John D'Emilio of the University of Illinois at Chicago, John Dittmer of DePauw University, Christina Greene of the University of Wisconsin, John Hardin of Western Kentucky University, and Robert Pratt of the University of Georgia—saved me from innumerable errors of fact and stylistic clunkers. Those that remain reflect my poor judgment in not heeding their suggestions. Nancy Hewitt, as always, served as sounding board, reader, cheerleader, and amazing friend. Many thanks to you all.

Steven F. Lawson

Contents

PART ONE

Introduction:
Setting the Agenda of the
Civil Rights Movement

In June 1966, President Lyndon B. Johnson convened a White House Conference on Civil Rights. The meeting came at a crossroads for the civil rights movement. After two years of astonishing legislative triumphs that secured passage of the 1964 Civil Rights Act and the 1965 Voting Rights Act, racial polarization gripped the nation with the outbreak of urban rioting among blacks and a resulting white backlash. Amidst this turmoil, the 2,500 delegates attending the White House conference issued a glossy report, *To Fulfill These Rights,* which was strong on sentiment but weak on pledges of implementation. The title of the report echoed that of *To Secure These Rights,* a landmark book-length study written by a presidential committee appointed by Harry S Truman nearly twenty years before. If the 1966 document marked the approaching end of the freedom coalition, in 1947, *To Secure These Rights* loudly proclaimed the opening salvo of the federal government's campaign for civil rights.

In April 1945, when President Truman entered the White House after the sudden death of Franklin D. Roosevelt, his most immediate concern was to end the war against Germany and Japan. The Nazis surrendered in May, and in early August, Truman inaugurated the nuclear age with the dropping of atomic bombs on Hiroshima and Nagasaki. The devastating conflict that had raged for six years around

1

the globe finally ceased. Not as momentous as atomic weapons in reshuffling the balance of power in foreign affairs, the war nonetheless unleashed forces at home that catapulted African Americans and their struggle for civil rights into the political spotlight.

THE NEW DEAL COALITION FOR CIVIL RIGHTS

A decade before the war, Franklin D. Roosevelt's New Deal provided a measure of economic relief and political recognition for African Americans in fighting the Great Depression. New Deal agencies hired influential blacks including the educator Mary McLeod Bethune, the social scientists Ralph J. Bunche and Robert Weaver, and the historian Rayford Logan. They and their fellow black recruits worked hard to challenge programs administered at the local level by white southern segregationists to the disadvantage of African Americans. In 1936, African American voters in great numbers switched their allegiance from the Republican party of Lincoln to the Democratic party of Roosevelt.[1]

Working alongside the band of blacks who came to Washington were several sympathetic southern whites. Clark Foreman from Atlanta, who headed the National Youth Administration, appointed Bethune to a position in it. He believed racist policies that maintained conservative southern white officials in power not only harmed African Americans but also poor whites, whose racial prejudices had been manipulated to keep them from throwing in their economic lot with poor blacks. Southern white liberals encouraged black and white workers to organize unions and favored abolition of the poll tax requirement for voting in the South, which disfranchised the poor of both races. In addition to the fee necessary for voting, voters had to pay the poll tax well in advance of the election, often before the candidates were announced. Also, states such as Alabama made the tax cumulative: If voters skipped one or more elections, the next time they sought to cast a ballot they had to pay the back taxes.

In 1938, the New Deal inspired white liberals and blacks to form the Southern Conference for Human Welfare (SCHW), which held an integrated meeting in Birmingham, Alabama, in spite of opposition from Police Commissioner Eugene "Bull" Connor. Taking the lead in defying the city's segregation ordinance was the president's wife, Eleanor Roosevelt, who attended the meeting. When the police asked Mrs. Roosevelt to move from the black side of the room, where she was sitting, the First Lady picked up her chair and carefully placed it on the line drawn on the floor to separate whites and blacks. In straddling the racial demarcation line, she dramatically took her stand against Jim Crow.[2]

The SCHW spawned the National Committee to Abolish the Poll Tax, led by Jennings Perry, a Tennessee newspaper editor, and Virginia Durr, a fervent New Dealer from Birmingham, Alabama, and an activist in the women's division of the Democratic party. Deeply committed to economic and political reforms in the South, Durr had been a driving force behind the creation of the SCHW and worked tirelessly to round up presidential and congressional support to wipe out the suffrage tax. During the 1940s, the committee's efforts bore fruit in the introduction and passage of several anti–poll tax bills in the House of Representatives only to see them die in the Senate. Nevertheless, reformers achieved victories at the state level in Georgia and Tennessee, which eliminated the franchise levy.[3]

In the end, the efforts of the Roosevelt administration to advance black equality proved wanting. Primarily concerned with ending the Depression, Roosevelt considered economic recovery a higher priority than civil rights reform and refused to push for legislation to address racial inequality. He endorsed antilynching and anti–poll tax measures but did nothing substantial to engineer their congressional passage. To do so would have angered powerful southern white lawmakers whose support he needed to achieve his larger New Deal programs and his foreign policy objectives to help the Allies fight the fascists in Europe at the end of the 1930s.

THE IMPACT OF WORLD WAR II

Having largely avoided taking a firm stand on civil rights issues for nearly a decade, in 1941 Roosevelt faced a simmering confrontation that moved him off dead center. A. Philip Randolph, the head of the Brotherhood of Sleeping Car Porters, threatened to mobilize 100,000 African Americans to march on Washington to protest racial segregation and discrimination in the armed forces and bias against blacks in the hiring practices of the federal government and defense industries. The historian John Hope Franklin recalled some of the prejudice blacks faced in the military. His college-educated brother, a high school principal, was drafted into the army and encountered a white sergeant who told him in no uncertain terms that he would "dedicate his years . . . to seeing that [Franklin] did nothing more exalting than peel potatoes."⁴

With the United States on the threshold of entering World War II, Roosevelt preferred to avoid unfavorable publicity from a large demonstration of people protesting racial injustice in his own backyard. Urged on by Eleanor Roosevelt, the president met in June with Randolph and other civil rights leaders and subsequently issued an executive order creating a Fair Employment Practice Committee (FEPC) to investigate and publicize job discrimination. Randolph did not get a proclamation to abolish segregation in the military, but then again he had far fewer than 100,000 people to deliver to the nation's capital. Despite the compromise, this incident suggested the rising power of African Americans to exert pressure on the federal government and foreshadowed tactics that would emerge more fully in the late 1950s and 1960s.⁵

Though the march on Washington did not materialize, blacks fought a "Double V" campaign to achieve victory against Fascism abroad and racism at home. In 1942, a group of Chicago pacifists organized the interracial Congress of Racial Equality (CORE) and engaged in nonviolent sit-ins to integrate public accommodations in northern cities that continued to practice discrimination in spite of state laws that prohibited it. In 1943 and 1944, a group of female students at Howard University in Washington, D.C., one of the premier black institutions of higher learning, conducted sit-ins against cafeterias that barred blacks in the nation's capital. Although these pathbreaking demonstrations did not spawn a wave of protests throughout the country, they did indicate the rising anger of African Americans about racial inequality and the expectation that they could do something to overturn it.⁶

In 1943, anger spilled over into violence. More than 240 racial disturbances erupted in forty-eight cities around the country. Most of the problems stemmed from increasingly close contact between blacks and whites in transportation systems, recreational facilities, employment, and housing resulting from wartime migration within and outside the South and the stationing of black servicemen at southern military bases. Forced to compete for the short supply of affordable housing, crowded onto municipal buses, and in search of beaches and amusement parks where they could relax and forget their troubles, blacks and whites clashed while staking out their territory in contested public spaces. In Detroit alone, thirty-four people were killed, seven hundred injured, and $200 million in property destroyed. On the West Coast, where the population of African Americans had swelled by

33 percent during the war, fights broke out in Seattle, Portland, Oakland, and Los Angeles between blacks and whites.[7]

The war instilled in many African Americans an invigorated sense of pride and determination to reclaim their citizenship rights. If they could serve their country and risk dying for it, they deserved to be treated equally. Approximately a million African Americans, including 4,000 women, entered the armed forces, and about half were stationed overseas. The military taught them how to use weapons to fight the enemy and indoctrinated them in the wartime aim of crushing dictators who preached racist doctrines and trampled on democratic principles. African Americans took great pride in the elite group of soldiers that constituted the Tuskegee Airmen. The Airmen's combat record in the air war over Europe was exemplary, and black pilots exhibited skills surpassed by none in fighting the Nazis. If Hitler's *Luftwaffe* did not scare them, neither did racist white military commanders in the United States. At bases in Alabama, South Carolina, Michigan, and Indiana, black pilots staged demonstrations challenging their exclusion from or segregation in dining and recreational facilities at military posts.[8]

The National Association for the Advancement of Colored People (NAACP), founded in 1909, remained the leading organization challenging white supremacy. In 1944, the NAACP persuaded the Supreme Court to declare unconstitutional the white primary in a case from Texas, *Smith v. Allwright*. In the South, where the Democratic party had reigned supreme since the end of Reconstruction and Republicans were identified with the northern victors of the Civil War, winners of Democratic primary contests routinely triumphed at the general election. By preventing blacks from participating in these Democratic primary elections, whites deprived them of the only meaningful opportunity to cast a ballot in the South. Capping a twenty-year legal battle, the NAACP, led by its chief attorney, Thurgood Marshall, convinced the judiciary that the white Democratic primary in Texas denied African Americans the vote in violation of the Fifteenth Amendment. Because the rest of the southern states also employed Democratic white primaries, the decision in *Smith v. Allwright* had widespread impact. In 1944, approximately 5 percent of southern blacks were registered to vote; by 1948, the percentage had more than doubled.[9] Additional legal challenges to racial discrimination in teacher salaries and segregation on interstate transportation systems not only succeeded in the courts but also accrued rich dividends for the NAACP in the astonishing growth of its wartime membership from 50,000 to 450,000.[10]

The war also encouraged white moderates and liberals in the South to attack racial discrimination. In 1944, a group of whites and blacks formed the Southern Regional Council (SRC) in Atlanta. The SRC functioned as an educational forum rather than an action group, but it supported efforts to expand the suffrage to blacks and poor whites.[11] In addition, labor unions affiliated with the Congress of Industrial Organizations (CIO) conducted organizing drives to sign up white and black workers and achieved some success in Memphis, Tennessee, and Winston-Salem, North Carolina. These campaigns emphasized not only extending voting rights through abolition of the poll tax but also economic reforms that would increase the power and opportunity of workers to obtain a decent standard of living. Union halls became a place where blacks and whites could come together to initiate voter registration drives.[12] Though southern white dissenters remained a definite minority and continued to face great obstacles, they had some reason to be encouraged that World War II had set in motion forces that would democratize the South.

Smith v. Allwright and the anti–poll tax campaign fostered voter registration drives that mobilized black women to participate alongside men. Because suffrage drives were often a community affair, women played a leading role as key members of churches, civic clubs, and professional associations. Shortly after the war, perhaps the best-organized effort occurred in Atlanta, Georgia. Though men gained most of the publicity and credit for its success in adding the names of 18,000 blacks to the voter rolls, female teachers and domestic workers joined together to ring door bells and conduct house-to-house canvassing of potential registrants. Narvie J. Harris, a black teacher, used the Parent-Teachers Association (PTA) chapter she had founded to help educate students as well as parents to the importance of the vote in achieving full citizenship. Atlanta's black women, like their counterparts throughout the South, sought to extend the ballot chiefly to improve the conditions of their families and obtain jobs, health care, decent housing, and safer streets.[13]

Together with Franklin D. Roosevelt's New Deal, World War II helped reshape traditional thinking about the role of the federal government in promoting economic security and protection of basic civil rights. The antigovernment bias that had characterized Americans for much of their history diminished as the federal government used its considerable power to fight first the Great Depression and then the Second World War. In the process, groups that had suffered abuses at the hands of government, such as organized labor and African Americans, came to believe that Washington could protect their civil rights and civil liberties.[14]

POSTWAR VIOLENCE

When the war ended in August 1945, the biggest threat to the racial status quo came from black veterans returning home expecting to find a new day for democracy. Similarly, mothers and sisters of black veterans were proud of the achievements of their husbands, fathers, and sons. In Columbia, Tennessee, thirty-seven-year-old Gladys Stephenson, a domestic worker whose eldest son James served in the Navy, exhibited the self-respect that World War II fostered. In late February 1946, she stood up to a clerk in a radio repair shop who refused to fix a radio that she wanted her son James to have after returning from the military. Her unwillingness to follow the code of southern etiquette and defer to a white man set in motion a chain of events that precipitated a race riot in her town.[15]

The white clerk, Billy Fleming, also a veteran, did not take kindly to Gladys Stephenson's complaint that the repair shop had not treated her fairly. Before she and her son could exit the building, Fleming attacked James Stephenson from behind, and the two began to slug it out, crashing through windows and tumbling into the street. Gladys Stephenson then picked up a shard of glass and delivered a glancing blow to Fleming's shoulder. Several bystanders managed to break up the brawl, and the police arrived shortly to arrest the Stephensons, but not Fleming, for attempted murder. Rumors about the incident quickly circulated through Columbia and surrounding Maury County, the site of two lynchings over the previous twenty years. The sheriff, who had a good relationship with local blacks, released the Stephensons into the custody of African American civic leaders for their own protection. They returned to the black section of town called the "Bottom," where armed residents stood guard against white marauders coming to retrieve the mother and son.

On the evening of February 25, amidst a great deal of confusion, city police officers moved into the area, precipitating an exchange of gunfire that wounded four officers. With the situation spiraling out of control, the sheriff called upon the state governor to send in reinforcements. Rather than restoring calm, the Highway Patrol roared into the Bottom and shot up and ransacked black business establishments and social clubs, beating up and wounding several residents. In the early morning hours of February 26, the Patrol, joined by members of the Tennessee State Guard, finally brought a halt to the hostilities. They took 100 blacks into custody, confiscated their weapons, and incarcerated them in the local jail. Two of those held were shot and killed by the police while under questioning, accounting for the two fatalities that occurred during the "Columbia riot." Eventually, twenty-eight black Columbians were indicted on attempted murder charges; ironically, the Stephensons, whose actions (along with Fleming's) had ignited the fracas, never stood trial.[16]

The Columbia incident, among others, demonstrated that although the war had brought African Americans some notable gains, the United States had a long way to go before it truly became the land of liberty and justice for all. Proof of this was unfortunately abundant. On February 13, two weeks before the Columbia clash, a black veteran named Isaac Woodard, still in his military uniform, was riding a Greyhound bus from Camp Gordon, Georgia, to his apartment in New York City's East Bronx. In Batesburg, South Carolina, Woodard got off the bus to clean himself up in the segregated washroom and took more time than the driver thought reasonable. The Greyhound operator called the police to arrest Woodard for disturbing the peace. The officers did not like Woodard's attitude; they beat him severely and poked him in the eyes with a nightstick, leaving the former soldier blind.

Five months later, two other atrocities occurred. In Monroe, Georgia, on July 25, 1946, a black veteran, Roger Malcolm, his wife, and his sister-in-law and her husband, were gunned down and killed by the Ku Klux Klan. Malcolm had just been released from jail for stabbing his white employer, who had tried to flirt with Malcolm's wife. Not only did Malcolm not remain submissive, but he represented to the Klan "bad Negro" veterans who returned from the war and were "getting out of their place." On August 8, still another black ex-G.I., John C. Jones, and his cousin, Albert Harris, were released from jail in Minden, Louisiana, after having been arrested for loitering. That day a group of whites in cahoots with a deputy sheriff attacked the pair and blowtorched Jones to death, though Harris managed to survive the beating and escaped.[17]

PRESSURE FOR REFORM

African Americans refused to remain silent in the wake of this brutality. The NAACP and its allies mobilized to obtain federal action to protect blacks from mob violence. Along with the SCHW and the CIO, the

NAACP came to the legal defense of the black Columbians facing murder charges and succeeded in winning unprecedented acquittals before an all-white jury for twenty-three of twenty-five defendants. Activists did not concentrate on litigation alone. They took their concerns directly to Washington and engaged in a series of public protests. On July 29, 1946, the National Negro Congress, a group sympathetic to the Communist party, led a march of more than 1,000 people in front of the White House, after which a presidential assistant met with its leaders. The following day, a delegation of fifty NAACP women continued the picketing by carrying signs reading "Speak! Speak! Mr. President" and "Where is Democracy?" In response to the Monroe murders, some 400 members of the National Association of Colored Women paraded at the White House and called for an end to lynching. In August, mass meetings were held in New York City and Washington, D.C., attracting 15,000 people each. NAACP executive secretary Walter White summed up the sentiment of the protesters: "A dread epidemic is sweeping the country, and especially the Deep South. . . . This disease rampant in our land is a rabies of the spirit, a mob sickness." To find a cure for this illness, on August 6, the NAACP and some forty civil rights, labor, religious, and veterans' groups created the National Emergency Committee Against Mob Violence (NECAMV).[18]

Black advocates had good reason to believe their complaints would receive a sympathetic hearing from the federal government. First, wretched scenes of Allied soldiers liberating Nazi concentration camps put the spotlight on the wartime victims of racial chauvinism. The 1944 publication of *An American Dilemma,* by the Swedish economist Gunnar Myrdal and a distinguished team of researchers sponsored by the Carnegie Foundation, revealed the horrors of the nation's own malignant racism, which deeply scarred its black citizens. As the wartime alliance between the United States and the Soviet Union dissolved into a bitter cold war rivalry for global supporters, the treatment of African Americans became a matter fraught with international implications. Racist incidents would hamper American diplomats in their battle to win the allegiance of people of color throughout the world, whose power was beginning to emerge through decolonization and national liberation struggles.[19]

Second, blacks were gaining political muscle to back up their ideological arguments against continued inequality. The acquisition of the right to vote proceeded steadily but slowly in parts of the South following the eradication of the white primary. In the North, where blacks could freely exercise the ballot, the electoral power of their communities had increased through wartime migration from the South. Hundreds of thousands of blacks who left their homes in the South congregated in the major cities in the North and West that offered them the possibility of jobs. The black population swelled in states rich in electoral votes—New York, New Jersey, Ohio, Pennsylvania, Michigan, Illinois, and California—which heavily influenced the outcome of presidential contests. For Democrats, maintaining black allegiance to Roosevelt's New Deal Coalition proved particularly critical.

HARRY S TRUMAN

Upon taking office, President Harry S Truman immediately encountered an array of foreign and domestic problems that would have vexed FDR. Truman lacked his predecessor's charisma, but he displayed greater sensitivity toward civil rights than had the more popular and experienced Roosevelt. Indeed, when Truman left the presidency in 1953, he had cemented the loyalty of black voters to the Democratic party and set the agenda for civil rights that guided the nation over the next two decades.

Truman's role as a supporter of civil rights had not come easily. His Missouri ancestors had been slaveholders and supporters of the Confederacy, and his mother denounced Abraham Lincoln throughout her long life. Nevertheless, during the 1920s as Truman began his ascent into politics in his hometown of Independence, Missouri, he did not flinch from denouncing the revived Ku Klux Klan, which played an active role in electing candidates to office. Truman, who as a captain in World War I had led a unit largely made up of Irish Catholics, detested the Klan's religious bigotry and intolerance. He moved up the political ladder by joining forces with the political machine run by the Kansas City boss, Tom Pendergast, who courted black votes and helped Truman get elected to the Senate in 1934. Running for reelection in 1940, Truman articulated his core principles as well as those that would gain wide currency in the approaching war. "I believe," he declared in Sedalia, Missouri, "in the Constitution and the Declaration of Independence. In giving the Negroes the rights which are theirs we are only acting in accord with our own ideals of a true democracy."[20]

Truman contended that the federal government had an obligation to use its power to eliminate obstacles to equal opportunity when state and local authorities refused to do so. By the time he became president in 1945, Truman had gone on record in support of legislation for a permanent Fair Employment Practice Committee, to extend voting rights, and to punish lynchers. Truman was not a reformer by temperament or vocation; rather, as a successful politician, he understood that he had to shape his convictions to meet the realities of the legislative arena. In this way, politics both constrained and constructed his vision. On the one hand, he encountered a Congress in which a conservative coalition of lawmakers had succeeded in blocking extension of the New Deal since the late 1930s. In the virtually one-party Democratic South, Democratic congressional incumbents had established seniority, which placed them in a position to chair important committees and to block reform legislation initiated by the president. On the other hand, Truman faced an electorate in which the strength of African Americans was expanding.

To resolve these political tensions, President Truman "recognized the trends and pressures and adjusted to them, sensing the need to maintain a rough equilibrium between shifting powers."[21] For example, he started out by continuing his commitment to the FEPC and then backed off. On November 21, 1945, the chief executive had a golden opportunity to give some meaningful enforcement power to the agency when the government took over Washington, D.C.'s Capital Transit Company during a crippling strike. However, he refused to authorize the FEPC to interfere with the company's racially discriminatory practices. In response, Charles H. Houston, the former chief legal officer of the NAACP and a member of the FEPC, resigned in outrage.[22]

Truman also vacillated with respect to anti–poll-tax legislation. In early 1946, he endorsed the efforts of Congress to eliminate the poll tax. After the House passed a bill, he refrained from marshaling his forces in the Senate to rescue the measure from the clutches of diehard southern enemies. In fact, Truman undercut reformers by declaring publicly that the states would have to work out the problem for themselves. Privately, he confided to one of the bill's opponents: "There never was a law that could be enforced if the people didn't want it enforced."[23] The president was undoubtedly correct about the dismal prospects of overcoming a filibuster, the Senate's waging of endless debate, which required a two-thirds vote to shut off.[24] Moreover, there were other vital problems of postwar economic reconversion and foreign policy that he had to address. Still, Truman, who believed that "the president can do nothing unless he is backed by public opinion," so far had not taken the opportunity to use his presidential resources to help educate the American people concerning civil rights.[25]

Furthermore, Truman's sense of equality did not impel him to challenge segregation. The president asserted that his "appeal for equal economic and political rights for every American citizen had nothing at all to do with the personal or social relationships of individuals or the right of every person to choose his own associates."[26] In early 1947, Truman crossed a CORE picket line at Washington's National Theatre that had been set up to protest the theater's refusal to admit blacks. He believed that the primary problem with the formula of "separate but equal" was that the states accepted the first part of the equation but not the second.[27] His moral convictions notwithstanding, the president, as the historian Barton Bernstein has commented, "shared the views of many decent men of his generation and thought that equality before the law could be achieved within the framework of 'separate but equal.'"[28]

CREATION OF THE PRESIDENT'S COMMITTEE ON CIVIL RIGHTS

Truman was continually forced to balance his moral and political concerns because civil rights advocates applied concerted pressure on him to act. On September 19, 1946, in the wake of the Columbia riot, the vicious assault on Isaac Woodard, and the murders in Georgia and Louisiana, the coalition of organizations composing the National Emergency Committee Against Mob Violence met with the president at the White House. Led by representatives from the NAACP, the Urban League, the Federal Council of Churches, the American Federation of Labor (AFL), and the CIO, the delegation reminded Truman that "Negro veterans of the late war for human freedom have been done to death or mutilated with a savagery unsurpassed even at Buchenwald."[29] Although the president was already aware of the postwar horrors in the South, he reportedly replied: "My God! I had no idea that it was as terrible as that! We've got to do something!"[30]

The solution that Truman devised combined moral outrage with political calculation. The idea to set up a national committee to reduce racial conflicts had been kicking around the White House since the outbreak of rioting in 1943. Nothing had come of it, but one of its proponents, David Niles, an assistant to Roosevelt and then Truman, revived the proposal during the meeting with the NECAMV. In consultation with Walter White, the NAACP's executive secretary, Truman decided to create a committee through executive order rather than seek legislation that would be derailed by a Senate filibuster.[31] In this way, the president accomplished a number of objectives: He satisfied civil rights advocates whose goals and methods he agreed with; he took political pressure off himself and transferred it to a committee; he avoided direct confrontation with southern Democratic lawmakers; and he established a forum to begin educating the public on the need to extend equality under the law.

Truman responded positively to the NECAMV because it reflected the kind of African American leadership with which he felt comfortable. In particular, the president found groups such as the NAACP and the Urban League responsible in presenting their case for equality. The National Urban League, founded in 1911, was almost as old as the NAACP and more conservative. Instead of protest, the league focused on negotiating with businesspeople and civic leaders to improve opportunities in black employment, housing, and welfare. Eleanor Roosevelt had worked closely with these organizations, and it was natural for Truman to cloak himself in his predecessor's mantle as much as possible to enhance his political legitimacy. In contrast, he had far more difficulty dealing with more militant African American leaders. Four days after he met with the NECAMV, on September 23, the president sat down to confer with Paul Robeson, the gifted athlete, singer, and actor, and a delegation of representatives from the National Negro Congress, the SCHW, and the National Council of Negro Women. Robeson, the National Negro Congress, and the SCHW represented the left wing of the civil rights spectrum, and they had worked closely with Communists. The meeting proved a disaster, as delegates charged that lynching in the South was the moral equivalent of the crimes of Nazi war criminals then being prosecuted at the Nuremberg Trials. Truman somehow interpreted such comments as a "threat," but his pique must have been aroused by something more than the content of the comments. After all, he had heard similar remarks from the NECAMV. Perhaps Truman was upset by the tone of the comments as well as by the people who were delivering them. Clearly, Robeson and his associates did not represent the *responsible* brand of black leadership he found compatible in groups such as the NAACP.[32]

Nevertheless, Truman responded favorably to rising black activism, even though some of it came from elements he disliked. He kept in close touch with Attorney General Tom Clark about the Justice

Department's investigations of postwar lynchings. The department brought a federal indictment against Isaac Woodard's assailant and tried him before an all-white South Carolina jury, which took a brief half hour to find him not guilty. The president and attorney general agreed that a case-by-case effort to prosecute racial violence was not enough and concluded that a national civil rights committee must be established not only to study lynching but also to explore solutions to a broad range of civil rights problems. By mid-October, Clark had drafted language for an executive order to create a civil rights committee.[33] The president waited until early December to deliver the proclamation to work out some of the necessary details for its operations and perhaps to avoid any unnecessary political fallout before the November congressional elections. However, the voters elected a Republican majority to run the Eightieth Congress.

On December 5, Truman issued Executive Order 9808, creating the President's Committee on Civil Rights (PCCR). Couching his language in Roosevelt's wartime rhetoric, he declared: "Today, Freedom from Fear, and the democratic institutions which sustain it, are again under attack." Rather than focusing solely on mob violence, he instructed the committee "to make recommendations with respect to adoption or establishment by legislation or otherwise of more adequate means and procedures for protection of civil rights of the people of the United States."[34]

If in Truman's political calculations the formation of the committee would satisfy his civil rights constituency without unduly angering the South, for the most part he was right. Most major black newspapers welcomed the executive order, and the *Kansas City Call* praised the committee's establishment as "salutary and potentially of great value to the welfare of millions of Americans." The southern press mostly ignored the executive order, and some even praised it for investigating the horrible crime of lynching.[35] For the time being, the committee operated under the political radar.

COMMITTEE MEMBERS

Truman's appointments to the committee reinforced his desire to minimize controversy and maximize credibility. One of the president's aides, Phileo Nash, recalled the administration's thinking in cobbling together what was described as a "Noah's ark," a committee of pairs: "We were so meticulous to get balance that we wound up with two of everything; two women, two southerners, two business [leaders], two labor [leaders] . . . , it was a carefully balanced commission."[36] The list also included two African Americans, and for its era, the agency had a decidedly liberal cast to it. Three of its members had participated in the National Emergency Committee Against Mob Violence, and the names of six of fifteen appointees had appeared on a list submitted by the NAACP's Walter White to the president. True, the group did not include more militant African American activists, such as A. Philip Randolph, W. E. B. Du Bois, Mary Church Terrell, and Charles Hamilton Houston, but neither did it contain a single southern proponent of white supremacy. The two white representatives from Dixie, Dorothy Tilly and Frank Porter Graham, were considered liberal on racial matters.[37]

Given the subject matter before the committee, the black and southern delegates had to be carefully chosen for they had the clearest personal stakes in the outcome. The two black appointees reflected the careful White House selection process. Truman had a clear preference for the leadership displayed by the NAACP and the Urban League, yet the appointees could not be too closely identified with these organizations lest they be perceived as too partisan. Seeking so-called responsible Negroes, the administration tapped two African Americans with ties not only to civil rights groups but also to the corporate and academic worlds.

Sadie T. M. Alexander was born in Philadelphia and had graduated with a Ph.D. in economics and a law degree from the University of Pennsylvania. After working briefly as an actuary for the black-owned North Carolina Mutual Life Insurance Company, she met her husband, Raymond Pace Alexander, a Harvard Law School graduate, and returned to Philadelphia to practice law with him. Sadie Alexander served on Philadelphia's Commission on Human Relations and from 1943 to 1947 she was secretary of the National Bar Association, the professional association of African American lawyers who until the 1940s had been denied admission into the segregated American Bar Association. On the board of the National Urban League and the National Advisory Council of the American Civil Liberties Union (ACLU), the forty-nine-year-old Alexander had worked closely with the National Council of Negro Women, founded by Mary McLeod Bethune.[38]

The second African American on the PCCR, Channing H. Tobias, came from a different background. Born in Augusta, Georgia, Tobias attended Paine College, a black institution in his home state. An ordained minister in the Colored Methodist Episcopal Church, he first traveled outside the South to receive divinity degrees at Drew Seminary in New Jersey and the University of Pennsylvania. After returning to Paine to teach, in 1923 he began working as senior secretary of the Colored Work Department of the YMCA. Although a critic of discrimination, he accepted this segregated position because he believed that blacks had to control their own social and cultural institutions until genuine equality was achieved. At the same time, he used his position within the black community to join in antiracist projects affiliated with the Commission on Interracial Cooperation and the SCHW. In 1943 he became a board member of the NAACP and three years later joined the National Emergency Committee Against Mob Violence delegation that helped persuade Truman to establish the PCCR. By the time the president appointed him to the committee, the sixty-five-year-old Tobias had become the first black director of the philanthropic Phelps-Stokes Fund, which aimed to improve educational opportunities for African Americans. Less outspoken than Alexander, he nonetheless blended "high ideals with pragmatism" and "unyielding determination with 'calm reasonableness.'"[39]

Truman balanced these appointments of African Americans not with southern whites opposed to racial change but with white liberals who advocated racial justice without attacking segregation directly. Frank Porter Graham graduated from the University of North Carolina (UNC) in 1905 and went on to become president of the university. "Dr. Frank," as he was affectionately known by students and faculty alike, staunchly defended academic freedom. Sought after by the federal government during the 1930s and 1940s, he headed the advisory council that established the Social Security Act and as a member of the War Labor Board advocated equal pay for black workers. The sixty-year-old educator walked a fine line as a racial progressive in the South. As the first president of the Southern Conference for Human Welfare, he delivered the keynote address at its inaugural Birmingham meeting and served on the board of the National Urban League. When Pauli Murray attempted to become the first black student to attend UNC in 1939, however, Graham politely turned her down. Rather than attacking Jim Crow directly, he stressed the importance of expanding the right to vote to disfranchised black southerners who could then use their ballots to bring political and economic democracy to the region.[40]

The second white southerner on the committee, Dorothy Tilly, shared Graham's approach to racial issues. Born in 1883 in Hampton,

Georgia, the daughter of a Methodist minister, Tilly graduated from junior college and actively pursued church work. During the 1930s, she directed a summer school program at Paine College to train African American women to become community leaders. In addition to her involvement with the Methodist church's outreach programs to aid African Americans, she belonged to the Commission on Interracial Cooperation and the Association of Southern Women for the Prevention of Lynching. Without challenging segregation, the latter group waged a vigorous campaign against mob violence in the South. In 1944, Tilly became director of the women's division of the Southern Regional Council.[41]

To chair the committee, Truman picked not an African American or a white southerner but a white northerner, Charles E. Wilson, one of two corporate executives on the committee. Born in 1886 into a poor family in New York City, Wilson rose from rags to riches. Dropping out of school and working at an electric company for three dollars a week, he climbed the ladder of success and became president of General Electric, where he earned $175,000 a year. A fiscal conservative who had opposed union organizing at General Electric, Wilson had experience working for the federal government during the 1930s in the National Recovery Administration and during World War II on the War Production Board. Although Wilson favored desegregation of the armed forces and served on the Commission on Universal Military Training, the president selected him less for his views on civil rights than because, as a leading corporate executive, the sixty-year-old Wilson gave the PCCR a stamp of legitimacy that would help create a consensus around its findings.[42]

The other corporate executive on the committee, Charles Luckman, had a similar career trajectory to Wilson's. Born in Kansas City and originally trained as an architect, Luckman switched to sales and moved up in the ranks of Lever Brothers to become its president in 1946 at the age of thirty-five. Unlike Wilson, this "boy wonder" of American business supported labor unions, collective bargaining, and social legislation. Combining business experience with a progressive outlook, Luckman believed that the committee could educate the public on civil rights much as his company marketed soap and toothpaste.[43]

Presumably to balance the two corporate titans, Truman chose a pair of labor union leaders. Like his executive counterparts, James Carey had pursued his dream of economic success but chose instead to apply his talents to organizing workers. Employed at a radio laboratory after graduating from high school in Philadelphia, during the

Great Depression Carey attended night school at Drexel Institute to study electrical engineering and then attended the University of Pennsylvania's Wharton School of Finance. He stayed in radio, but not in the management end; rather, in 1935, Carey became president of the United Electrical, Radio, and Machine Workers of America. He subsequently became active in the CIO and was elected secretary-treasurer of the national union. A staunch anti-Communist, he had lost control of the United Electrical union to left-wing opponents. Carey had previously tangled with General Electric's Wilson over collective bargaining issues, although he praised his former adversary and most likely agreed with him that the electrical workers' union had fallen into the wrong hands. More important for his work on the committee, the thirty-five-year-old Carey had chaired the CIO's Committee to Abolish Racial Discrimination and had attended the critical meeting against mob violence with Truman at the White House in September 1946.[44]

Boris Shiskin represented another labor success story. A Russian Jewish immigrant from Odessa, Shiskin settled in New York City in 1922 and matriculated at Columbia University. Upon graduation, he went to Washington, D.C., on a fellowship and wound up working for the AFL as an economist and housing expert. Although the CIO had broken away from the AFL in 1937 over philosophical differences, the forty-year-old Shiskin agreed with Carey about racial equality. Shiskin served as a consultant for a number of government bureaus during the era of the New Deal and World War II, and his most relevant qualification for the PCCR had been membership on the Fair Employment Practice Committee from 1942 to 1946.[45]

The remaining members of the committee were equally distinguished citizens from a variety of backgrounds that complemented each other and the rest of the group. John Dickey joined Graham as the second university president on the panel. A graduate of Dartmouth College and Harvard Law School, the thirty-nine-year-old Dickey became president of Dartmouth in 1945. He had not been involved in racial affairs, but he had served as director of the Office of Public Affairs in the State Department.[46] Also without any connection to civil rights, Francis P. Matthews was an Omaha, Nebraska, lawyer and a Catholic layman prominent in civic and educational affairs. As chair of the Board of Regents of his alma mater, Creighton University, he had a common interest in education with Dickey and Graham. As an officer in the U.S. Chamber of Commerce, he fit in well with Wilson and Luckman. Matthews authored a tough report on Communist infiltration in America for the Chamber of Commerce, and this put him squarely in line with the president's cold war ideology.[47] Despite its biblical namesake, the so-called Noah's ark committee had room for three members of the clergy. Recognizing the need for ecumenical balance, Truman appointed a Jew, a Catholic, and a Protestant. Rabbi Roland Gittelsohn had been a decorated chaplain with the Marines at the Battle of Iwo Jima. A native of Cleveland, he presided over a synagogue on Long Island, New York. His dedication to racial and religious cooperation reflected the orientation of the committee.[48] The Episcopal bishop, Henry Knox Sherrill, had volunteered as a chaplain overseas during World War I, and during the Second World War he chaired the Commission on Chaplains in the Army and Navy. Born in Brooklyn, he spent many years as head of the Massachusetts diocese before moving to the top of the Episcopal hierarchy. There was little in his background that focused on civil rights.[49] Not so with Bishop Francis J. Haas, dean of Catholic University's School of Social Service. He had close ties to the Roosevelt administration, and FDR had dispatched Haas, to no avail, to try and heal the cleavage between the AFL and CIO. In 1943, Roosevelt appointed Haas to chair the FEPC, on which Shiskin and Graham sat, and Haas conducted hearings on racial discrimination in the railroad and defense industries. His tenure quickly came to an end when the Catholic church appointed him bishop of Grand Rapids, Michigan.[50]

The remaining two members had solid liberal credentials. Franklin D. Roosevelt Jr. was appointed vice-chair of the PCCR. The son of the president, a graduate of Harvard with a University of Virginia law degree, and a decorated naval officer during World War II, Roosevelt had joined the American Veterans' Committee, a liberal alternative to the American Legion. He also became a founding member of Americans for Democratic Action, a group that embraced both social reform and anti-Communism. Roosevelt's greatest asset for Truman was his name and lineage, which connected Truman to the legacy of his predecessor.[51] A liberal anti-Communist like FDR Jr., Morris Ernst had more humble origins than his colleague. Born in Alabama but raised in New York City, Ernst graduated from Williams College, went into the family furniture business, and worked his way through New York University Law School at night. He became co-council for the ACLU and won a number of high-profile cases involving censorship and birth control. In later years, Ernst became preoccupied with the perceived Communist menace and reconciled his civil libertarianism with fervent support of the House Committee on Un-American Activities (HUAC). He bragged about his close relationship with FBI director J. Edgar Hoover, and defended him from criticism by fellow civil libertarians who did not share Ernst's passion for purging Communists.[52]

The committee's staff, which had the difficult task of researching and writing the report, were strong advocates of federal intervention to expand civil rights. The committee's director, Robert K. Carr, taught in the government department at Dartmouth, where Dickey was president, and had authored a recent study on the Civil Rights Section (CRS) of the Justice Department. Created in 1939, the CRS operated as a stepchild in the department, short on funds and lacking sufficient legal authority to defend minorities from civil rights violations. Eleanor Bontecou, an attorney in the CRS, lamented the attitude of her Justice Department colleagues: "They looked upon us as . . . 'do-gooders' and what not."[53] Carr's study concluded that the CRS needed sufficient power not just to protect civil rights but also to increase the scope of the constitutional rights afforded to citizens threatened by racial discrimination. Carr had one black assistant, Frances Williams, an alumna of Mount Holyoke College and the University of Chicago. She was involved in the YWCA, a training ground for future black and white female civil rights activists, and had served as a race relations advisor in the Office of Price Administration. Nancy Wechsler, who held the post of committee counsel, was active in the Americans for Democratic Action. Milton D. Stewart, a former journalist who had studied economics and social philosophy at New York University, directed research.[54]

More than a Noah's ark, the PCCR consisted of people with overlapping and multiple identities. For example, Dorothy Tilly was a southerner and a woman; Sadie Alexander was an African American, woman, and lawyer; Channing Tobias was a southerner, African American, and member of the clergy; Morris Ernst was a civil liberties lawyer, anti-Communist, and Jew; Bishop Haas was a Catholic, northerner, and college dean; Frank Graham was a southerner, Protestant, and college president. Whatever similarities or differences existed among them, committee members approached their task seriously and were determined to take President Truman at his word, not just to inventory the state of civil rights in America but also to come up with concrete recommendations to secure those rights. It was as good a committee as this chief executive could assemble, a concerned but cautious body, steady but progressive.

President Truman, seated, is surrounded by the members of his Committee on Civil Rights. Dubbed "Noah's ark" for its composition, the group consisted of two women, two African Americans, two southerners, two college presidents, and two corporate chief executives. Sadie Alexander appears at Truman's right; Dorothy Tilly is directly behind the president.
Bettmann/Corbis.

THE COMMITTEE AT WORK

The PCCR approached its task with a certain amount of ambiguity. Truman used the terms *civil rights* and *civil liberties* interchangeably with racial discrimination and religious bigotry. Whereas today we think of civil rights as those covered under the Thirteenth, Fourteenth, and Fifteenth Amendments of the Constitution and civil liberties as deriving from the Bill of Rights, in Truman's era the categories were more fluid. Presidential aide Phileo Nash remembered that the "use of the word 'civil rights' . . . came about in the course of our staff studies. We thought it advisable to find a term that was slightly fresh, and the word civil rights was not used for this function at that time."[55] This left the committee some leeway to chart its own course in exploring civil rights. Its members agreed that republican governments had been established to secure and protect four inalienable rights. The right to safety and security of the person meant that society could not imprison or execute citizens without due process of law. The right to citizenship conferred the right to vote and to serve in the military in defense of the country. The right to freedom of conscience and expression depended on the free marketplace of ideas. The right to equal opportunity gave individuals the chance to develop their talents and reap their rewards.[56]

Although the PCCR blazed new trails, it did have an important guidepost to help direct it. The publication in 1944 of Gunnar Myrdal's *An American Dilemma* not only provided a massive amount of factual information about race relations, but it also furnished a framework to interpret the data, one that postwar liberals adopted in approaching civil rights. Myrdal conceived of the racial problem as a moral conundrum stemming from the gap between the American creed of equal opportunity and the reality of discrimination. When well-meaning Americans came to see the disjuncture between their core values and their bigoted behavior, Myrdal believed, their consciences would lead them to modify their behavior and conform to democratic principles. Despite cataloging a long list of injustices, *An American Dilemma* optimistically concluded that through a combination of federal intervention and popular education the campaign against prejudice could succeed.[57] Although the committee cited Myrdal only once in its final report, the document produced by the PCCR was infused with his central assumptions. Myrdal's words reverberated in the PCCR's statement that "the pervasive gap between our aims and what we actually do is creating a kind of moral dry rot which eats away at the emotional and rational bases of democratic beliefs."[58]

The PCCR spent most of the year preparing its findings. The group decided to maintain a low profile while performing its task. It held public hearings in Washington, D.C., which drew approximately forty witnesses, but decided against going on the road to various racial hot spots around the country. Instead, the group solicited written comments from 184 organizations and 102 individuals and received a huge number of responses. The staff provided committee members with over three hundred pages of reports, countless printed publications, and more than a thousand pages of transcriptions of committee hearings and deliberations.[59] Although the committee sought to avoid publicity, it did operate to take "Truman off the hot seat," as one of his aides put it. The president's assistants kept in close touch with the committee, and in early 1947, when a brutal lynching occurred in South Carolina, the administration had the committee investigate it, thereby shifting pressure from civil rights groups off the White House.[60]

Committee meetings, a total of ten in all, were generally well attended, and Wilson proved a congenial chair, open to all sides of an issue. At the February 6 meeting in Washington, white committee members learned firsthand of the pervasiveness of racial discrimination. When Sadie Alexander went with her colleagues for a meal at a restaurant, she was refused service. "I never thought this could happen to a woman like you," a shocked Wilson commiserated with her. Washington, D.C., hotels were also segregated, but the committee staff convinced the Statler Hotel to accommodate Alexander and Tobias.[61] This would be just the beginning of Wilson's and the panel's education.

The first witnesses to testify before the committee did so behind closed doors. Assistant Attorney General Turner Smith, head of the Justice Department's Civil Rights Section, catalogued the complaints his bureau had received. Lynching topped the list, followed by Klan intimidation and discrimination in voting, transportation, public accommodations, and law enforcement. Smith's boss, Attorney General Tom Clark, who had prosecuted high-visibility racial crimes, nevertheless told the committee that moral education was the most important factor in combating bias. He did not discount the necessity for legislation to punish unacceptable behavior, however. Clark called upon the group to recommend beefing up the U.S. Criminal Code, specifically Title 18, Sections 51 and 52, which Congress had enacted during Reconstruction but which the courts had interpreted narrowly as an enforcement instrument against lynching and mob violence.[62]

J. Edgar Hoover endorsed Clark's remarks about the value of education to change people's behavior, but he was far less sympathetic to civil rights than was Clark. The FBI director commanded enormous power in Washington as well as a public relations network that bolstered his image as the nation's number one G-man. He maintained close contacts with white southern police, and the FBI relied on local law enforcement officials to perform its high-priority duties of apprehending car thieves, kidnappers, and bank robbers. It was true that current federal laws on the books made it difficult, as Clark pointed out, to convict civil rights violators. The FBI director proved uncharacteristically timid, however, when it came to civil rights. He employed only three blacks on the bureau payroll, not as investigative agents, but as his personal chauffeur and menial office help. Hoover held a dim view of the moral character of African Americans, and when members of the PCCR inquired why the FBI had not sent a black agent to investigate the murders in Monroe, Georgia, Hoover revealed a great deal about his racial attitudes. He asserted that "the local Negro I think would be more *disinclined* to talk to [a black agent] because the particular type of Negro living in Monroe was a very ignorant type of Negro." [emphasis in original][63]

Two months later in April, representatives of civil rights groups had their turn before the committee, this time in open hearings. In contrast to government witnesses, they made a stronger case for federal legislation than for education as the main weapon in attacking racial discrimination. The NAACP's Walter White spoke to listeners of the Mutual Radio Network, which broadcast the hearings live. Referring to the practitioners of racial violence and white supremacist politicians in the South, he passionately declared: "Hitler is presumably dead, but his spirit lives on in America today." He suggested legislation as the "only tool to implement the struggle to gain full citizenship." Lester Granger, director of the Urban League, pointed out that in addition to enacting legislation aimed at the South, Washington had a responsibility to clean its own house by removing barriers to black employment within the federal government. As a result of expansion during the New Deal and World War II, the federal government had become one of the major employers in the United States.[64] The parade of civil rights advocates appearing before the committee (the committee did not hear from outright opponents) supported urging the federal government to come up with new remedies to deal with racial inequality without denying the value of education.

THE FIRST FREEDOM RIDES

Civil rights advocates did not confine their complaints solely to the president's committee. In the spring of 1947, a small group of activists that had experimented with nonviolent, direct-action protests during World War II launched a campaign to challenge segregated seating on interstate buses. The previous year the Supreme Court had banned such segregation, but the transportation companies continued to comply with state laws that required black and white passengers to occupy separate sections on buses. In April 1947, while representatives of the NAACP and other civil rights organizations appeared before the PCCR, the Congress of Racial Equality and the Fellowship of Reconciliation, a Christian pacifist organization, sponsored teams of integrated riders to see whether they could travel unmolested through Virginia, North Carolina, Tennessee, and Kentucky. George Houser, the executive secretary of CORE, had come up with the idea along with Bayard Rustin, a black conscientious objector from West Chester, Pennsylvania, who had served a prison term for refusing to cooperate with the draft during World War II.[65] They believed that they had the greatest chance of success in these upper-South states.

Embarking from Washington, D.C., on April 9, on what they called the "journey of reconciliation," eight blacks and eight whites divided into two groups and rode Greyhound and Trailways buses into Dixie. They first encountered trouble as the buses headed from Virginia into North Carolina. A driver asked Rustin, one of the black passengers, to vacate his seat in the front of the bus and move to the rear. Rustin, an advocate of Gandhian nonviolence, politely refused to comply.

The driver backed off, and the journey continued uneventfully until the buses rolled into Chapel Hill, North Carolina, a usually quiet and progressive college town. Here four of the passengers, including Rustin and James Peck, a white man, were arrested for failing to move into designated segregated sections on the bus. As they made their way from the bus into the station, violence flared as a group of taxi drivers attacked Peck. The arrested travelers posted bail and took refuge at the home of the Reverend Charles Jones, a white Presbyterian minister with ties to the Fellowship of Reconciliation. After receiving threatening phone calls at his house, the group resumed its trip into Tennessee, Kentucky, and back through North Carolina and Virginia. The bus drivers insisted on segregated seating, but the passengers refused to cooperate. Although no further violence broke out, a total of twelve riders were taken into custody for refusing to comply with segregation orders. On April 23, the journey ended as both a testimony to the interracial travelers' courage and the unwillingness of southern transportation authorities to obey the 1946 Supreme Court ruling against interstate bus segregation. Indeed, little had changed, and the following year Rustin and one of his white companions were convicted of violating North Carolina's segregation law and served twenty-two days on a prison chain gang.[66]

THE COMMITTEE DELIBERATES

Although President Truman did not comment publicly on the violations of federal law that the freedom riders experienced, he did lend his support to those civil rights advocates with whom he had developed a close relationship. He favored the moderate approach of the NAACP, which promoted equality through lawsuits and legislation, rather than that of militant groups like CORE, which practiced civil disobedience. On June 29, 1947, he became the first chief executive to deliver an address to the NAACP. The setting fit the occasion well, as Truman spoke to a crowd of more than fifteen thousand at the Lincoln Memorial. His words carried even farther as they were broadcast live on national radio. His speech, drafted in large part by Robert Carr and Milton Stewart, reflected the thinking of the PCCR staff. Truman told his audience that the nation could not afford to wait any longer to remedy its racial evils and that the federal government must become the "friendly vigilant defender of the rights and equalities of all Americans." African Americans deserved no less, but it was also essential to the country's cold war struggle with the Soviet Union "that we have been able to put our own house in order."[67] Truman delivered the most powerful speech on civil rights of any president before him. The chief executive recognized that he had come a long way from his racist upbringing in small-town Missouri. He confided to his sister that he knew "Mama won't like what I have to say because I wind up quoting old Abe [Lincoln]. But, I believe what I say."[68]

The day after Truman's remarks, which Rabbi Gittelsohn praised as "beautiful," the PCCR met at Dartmouth College to draft its report. The committee easily reached agreement on most proposals. Numerous witnesses had pointed out the fundamental importance of the right to vote as the cornerstone for achieving first-class citizenship and ensuring personal safety. Sadie Alexander wanted to go further than her colleagues by recommending her "pet" project: invoking the Fourteenth Amendment to reduce congressional representation of those states that denied citizens the right to vote. The committee rejected this proposal as "impractical" and worried that some southern states would accept the reduction in representation to keep blacks from the suffrage.[69] The committee also sketched out support for desegregation of interstate transportation, public accommodations, and the military. It favored strengthening sections 51 and 52 of the federal criminal code to enhance the power of the Justice Department to prosecute civil rights crimes. The committee drew up strong proposals against lynching and for desegregation of Washington D.C., the creation of a permanent FEPC, and the reorganization of the Civil Rights Section of the Justice Department.

The PCCR had much more difficulty in deciding what to do about public school segregation, elimination of federal grants to segregated institutions, the performance of the FBI in civil rights investigations, and the federal loyalty programs. School desegregation posed the greatest problem for Tilly and Graham, the two white southern committee members. Both liberals, they nonetheless believed in placing the emphasis on the right to vote, because as Tilly feared, "the South will stay ignorant before it will be forced to having non-segregated schools." They cautioned that federal action in this area would precipitate fierce white opposition and endanger otherwise hopeful progress in race relations in the postwar South.[70] The committee also squabbled over the closely related issue of earmarking federal funds for education only for those schools that prohibited segregation and discrimination. Tilly and Graham received support from the other college president, Dickey, and from Bishop Sherrill and Luckman, all of whom agreed that cutting off grants to segregated southern schools would harm black and white children alike. On the other side, the strongest support for the measure came from Alexander, Tobias, Ernst, and Gittelsohn. Shiskin, Matthews, and Roosevelt eventually provided them with the majority in favor of the school desegregation recommendations.[71]

The PCCR also vigorously debated an issue related more to civil liberties than civil rights. On March 21, 1947, Truman issued an executive order establishing a federal loyalty board to investigate the background of government employees for ties to subversive organizations, particularly the Communist party and affiliated groups. The loyalty board's deliberations showed little regard for due process, and the definition of what constituted disloyalty remained vague. At the same time, the House Committee on Un-American Activities was conducting its own investigation into the influence of Communism in the Hollywood movie industry, and had punished ten witnesses who refused to answer its questions satisfactorily. Many civil libertarians regarded these investigations into political beliefs as a violation of the First Amendment's protection of freedom of speech—or in this case freedom not to speak—and freedom to join whatever groups one pleased. Ernst, although a strong advocate of civil rights protection, was a self-professed red-baiter. He drew a distinction between free speech advocacy, which as an ACLU lawyer he favored, and the behavior of totalitarian groups such as the Communist party, which tried to inhibit the free flow of information about itself from reaching the public. Thus, he recommended full disclosure of the names of officers and members of political groups who used the federal mails, a policy he argued would flush Communists out in the open. Ernst succeeded in getting his recommendation through the committee, but the president's loyalty program and HUAC's investigative forays upset some of his colleagues, who insisted on issuing words of warning in its report about potential threats to civil liberties.[72]

Ernst also had another reservation, this time more closely linked to civil rights. An outspoken admirer of J. Edgar Hoover, Ernst did not share his fellow committee members' criticism of the FBI's role in racial affairs and its reluctance to work more closely with the Civil Rights Section to enforce laws already on the books. Ernst insisted, with Hoover's backing, that the PCCR soften its criticism of the FBI, and although he succeeded in securing a draft with less harsh language, he could not prevent the committee from expressing its concern that the agency was not living up to its usual high standards with respect to civil rights. The committee also recommended elevating the CRS to a more substantial division status in the Justice Department.[73]

After the PCCR met in early September to iron out some of its disagreements, the staff proceeded to write the final version of the report. Tilly and Graham warned that some of the language concerning the South seemed too one-sided. They persuaded Carr to modify some offensive sentences and pointed out that racial discrimination was not just a southern problem but a national problem as well. For example, although the committee shared Gunnar Myrdal's views about the failure of the country to live up to its democratic creed, the final report was edited to eliminate a passage from *An American Dilemma,* which highlighted the "pattern of violence against Negroes in the South."[74] Also, some committee members were troubled about the presentation of the wartime treatment of Japanese Americans who had been removed from the West Coast and placed in internment camps. Ernst participated in prosecution of the cases that defended the evacuation and incarceration of Japanese Americans; Dickey held a position in the State Department; and FDR Jr. was the son of the president who promulgated the orders for detention. In the end, the report did not attack the decision to evacuate and intern Japanese Americans, but it did support compensation for its victims.[75] Nevertheless, despite attempts to soften aspects of the report, the PCCR chose to focus on "the bad side of our record—on what might be called the civil rights frontier."[76]

THE REPORT

Truman received *To Secure These Rights,* the committee's report, on October 29, 1947.[77] He may not have expected the far-ranging recommendations that emerged from his carefully balanced committee, but he did not flinch from endorsing them. Congratulating the panel members for doing "a good job . . . what I wanted you to do," he hailed the report as "an American charter of human freedom in our time" and "a guide for action." The president wanted the document to inspire "men of good will everywhere [who] are striving under great difficulty to create a worldwide moral order." He pledged that the federal government would strive to protect individual freedom based on "equal freedom under just laws."[78]

The text of the report spells out in detail the liberal vision for expansion of civil rights in the years after World War II. The report's emphasis on the duty of the federal government to protect individuals from racial discrimination contained the basis of the liberal credo for decades to come. The report asserted that Washington "cannot afford to delay action until the most backward community has learned to prize civil liberty and has taken adequate steps to safeguard the rights of every one of its citizens." Furthermore, liberals contended that rights belonged to individuals and not to groups. Accordingly, blacks were entitled to equal treatment and, like all Americans, they should "tolerate no restrictions upon the individual which depend upon irrelevant factors such as his race, his color, his religion, or the social position to which he is born."[79] This conception of civil rights would last into the mid-1960s. At that time, in response to the persistence of racism, civil rights activists called for affirmative action to treat African Americans as a racial group rather than merely as individuals and to compensate them for the consequences of white supremacy.

To Secure These Rights also reflected the liberal belief that bolstering civil rights stemmed from moral, diplomatic, and economic considerations. The report took a page from *An American Dilemma* by stating the PCCR's faith "that the greatest hope for the future is the increasing awareness by more and more Americans of the gulf between our civil rights principles and our practices."[80] The cold war heightened this awareness. In the struggle against the Soviet Union, the United States could not afford to tolerate racial discrimination within its borders and expect the rest of the world to believe its political and economic systems were superior to those of its Communist adversary. The report also catalogued ways in which racial prejudice hampered growth of the American economy. Bias cost the economy money in markets that were closed to black consumers, in the depression of minority wages, in higher expenditures to operate segregated facilities, and in reduced production that resulted from restricted markets and a reduction of purchasing power. Furthermore, the economy lost millions of dollars from racial disturbances.[81]

The thirty-four recommendations that appear in the report established the agenda for civil rights reforms for a generation to come. In addition to attacking disfranchisement and advocating the strengthening of federal law enforcement machinery against racial crimes such as lynching, the document proposed to dismantle segregation throughout American society. It condemned racial separation in housing, interstate transportation, public accommodations, the military, and employment. Most remarkable of all was the stand it took against school segregation. In challenging Jim Crow, the PCCR took aim at the ideology of white supremacy itself. "The separate but equal doctrine," the report chided, "is inconsistent with the fundamental equalitarianism of the American way of life in that it marks groups with the brand of inferior status. . . . There is no adequate defense of segregation."[82] Seven years later, in 1954, the U.S. Supreme Court would reach the same conclusion in its historic *Brown v. Board of Education* ruling.

The report did not frame civil rights in merely legal terms, although it did emphasize them. Those who supported expansion of the suffrage, for example, did not view it as an end in itself. They expected newly enfranchised blacks and whites to join together and use their ballots to alter power relationships in the South and extend economic democracy to the most impoverished region in the country. However, in protecting the lives of minorities, the federal government would have to provide more than political and legal rights; it would have to improve opportunities for equal education and employment. The report addressed some of these issues by recommending laws to promote increased opportunities for African Americans in employment, education, housing, and health services.[83]

To Secure These Rights reflected and reinforced the larger movement for racial equality that was gaining strength in postwar America. In January 1947, a group of black Mississippians, many of them veterans, challenged the right of Senator Theodore Bilbo to take his seat in the new Eightieth Congress. Represented by the NAACP, they charged that Bilbo had prevented blacks from voting by stirring up racial hatred and advising local officials to keep African Americans from casting their ballots. They achieved some success, as the Senate temporarily blocked Bilbo from taking his seat pending an investigation, and the conflict was resolved when the Mississippi senator soon died from cancer. In May 1947, another presidential commission released a report that called for an end to military segregation. In Clarendon County, South Carolina, blacks began a campaign to obtain buses from the local board of education to take their children to school, which the doctrine of "separate but equal" had yet to provide them. Their efforts culminated a few years later in a full-scale drive against segregated schools. A week before the PCCR issued its findings, the NAACP submitted a petition, drafted by W. E. B. Du Bois, to the United Nations asking its Commission on Human Rights to investigate racism in the United States. Although the UN declined to interfere, largely at the U.S. delegation's insistence, the petition demonstrated the increased militancy of African Americans and further publicized their grievances.[84] Thus, the PCCR's report converged with escalating attempts by African Americans on the local, national, and international levels to destroy Jim Crow.

REACTIONS TO THE REPORT

To Secure These Rights exceeded civil rights activists' highest expectations. Walter White considered the report "the most uncompromising and specific pronouncement by a governmental agency on the explosive issue of racial and religious bigotry which has ever been issued." The African American press generally agreed. The Chicago *Defender* praised it as a "new blueprint for freedom," and the *Afro-American* declared it "one of the most significant documents of all time." The only hesitation some newspapers expressed was about whether the president and Congress would follow through on translating the committee's recommendations into law.[85]

To encourage public support, black newspapers serialized the report and were joined in this enterprise by liberal periodicals. The American Jewish Congress distributed some two hundred thousand summaries of the report. Workshops were organized to discuss the committee's handiwork, and Dorothy Tilly persuaded the Southern Regional Council to initiate one in Atlanta. *To Secure These Rights* also reached people's hands through the government's printing of twenty-five thousand copies, and the publisher Simon & Schuster sold another thirty-six thousand copies for a dollar each. Through all these outlets, over a million copies of the report were distributed.[86]

The report, however, did not please everyone. Southerners, who had remained relatively quiet when the PCCR was formed, blasted the document. A correspondent from Virginia angrily wrote Truman several days after its release: "If you do away with segregation, allow negro [*sic*] children in white schools, churches, etc. you might as well drop a few bombs on us and not prolong the agony." These comments generally summed up the reaction of white southern politicians and the press. They heaped vitriol on Tilly and Graham, calling them "traitors and dupes," regardless of the fact that they had opposed the recommendations on school desegregation.[87] It did not matter, because the appearance of the report pushed moderates to the sidelines and propelled reactionaries to the forefront.

TRUMAN'S RESPONSE
AND THE ELECTION OF 1948

Given the outburst from the South, Truman faced rough treatment in submitting civil rights proposals to Congress. The problem was not so much that conservative Republicans were in control of the Eightieth Congress, but that powerful southern Democrats could block attempts to pass legislation by undertaking a filibuster in the Senate, the graveyard of civil rights bills.

Truman was forced to spend a great deal of political capital to mobilize support for his program. With a cold war to fight at home and abroad, the president could not afford to antagonize southern lawmakers whose support he needed for these higher priority efforts. Accordingly, Truman devised a strategy to appeal to his civil rights backers without further alienating opponents. Looking ahead to running for president in 1948, the president and trusted political advisors such as Clark Clifford believed that he had to shore up his liberal New Deal base, including African Americans, by challenging Congress to enact proposals that he knew had no chance of passing. This strategy called for Truman to create a platform upon which to run for reelection and to blame the Republican leadership in Congress for failing to act on his proposals. His counselors guessed that although there would be a great deal of grumbling from southern segregationists, Dixie's white Democrats would remain faithful to the party as they had since the Civil War.[88]

From February through July 1948, Truman and the southern Democrats engaged in a political dance: For every two steps forward the president moved, he took one step back. On February 2, he delivered a special message to Congress in which he proposed a ten-point program based on the PCCR's findings. In addition to antilynching, anti–poll tax, and FEPC bills, the president called for ending segregation in interstate transportation, upgrading the Civil Rights Section into a division of the Justice Department, creating a Civil Rights Commission, establishing home rule and antidiscrimination measures for the District of Columbia, and adjudicating financial claims by Japanese Americans resulting from their wartime evacuation. The chief executive omitted the most politically incendiary features of *To Secure These Rights:* school desegregation and the ban on federal grants to segregated institutions. It did not matter, however, as Truman knew, because none of the measures, even the least controversial, had a chance of passing. Truman recorded in his diary: "I send the Congress a Civil Rights message. They will no doubt receive it . . . coldly. But it needs to be said."[89]

He proved correct. His bills never made it out of the Senate; nor did he fight particularly hard for them in the face of fierce southern opposition. Indeed, the president went to the Democratic National Convention in July prepared to accept a civil rights plank that wasn't too offensive to the South and fell far short of his own program. However, again he shifted direction. Once Hubert H. Humphrey, a Democrat running for the Senate from Minnesota, engineered a liberal-labor coalition of delegates to replace the weak civil rights platform with a very strong one, Truman easily capitulated.[90]

Political events altered his game plan. The acceptance of the strong civil rights standard pushed representatives from Mississippi and Alabama to leave the convention and form the State's Rights, or Dixiecrat, party, nominating Governor Strom Thurmond of South Carolina for president and Governor Fielding Wright of Mississippi for vice president.[91] Even more worrisome, on his left, Truman faced the Progressive party nominee, Henry Wallace, an original New Dealer who appealed to many in the liberal wing of the party and had support from the Communist party. In the South, Wallace campaigned before blacks and whites standing side by side and forcefully denounced disfranchisement and Jim Crow.[92] Although there were still too few black voters in the South to make a difference, increasing numbers of African Americans in the North and West could affect the outcome of the election. These votes were not only up for grabs by Wallace, but also by the Republican candidate, Thomas E. Dewey, the reform governor of New York who spoke out in favor of civil rights.

Truman worried more about Dewey and Wallace than about Thurmond. To forestall any erosion of the northern black support he needed, the president responded in several ways. He called Congress into special session on July 26 to consider once again his civil rights proposals, which he knew were doomed from the beginning. No one

doubted the political motivations behind this move. He sought to em-
barrass the Republicans, and in turn their party standard-bearer, Dewey,
for failing to enact his proposals. He also engaged in red-baiting Wallace by accusing him of being a front man for the Communists.

Truman could not afford to depend solely on rhetoric, however, to
shore up African American backing. For several months, A. Philip
Randolph, who was no stranger to manipulating presidents, threatened to lead a mass civil disobedience movement of young black
males against the cold war military draft unless Truman acted to eliminate segregation in the armed forces. Randolph's demand took on
greater weight because the president's own civil rights committee had
endorsed desegregation of the military. Like Roosevelt, Truman
wanted to avoid a protest that would underscore America's continuing
racial discrimination and hurt the administration's diplomatic efforts.
Randolph's gambit, backed by the new-found political strength of
African Americans, worked. Truman issued two executive orders man-
dating the desegregation of the armed forces and the elimination of
racial discrimination in federal government employment. Thus, Randolph completed what he had started six years earlier.[93]

Truman's calculations paid off. Only four southern states—Mississippi, Alabama, South Carolina, and Louisiana—defected to Thurmond. Thanks to Truman's appeal to black voters, Wallace made a
poor showing among them. Dewey's lackluster campaigning and Truman's claims that a Republican return to the White House would lead
to another depression bolstered the president's victory.[94]

THE CIVIL RIGHTS REPORT
AND TRUMAN'S LEGACY

Truman's 1948 presidential victory did not provide the legislative mandate the president needed for his civil rights program to triumph.
Below the surface little had changed in Congress. Democrats replaced
Republicans as the majority party, but southern Democrats who
gained from this triumph used their seniority to chair important committees and the filibuster to thwart whatever civil rights measures
Truman sent them. Furthermore, Truman's cold war concerns, particularly with the outbreak of the Korean War in 1950, helped disrupt the
solidarity of civil rights advocates. To affirm ideological purity, liberal
and labor groups, including the NAACP, the ACLU, and the CIO,
purged their ranks of suspected Communists and left-wing associates.

Many of the interracial bands of activists who had joined the Southern Conference for Human Welfare and the Henry Wallace presidential campaign to try to democratize the South suffered a blow during the Communist witch hunts, from which it was hard to recover. Anti-Communist liberals often played into the hands of conservatives, who used the fear of subversion to stop any civil rights reform whatsoever. The cold war did not halt the civil rights movement altogether; rather, it served to reduce the number of opportunities for change, particularly economic, and labor-related reforms that could be smeared with the red taint of communism.

Despite considering the cold war a more urgent priority, Truman did not stop pursuing racial justice. His administration had other weapons at its disposal to circumvent the obstructionist Congress, and the president quietly deployed them in a few notable instances. He approved the Justice Department's filing of briefs on behalf of the NAACP and supported black plaintiffs in their efforts to overturn racially restrictive housing covenants. Many homeowners had placed these discriminatory stipulations in their deeds, which bound them to sell their property to Caucasians only. Local courts had enforced them as legal contracts. The PCCR had received complaints about these restrictive agreements and recommended their elimination. In 1948, the Supreme Court ruled that the covenants could not be constitutionally implemented under the Fourteenth Amendment. In addition, over the next few years, Truman's Justice Department joined with the NAACP to lodge judicial challenges to racial segregation in interstate transportation and public schools and colleges.[95]

When Truman retired in 1953, he had accomplished more than any other president before him and most of those who came after him in establishing federal support for civil rights. Roy Wilkins of the NAACP wrote him that "no chief Executive in our history has spoken so plainly on this matter as yourself, or acted so forthrightly."[96] Inspired by moral concerns and tempered by political reality, Truman lined up behind the concept of racial equality and helped thrust it on the public agenda.

Undeniably, human decency motivated him, but the president responded largely because the political landscape was changing significantly. Truman reacted to a rising social movement that a chief executive could no longer afford to ignore. Wartime and postwar ideology, diplomacy, and demographics had strengthened the position of African Americans seeking to eliminate white supremacy. There was nothing predestined to guarantee success; white Americans who held power, no matter how sensitive to their plight, would not take bold action unless black activists applied pressure and gained visibility at the national and international levels. This pattern became evident in the 1940s and would continue for two decades. Progress occurred in fits and starts, but as long as civil rights advocates, black and white alike, combined political power with appeals to moral conscience, the struggle for equality moved forward. Reports as forward-looking and eloquent as *To Secure These Rights* could not by themselves produce social change. Rhetoric and good intentions were not enough; it took power wielded by a determined mass movement and applied on sympathetic but cautious national officials to topple Jim Crow.

Harry S Truman and A. Philip Randolph were still alive when President Lyndon B. Johnson signed into law the Civil Rights Act of 1964 and the Voting Rights Act of 1965. Both men, as well as scores of anonymous black women and men, had helped provide the foundation upon which these twin legislative towers had been built. When civil rights forces sufficiently pressured the national government to fight on their side, both Randolph and Truman saw fulfilled much of what they had tried to accomplish in the 1940s. Over the years, Truman's chief civil rights legacy remained the creation of the President's Committee on Civil Rights and its heralded report. In some 176 pages, *To Secure These Rights* provided a detailed inventory of the civil wrongs done to African Americans and offered a road map for the country to follow to remedy them. Reading the report today, we should appreciate the insight of the committee at a time when segregation and disfranchisement reigned supreme. Yet more than half a century after publication of the report and four decades after passage of landmark civil rights acts, there remains a need to reflect on how the nation, now that it has secured fundamental civil rights for African Americans, intends finally to fulfill them.[97]

NOTES

[1]Harvard Sitkoff, *A New Deal for Blacks: The Emergence of Civil Rights as a National Issue, the Depression Decade* (New York: Oxford University Press, 1978); Nancy J. Weiss, *Farewell to the Party of Lincoln: Black Politics in the Age of FDR* (Princeton: Princeton University Press, 1983), *passim.*

[2]Patricia Sullivan, *Days of Hope: Race and Democracy in the New Deal Era* (Chapel Hill: University of North Carolina Press, 1996), 24–26, 98–101.

[3]Steven F. Lawson, *Black Ballots: Voting Rights in the South, 1944–1969*, 2nd ed. (Lanham, Md.: Lexington Books, 1999), 62ff.

[4] John Hope Franklin, "A Half-Century of Presidential Race Initiatives: Some Reflections," *Journal of Supreme Court History* 24 (1999): 226.

[5] Herbert Garfinkel, *When Negroes March* (New York: Atheneum, 1969).

[6] James Farmer, *Lay Bare the Heart* (New York: Arbor House, 1985), 97ff; August Meier and Elliott Rudwick, *CORE: A Study of the Civil Rights Movement, 1942–1968* (New York: Oxford University Press, 1973), 13–14; and Pauli Murray, *The Autobiography of a Black Activist, Feminist, Lawyer, Priest, and Poet* (Knoxville: University of Tennessee Press, 1989), 202–208.

[7] Dominic Capeci Jr., *Race Relations in Wartime Detroit: The Sojourner Truth Housing Controversy of 1942* (Philadelphia: Temple University Press, 1984), *passim;* Quintard Taylor, *In Search of the Racial Frontier: African Americans in the American West, 1528–1990* (New York: Norton, 1998), 251, 262, 271.

[8] Lynn Homan and Thomas Reilly, *Black Knights: The Story of the Tuskegee Airmen* (Gretna, La.: Pelican Publishing, 2001), 179, 186, 192; Lawrence Scott and William M. Womack Sr., *Double V: The Civil Rights Struggle of the Tuskegee Airmen* (East Lansing: Michigan State University Press, 1992), 195–96, 203–209; 231–48.

[9] *Smith v. Allwright*, 321 U.S. 649 (1944); Darlene Clark Hine, *Black Victory: The Rise and Fall of the White Primary in Texas* (New York: KTO Press, 1979); Steven F. Lawson, *Running for Freedom: Civil Rights and Black Politics in America Since 1941*, 2nd ed. (New York: McGraw-Hill, 1997), 81.

[10] The bus transportation victory came in *Morgan v. Virginia*, 328 U.S. 373 (1946).

[11] Sullivan, *Days of Hope*, 163–66; John Egerton, *Speak Now Against the Day* (Chapel Hill: University of North Carolina Press, 1994), 310–16.

[12] Robert Korstad and Nelson Lichtenstein, "Opportunities Lost and Found: Labor Radicals and the Early Civil Rights Movement," *Journal of American History* 75 (Dec. 1988): 786–811; Michael Honey, *Southern Labor and Black Civil Rights: Organizing Memphis Workers* (Urbana: University of Illinois Press, 1993), *passim.*

[13] Kathryn Nasstrom, "Down to Now: Memory, Narrative, and Women's Leadership in the Civil Rights Movement in Atlanta, Georgia," *Gender & History* 11 (Apr. 1999): 123, 125; Lawson, *Black Ballots*, 125.

[14] Jerold Auerbach, *Labor and Liberty* (Indianapolis: Bobbs-Merrill, 1966), *passim.*

[15] Gayle Williams O'Brien, *The Color of the Law: Race, Violence, and Justice in the Post–World War II South* (Chapel Hill: University of North Carolina Press, 1999), 7–10.

[16] The account in these two paragraphs is taken from O'Brien, *Color*, chapter 1.

[17] Quote comes from William C. Berman, *The Politics of Civil Rights in the Truman Administration* (Columbus: Ohio State University Press, 1970), 47; William E. Juhnke, "Creating a New Charter of Freedom: The Organization and Operation of the President's Committee on Civil Rights, 1946–1948 (unpublished doctoral dissertation, University of Kansas, 1974), 1, 20–21, 24; Michael R. Gardner, *Harry Truman and Civil Rights: Moral Courage and Political Risks* (Carbondale: Southern Illinois University Press, 2002), 17–18.

[18] White quote in Juhnke, "Creating," 24; see also Juhnke, 23; Berman, *Politics of Civil Rights*, 47; Donald R. McCoy and Richard T. Reutten, *Quest and Response: Minority Rights and the Truman Administration* (Lawrence: University of Kansas Press, 1973), 45–46.

[19] Gunnar Myrdal, *An American Dilemma: The Negro Problem and Modern Democracy* (New York: Harper and Brothers, 1944); Mary L. Dudziak, *Cold War Civil Rights: Race and the Image of American Democracy* (Princeton: Princeton University Press, 2001), chapter 1; see also Thomas Borstelmann, *The Cold War and the Color Line: American Race Relations in the Global Arena* (Cambridge, Mass.: Harvard University Press, 2002).

[20] Gardner, *Harry Truman*, 88.

[21] McCoy and Reutten, *Quest*, 16.

[22] Ibid., 22–23.

[23] Lawson, *Black Ballots*, 78.

[24]The Senate rule to close debate is called *cloture*. Today it requires a three-fifths instead of two-thirds vote of the upper chamber.

[25]William E. Juhnke, "President Truman's Committee on Civil Rights: The Interaction of Politics, Protest, and Presidential Advisory Commissions," *Presidential Studies Quarterly* 19 (1989): 594.

[26]Harry S. Truman, *Memoirs: Years of Trial and Hope,* vol. 2 (Garden City, N.Y.: Doubleday & Company, 1956), 183.

[27]"Separate but equal" was the doctrine the Supreme Court had pronounced in 1896 in the case of *Plessy v. Ferguson.* Its effect was to provide legal sanction for racial segregation.

[28]Barton J. Bernstein, "The Ambiguous Legacy: The Truman Administration and Civil Rights," in Barton J. Bernstein, ed., *Politics and Policies of the Truman Administration* (Chicago: Quadrangle Books, 1970), 272; Berman, *Politics of Civil Rights,* 60–61; Harvard Sitkoff, "Years of the Locust: Interpretations of Truman's Presidency Since 1965," in Richard S. Kirkendall, ed., *The Truman Period as a Research Field: A Reappraisal, 1972* (Columbia: University of Missouri Press, 1974), 102; McCoy and Reutten, *Quest,* 29. Gardner, *Harry Truman,* 40, makes the moral and political dimensions either/or propositions, and overemphasizes the former. Indeed, in the early 1960s, the retired president spoke out against sit-in demonstrators and freedom riders for their confrontational protests against segregation.

[29]Juhnke, "Creating," 33.

[30]McCoy and Reutten, *Quest,* 48.

[31]Ibid., 48, 49; Berman, *Politics of Civil Rights,* 51–52; Gardner, *Harry Truman,* 16.

[32]Juhnke, "Creating," 37; McCoy and Reutten, *Quest,* 48.

[33]Gardner, *Harry Truman,* 16, 18; Berman, *Politics of Civil Rights,* 53; McCoy and Reutten, *Quest,* 51; Juhnke, "Creating," 41.

[34]*To Secure These Rights: The Report of the President's Committee on Civil Rights* (Washington, D.C.: Government Printing Office, 1947), 34 (hereafter cited as *TSTR*). Pages refer to those in the text of the report reprinted in this volume.

[35]Berman, *Politics of Civil Rights,* 56–57; Juhnke, "Creating," 43; McCoy and Reutten, *Quest,* 53.

[36]Gardner, *Harry Truman,* 23, for the Nash quote. According to committee member John Dickey: "It was a typically Truman kind of Committee, not very far out on the edges." Quoted in Juhnke, "Creating," 60.

[37]Juhnke, "Creating," 41; Bernstein, "Ambiguous," 278.

[38]Nancy Elizabeth Fitch, "Sadie Tanner Mossell Alexander," in John A. Garraty and Marc C. Carnes, eds., *American National Biography* (hereafter cited as *ANB*), vol. 1, (New York: Oxford University Press, 1999), 278; Gardner, *Harry Truman,* 245.

[39]Sandra Opdycke, "Channing Heggie Tobias," in *ANB,* vol. 21, 711–12 (the quote is on p. 712).

[40]William E. Leuchtenburg, "Frank Porter Graham," in *ANB,* vol. 9, 377; Murray, *Autobiography,* 114–16, 122–23. Instead, Murray went to Howard University, where she campaigned against segregated restaurants in Washington, D.C. She became a lawyer, poet, and feminist. Graham was appointed to fill a vacancy to the U.S. Senate from North Carolina in 1949, and when he stood for election in 1950, he lost the Democratic primary to a candidate who used Graham's associations with the SCHW and the PCCR to smear him. Warren Ashby, *Frank Porter Graham: A Southern Liberal* (Winston-Salem: John F. Blair, Publisher, 1980), 224–29.

[41]Marilyn Elizabeth Perry, "Dorothy Eugenia Rogers Tilly," in *ANB,* vol. 21, 676; Morton Sosna, *In Search of the Silent South: Southern Liberals and Race Relations* (New York: Columbia University Press, 1977), 150–55; Jacquelyn Dowd Hall, *Revolt Against Chivalry: Jesse Daniel Ames and the Women's Campaign Against Lynching* (New York: Columbia University Press, 1979), 217, 261, 332n13.

[42]Jacob Vander Meulen, "Charles Edward Wilson," in *ANB,* vol. 23, 557. Wilson also

served on the board of the "Freedom Train" project, which in 1947 transported original copies of the Declaration of Independence and the Constitution around the country for public viewing. He joined with the board in refusing to let the train stop in cities in the South, such as Birmingham and Memphis, which required racial segregation for those who came to inspect the documents. McCoy and Reutten, *Quest,* 74–75.

[43] Herbert Muschamp, "Charles Luckman," [obituary], *New York Times,* 28 Jan. 1999, C23; Juhnke, "Creating," 48.

[44] "James Barron Carey," in Gary M. Fink, ed., *Biographical Dictionary of American Labor* (Westport, Conn.: Greenwood Press, 1984), 144; Juhnke, "Creating," 49.

[45] "Boris Shiskin," *Washington Post,* [obituary], 14 June 1984, C7; Juhnke, "Creating," 50.

[46] Peter B. Flint, "John Sloan Dickey," [obituary], *New York Times,* 9 Feb. 1991; Juhnke, "Creating," 50–51.

[47] Lloyd J. Graybar, "Francis Patrick Matthews," in *ANB,* vol. 14, 720. In 1949, Truman appointed him secretary of the navy.

[48] David Stout, "Roland Bertram Gittelsohn," [obituary], *New York Times,* 15 Dec. 1995, B7; Tom Long, [obituary], *Boston Globe,* 15 Dec. 1995, 87.

[49] Donald S. Armentrout, "Henry Knox Sherrill," in *ANB,* vol. 19, 823.

[50] Thomas E. Blantz, "Francis Joseph Haas," in *ANB,* vol. 9, 761.

[51] Shelly L. Lemmons, "Franklin D. Roosevelt Jr.," in *ANB,* vol. 18, 826.

[52] Samuel Walker, "Morris Leopold Ernst," in *ANB,* vol. 7, 564–65.

[53] O'Brien, *Color,* 192; Robert K. Carr, *Federal Protection of Civil Rights: Quest for a Sword* (Ithaca: Cornell University Press, 1947).

[54] Juhnke, "Creating," 70–73.

[55] Gardner, *Harry Truman,* 15; Juhnke, "Creating," 79–80.

[56] *TSTR,* 52.

[57] David Southern, *Gunnar Myrdal and Black-White Relations: The Use and Abuse of an American Dilemma, 1944–1969* (Baton Rouge: Louisiana State University Press, 1987), 113, 115; Walter A. Jackson, *Gunnar Myrdal and America's Conscience: Social Engineering and Racial Liberalism, 1938–1987* (Chapel Hill: University of North Carolina Press, 1990), 276.

[58] *TSTR,* 158. See also 58.

[59] Juhnke, "Creating," 80, 112, 221; McCoy and Reutten, *Quest,* 82. Note the slight discrepancy in the numbers—the latter has ten more in each category.

[60] McCoy and Reutten, *Quest,* 81.

[61] Juhnke, "Creating," 82 (for quote), 92.

[62] McCoy and Reutten, *Quest,* 81–82.

[63] O'Brien, *Color,* 196.

[64] Juhnke, "Creating," 105 (for quote), 106; Juhnke, "President Truman's," 600.

[65] Daniel Levine, *Bayard Rustin and the Civil Rights Movement* (New Brunswick, N.J.: Rutgers University Press, 2000), 51.

[66] Ibid., 53–55, 60, 63; Catherine A. Barnes, *Journey from Jim Crow: The Desegregation of Southern Transit* (New York: Columbia University Press, 1983), 59–60.

[67] *Public Papers of the Presidents of the United States, Harry S. Truman, 1947* (Washington, D.C.: Government Printing Office, 1963), 311 (first quote), and 312 (second quote).

[68] Gardner, *Harry Truman,* 30.

[69] Transcript, decision paper #3, 30 June 1947, box 14, PCCR Papers, Harry S Truman Library (HSTL). Juhnke, "President Truman's," 602 (Gittelsohn quote); O'Brien, *Color,* 157, 246.

[70] McCoy and Reutten, *Quest,* 85; Juhnke, "Creating," 129–30; Transcript, proceedings of PCCR, 12–13 Sept. 1947, 809–10, box 14 HSTL. See remarks of Guy B. Johnson, director of the Southern Regional Council to the PCCR, 14 May 1947, in possession of author.

[71] Roosevelt apparently switched his vote to the winning side to carry the proposals. Wilson, as chair, did not vote. Juhnke, "Creating," 141–42, 145–46. There was also a close vote in favor of recommending enactment of a fair educational practice law for student admissions to public and private institutions. Dartmouth's Dickey spoke most vigorously against it.

[72] Juhnke, "Creating," 133, 135, 136; Walker, "Morris Ernst," 565. In the mid-1950s, Alabama, Florida, and Louisiana underscored the danger of Ernst's approach by trying to close down the NAACP for failing to reveal its membership lists. See Steven F. Lawson, "The Florida Legislative Investigation Committee and the Constitutional Readjustment of Race Relations, 1956–1963," in *An Uncertain Tradition: Constitutionalism and the History of the South,* Kermit L. Hall and James W. Ely, eds. (Athens: University of Georgia Press, 1989), 296–325, and Adam Fairclough, *Race and Democracy: The Civil Rights Struggle in Louisiana, 1915–1972* (Athens: University of Georgia Press, 1995), 195.

[73] Juhnke, "Creating," 172ff; McCoy and Reutten, *Quest,* 85; *TSTR,* 147–48.

[74] Juhnke, "Creating," 162.

[75] Southern, *Myrdal,* 116–17; Juhnke, "President Truman's," 605; Juhnke, "Creating," 134, 138, 160, 161, 162. Nor did the report include any recommendations about American Indians, who were considered a special case under the purview of the Bureau of Indian Affairs.

[76] *TSTR,* 46.

[77] The title of the report came from a phrase in the Declaration of Independence. The framers wrote that "to secure these rights" [of life, liberty, and the pursuit of happiness], "governments are instituted among men. . . ."

[78] *Public Papers, Truman, 1947,* 480.

[79] *TSTR,* 127 (first quote), 50 (second quote).

[80] Ibid, 59. Myrdal is quoted only once in the report. See p. 164.

[81] Ibid, 160ff.

[82] Ibid, 179.

[83] O'Brien, *Color,* 215; *TSTR,* 180–82; Bernstein, "Ambiguous," 280.

[84] Lawson, *Black Ballots,* 105–13; John Dittmer, *Local People: The Struggle for Civil Rights in Mississippi* (Urbana: University of Illinois Press, 1994), 2–9; Richard Kluger, *Simple Justice* (New York: Alfred A. Knopf, 1976), 13–17; Berman, *Politics of Civil Rights,* 65–66; Sitkoff, "Years of Locust," 102–03. Shortly after the report was issued, in November 1947, Rosa Lee Ingram of Georgia, a black tenant farmer and widow with twelve children, was beaten by a white man who attempted to assault her sexually. During the attack, two of Ingram's teenage sons came to her rescue; one swung the end of a rifle at the assailant's head and killed him. Ingram and two of her sons received a hurried and unfair trial and were convicted and sentenced to death. The sentences were commuted to life in prison. The case against this woman and her sons rallied protests from civil rights advocates, women's groups and Communists. In 1959 Ingram and her sons were paroled, and in 1964 the sentences were reduced to time already served. The incident shows that attacks on women mobilized African Americans to challenge the racist and sexist system of southern "justice." Jack Greenberg, *Crusaders in the Courts* (New York: Basic Books, 1964), 45, 530.

[85] Juhnke, "Creating," 195 (*Defender* quote), and 199; McCoy and Reutten, *Quest,* 92 (*Afro-American* quote).

[86] McCoy and Reutten, *Quest,* 92–93; Juhnke, "Creating," 200–201, 203; Southern, *Myrdal,* 118.

[87] Quoted in Gardner, *Harry Truman,* 62; Juhnke, "Creating," 197.

[88] Alonzo Hamby, *Man of the People: A Life of Harry S. Truman* (New York: Oxford University Press, 1995), 430–31. Gardner, *Harry Truman,* 90, disagrees that the Clifford memo was critical in shaping Truman's thinking on civil rights.

89 Robert H. Ferrell, ed., *Off the Record: The Private Papers of Harry S. Truman* (New York: Harper and Row, 1980), 122; Gardner, *Harry Truman*, 71, 77, 80.

90 Timothy N. Thurber, *The Politics of Equality: Hubert H. Humphrey and the African American Freedom Struggle* (New York: Columbia University Press, 1999), 61.

91 Kari Frederickson, *The Dixiecrat Revolt and the End of the Solid South, 1932–1968* (Chapel Hill: University of North Carolina Press, 2001), 150–86.

92 Sullivan, *Days of Hope,* 259–70. Wallace lauded the PCCR report, proclaiming it "the one bright spot in the Truman Administration," Sullivan, 245.

93 Paula F. Pfeffer, *A. Philip Randolph, Pioneer of the Civil Rights Movement* (Baton Rouge: Louisiana State University Press, 1990), 145–48.

94 Harold Gullen, *The Upset That Wasn't: Harry S. Truman and the Crucial Election of 1948* (Chicago: Ivan R. Dee, 1998).

95 *Shelley v. Kraemer,* 334 U.S. 1 (1948); Clement Vose, *Caucasians Only: The Supreme Court, the NAACP, and the Restrictive Covenant Cases* (Berkeley: University of California Press, 1959); *Henderson v. United States,* 339 U.S. 816 (1950); *Brown v. Board of Education,* 347 U.S. 483 (1954).

96 Roy Wilkins to Harry S Truman, 12 Jan. 1953, OF, folder 596, box 1509, HSTL.

97 In June 1997, President Bill Clinton created an advisory board, chaired by the distinguished historian John Hope Franklin, to his Initiative on Race in America. Despite its best efforts, the board's work went largely ignored and was overshadowed by scandals and the impeachment of the president. See John Hope Franklin, "A Half-Century of Presidential Race Initiatives: Some Reflections," *Journal of Supreme Court History* 24 (1999): 226–37.

PART TWO

To Secure These Rights

The Report of the President's Committee on Civil Rights

". . . to secure these rights governments are instituted among men . . ."
—THE DECLARATION OF INDEPENDENCE

ASSIGNMENT FROM THE PRESIDENT

MR. PRESIDENT:
This is the report which we have prepared in accordance with the instructions which you gave to us in your statement and Executive Order on December 5, 1946:

Freedom From Fear is more fully realized in our country than in any other on the face of the earth. Yet all parts of our population are not equally free from fear. And from time to time, and in some places, this freedom has been gravely threatened. It was so after the last war, when organized groups fanned hatred and intolerance, until, at times, mob action struck fear into the hearts of men and women because of their racial origin or religious beliefs.

Note: The publication of the text contains the spelling and punctuation as found in the original document. Errors of spelling and punctuation have not been corrected in order to preserve the report's authenticity.

Today, Freedom From Fear, and the democratic institutions which sustain it, are again under attack. In some places, from time to time, the local enforcement of law and order has broken down, and individuals—sometimes ex-servicemen, even women—have been killed, maimed, or intimidated.

The preservation of civil liberties is a duty of every Government—state, Federal and local. Wherever the law enforcement measures and the authority of Federal, state, and local governments are inadequate to discharge this primary function of government, these measures and this authority should be strengthened and improved.

The Constitutional guarantees of individual liberties and of equal protection under the laws clearly place on the Federal Government the duty to act when state or local authorities abridge or fail to protect these Constitutional rights.

Yet in its discharge of the obligations placed on it by the Constitution, the Federal Government is hampered by inadequate civil rights statutes. The protection of our democratic institutions and the enjoyment by the people of their rights under the Constitution require that these weak and inadequate statutes should be expanded and improved. We must provide the Department of Justice with the tools to do the job.

I have, therefore, issued today an Executive Order creating the President's Committee on Civil Rights and I am asking this Committee to prepare for me a written report. The substance of this report will be recommendations with respect to the adoption or establishment by legislation or otherwise of more adequate and effective means and procedures for the protection of the civil rights of the people of the United States.

Executive Order 9808 Establishing the President's Committee on Civil Rights

WHEREAS the preservation of civil rights guaranteed by the Constitution is essential to domestic tranquility, national security, the general welfare, and the continued existence of our free institutions; and

WHEREAS the action of individuals who take the law into their own hands and inflict summary punishment and wreak personal vengeance is subversive of our democratic system of law enforcement and public criminal justice, and gravely threatens our form of government; and

WHEREAS it is essential that all possible steps be taken to safeguard our civil rights:

Now, THEREFORE, by virtue of the authority vested in me as President of the United States by the Constitution and the statutes of the United States, it is hereby ordered as follows:

1. There is hereby created a committee to be known as the President's Committee on Civil Rights, which shall be composed of the following-named members, who shall serve without compensation:

    Mr. C. E. Wilson, chairman; Mrs. Sadie T. Alexander, Mr. James B. Carey, Mr. John S. Dickey, Mr. Morris L. Ernst, Rabbi Roland B. Gittelsohn, Dr. Frank P. Graham, The Most Reverend Francis J. Haas, Mr. Charles Luckman, Mr. Francis P. Matthews, Mr. Franklin D. Roosevelt, Jr., The Right Reverend Henry Knox Sherrill, Mr. Boris Shishkin, Mrs. M. E. Tilly, Mr. Channing H. Tobias.

2. The Committee is authorized on behalf of the President to inquire into and to determine whether and in what respect current law-enforcement measures and the authority and means possessed by Federal, State, and local governments may be strengthened and improved to safeguard the civil rights of the people.

3. All executive departments and agencies of the Federal Government are authorized and directed to cooperate with the Committee in its work, and to furnish the Committee such information or the services of such persons as the Committee may require in the performance of its duties.

4. When requested by the Committee to do so, persons employed in any of the executive departments and agencies of the Federal Government shall testify before the Committee and shall make available for the use of the Committee such documents and other information as the Committee may require.

5. The Committee shall make a report of its studies to the President in writing, and shall in particular make recommendations with respect to the adoption or establishment, by legislation or otherwise, of more adequate and effective means and procedures for the protection of the civil rights of the people of the United States.

6. Upon rendition of its report to the President, the Committee shall cease to exist, unless otherwise determined by further Executive Order.

HARRY S. TRUMAN.

THE WHITE HOUSE, *December 5, 1946.*

The Committee's first task was the interpretation of its assignment. We were not asked to evaluate the extent to which civil rights have been achieved in our country. We did not, therefore, devote ourselves to the construction of a balance sheet which would properly assess the great progress which the nation has made, as well as the short-comings in the record. Instead, we have almost exclusively focused our attention on the bad side of our record — on what might be called the civil rights frontier.

This necessary emphasis upon our country's failures should not be permitted to obscure the real measure of its successes. No fair-minded student of American history, or of world history, will deny to the United States a position of leadership in enlarging the range of human liberties and rights, in recognizing and stating the ideals of freedom and equality, and in steadily and loyally working to make those ideals a reality. Whatever our failures in practice have been or may be, there has never been a time when the American people have doubted the validity of those ideals. We still regard them as vital to our democratic system.

If our task were to evaluate the level of achievement in our civil rights record, mention would have to be made of many significant developments in our history as a nation. We would want to refer to the steady progress toward the goal of universal suffrage which has marked the years between 1789 and the present. We would want to emphasize the disappearance of brutality from our society to a point where the occurrence of a single act of violence is a shocking event precisely because it is so out of keeping with our system of equal justice under law. And we would want to point to the building of our present economy which surely gives the individual greater social mobility, greater economic freedom of choice than any other nation has ever been able to offer.

But our purpose is not to praise our country's progress. We believe its impressive achievements must be used as a stimulus to further progress, rather than as an excuse for complacency.

At an early point in our work we decided to define our task broadly, to go beyond the specific flagrant outrages to which the President referred in his statement to the Committee. We have done this because these individual instances are only reflections of deeper maladies. We believe we must cure the disease as well as treat its symptoms. Moreover, we are convinced that the term "civil rights" itself has with great wisdom been used flexibly in American history.

For our present assignment we have found it appropriate to consolidate some individual freedoms under a single heading, to omit others altogether, and to stress still others which have in the past not been given prominence. Our decisions reflect what we consider to be the nation's most immediate needs. Civil rights, after all, are statements of aspirations, of demands which we make on ourselves and our society. We believe that the principles which underlie them are timeless. But we have selected for treatment those whose implementation is a pressing requirement. Throughout our report we have made use of specific data for illustrative purposes.

This report deals with serious civil rights violations in all sections of the country. Much of it has to do with limitations on civil rights in our southern states. To a great extent this reflects reality; many of the most sensational and serious violations of civil rights have taken place in the South. There are understandable historical reasons for this. Among the most obvious is the fact that the greater proportion of our largest, most visible minority group—the Negroes—live in the South.

In addition to this seeming stress on the problems of one region, many of our illustrations relate to the members of various minority groups, with particular emphasis upon Negroes. The reasons are obvious; these minorities have often had their civil rights abridged. Moreover, the unjust basis for these abridgements stands out sharply because of the distinctiveness of the groups. To place this apparent emphasis in its proper perspective one need only recall the history of bigotry and discrimination. At various times practically every region in the country has had its share of disgraceful interferences with the rights of some persons. At some time, members of practically every group have had their freedoms curtailed.

In our time the mobility of our population, including minority groups, is carrying certain of our civil rights problems to all parts of the country. In the near future it is likely that the movement of Negroes from rural to urban areas, and from the South to the rest of the country, will continue. Other minority groups, too, will probably move from their traditional centers of concentration. Unless we take appropriate action on a national scale, their civil rights problems will follow them.

The protection of civil rights is a national problem which affects everyone. We need to guarantee the same rights to every person regardless of who he is, where he lives, or what his racial, religious or national origins are.

This report covers a broad field and many complex and controversial matters. It is not to be expected that every member of the Committee would personally put every statement just as it appears here. The report does represent a general consensus of the Committee except on those two specific matters where a substantial division of views is reported.

The Committee held a series of public hearings at which the spokesmen for interested groups made statements and were questioned. We heard some witnesses in private meetings. A number of staff studies gave us additional information. Hundreds of communications were received from interested private citizens and organizations who were anxious to help us with their information and advice.

From all of this and our own discussions and deliberations we have sought answers to the following:

(1) What is the historic civil rights goal of the American people?

(2) In what ways does our present record fall short of the goal?

(3) What is government's responsibility for the achievement of the goal?

(4) What further steps does the nation now need to take to reach the goal?

Our report which follows is divided into four sections which provide our answers to these questions.

Sadie T. Alexander	Charles Luckman
James B. Carey	Francis P. Matthews
John S. Dickey	Franklin D. Roosevelt, Jr.
Morris L. Ernst	Henry Knox Sherrill
Roland B. Gittelsohn	Boris Shishkin
Frank P. Graham	Dorothy Tilly
Francis J. Haas	Channing Tobias

Charles E. Wilson, *Chairman*

I

The American Heritage: The Promise of Freedom and Equality

In the time that it takes to read this report, 1,000 Americans will be born. These new Americans will come into families whose religious faiths are a roster of all those which men hold sacred. Their names will be strange and varied, echoes from every corner of the world. Their skins will range in color from black to white. A few will be born to riches, more to average comfort, and too many to poverty. All of them will be Americans.

These new Americans, drawn from all of the races of mankind, provide a challenge to our American democracy. We have a great heritage of freedom and equality for all men, sometimes called "the American way." Yet we cannot avoid the knowledge that the American ideal still awaits complete realization.

It was this knowledge which led the President to create this Committee; and the Committee's assignment has been primarily to discover wherein and to what extent we are presently failing to live up to that ideal. As we have said, this has meant that in its deliberations, and in this report, the Committee has focused its attention, not upon our achievements in protecting our heritage of civil liberties, but upon our shortcomings and our mistakes. These the Committee has not minimized nor has it evaded the responsibility of recommending remedial action. A later section of this report summarizes some of the concrete gains which we have made in the more secure protection of freedom and equality. Further evidence of our adherence to our great heritage in this field is the desire of our government to have our national record carefully scrutinized in an effort to expose our shortcomings and to find ways of correcting them.

If we are to judge with accuracy how far short we have fallen in living up to the ideals which comprise our American heritage of freedom and equality, we must first make clear what that heritage is.

THE IDEAL OF FREEDOM AND EQUALITY

The central theme in our American heritage is the importance of the individual person. From the earliest moment of our history we have believed that every human being has an essential dignity and integrity which must be respected and safeguarded. Moreover, we believe that the welfare of the individual is the final goal of group life. Our American heritage further teaches that to be secure in the rights he wishes for himself, each man must be willing to respect the rights of other men. This is the conscious recognition of a basic moral principle: all men are created equal as well as free. Stemming from this principle is the obligation to build social institutions that will guarantee equality of opportunity to all men. Without this equality freedom becomes an illusion. Thus the only aristocracy that is consistent with the free way of life is an aristocracy of talent and achievement. The grounds on which our society accords respect, influence or reward to each of its citizens must be limited to the quality of his personal character and of his social contribution.

This concept of equality which is so vital a part of the American heritage knows no kinship with notions of human uniformity or regimentation. We abhor the totalitarian arrogance which makes one man say that he will respect another man as his equal only if he has "*my* race, *my* religion, *my* political views, *my* social position." In our land men are equal, but they are free to be different. From these very differences among our people has come the great human and national strength of America.

Thus, the aspirations and achievements of each member of our society are to be limited only by the skills and energies he brings to the opportunities equally offered to all Americans. We can tolerate no restrictions upon the individual which depend upon irrelevant factors such as his race, his color, his religion or the social position to which he is born.

GOVERNMENT AND FREEDOM

The men who founded our Republic, as those who have built any constitutional democracy, faced the task of reconciling personal liberty and group authority, or of establishing an equilibrium between them. In a democratic state we recognize that the common interests of the people must be managed by laws and procedures established by majority rule. But a democratic majority, left unrestrained, may be as ruthless and tyrannical as were the earlier absolute monarchs. Seeing this clearly, and fearing it greatly, our forefathers built a constitutional system in which valued personal liberties, carefully enumerated in a Bill of Rights, were placed beyond the reach of popular majorities. Thus the people permanently denied the federal government power to interfere with certain personal rights and freedoms.

Freedom, however, as we now use the term, means even more than the traditional "freedoms" listed in our Bill of Rights—important as they are. Freedom has come to mean the right of a man to manage his own affairs as he sees fit up to the point where what he does interferes with the equal rights of others in the community to manage their affairs—or up to the point where he begins to injure the welfare of the whole group. It is clear that in modern democratic society a man's freedom in this broader sense is not and cannot be absolute—nor does it exist in a vacuum—but instead is hedged about by the competing rights of others and the demands of the social welfare. In this context it is government which must referee the clashes which arise among the freedoms of citizens, and protect each citizen in the enjoyment of the maximum freedom to which he is entitled.

There is no essential conflict between freedom and government. Bills of rights restrain government from abridging individual civil liberties, while government itself by sound legislative policies protects citizens against the aggressions of others seeking to push their freedoms too far. Thus in the words of the Declaration of Independence: "Man is endowed by his Creator with certain inalienable rights. Among these are life, liberty, and the pursuit of happiness. To secure these rights, *governments are instituted among men.*"

THE ESSENTIAL RIGHTS

The rights essential to the citizen in a free society can be described in different words and in varying orders, The three great rights of the Declaration of Independence have just been mentioned. Another noble statement is made in the Bill of Rights of our Constitution. A more recent formulation is found in the Four Freedoms.

Four basic rights have seemed important to this Committee and have influenced its labors. We believe that each of these rights is essential to the well-being of the individual and to the progress of society.

I. The Right to Safety and Security of the Person

Freedom can exist only where the citizen is assured that his person is secure against bondage, lawless violence, and arbitrary arrest and punishment. Freedom from slavery in all its forms is clearly necessary if all men are to have equal opportunity to use their talents and to lead worthwhile lives. Moreover, to be free, men must be subject to discipline by society only for commission of offenses clearly defined by law and only after trial by due process of law. Where the administration of justice is discriminatory, no man can be sure of security. Where the threat of violence by private persons or mobs exists, a cruel inhibition of the sense of freedom of activity and security of the person inevitably results. Where a society permits private and arbitrary violence to be done to its members, its own integrity is inevitably corrupted. It cannot permit human beings to be imprisoned or killed in the absence of due process of law without degrading its entire fabric.

2. The Right to Citizenship and its Privileges

Since it is a purpose of government in a democracy to regulate the activity of each man in the interest of all men, it follows that every mature and responsible person must be able to enjoy full citizenship and have an equal voice in his government. Because the right to participate in the political process is customarily limited to citizens there can be no denial of access to citizenship based upon race, color, creed, or national origin. Denial of citizenship for these reasons cheapens the personality of those who are confined to this inferior status and endangers the whole concept of a democratic society.

To deny qualified citizens the right to vote while others exercise it is to do violence to the principle of freedom and equality. Without the right to vote, the individual loses his voice in the group effort and is subjected to rule by a body from which he has been excluded. Likewise, the right of the individual to vote is important to the group itself. Democracy assumes that the majority is more likely as a general rule to make decisions which are wise and desirable from the point of view of the interests of the whole society than is any minority. Every time a qualified person is denied a voice in public affairs, one of the components of a potential majority is lost, and the formation of a sound public policy is endangered.

To the citizen in a democracy, freedom is a precious possession. Accordingly, all able-bodied citizens must enjoy the right to serve the nation and the cause of freedom in time of war. Any attempt to curb the right to fight in its defense can only lead the citizen to question the worth of the society in which he lives. A sense of frustration is created which is wholly alien to the normal emotions of a free man. In particular, any discrimination which, while imposing an obligation, prevents members of minority groups from rendering full military service in defense of their country is for them a peculiarly humiliating badge of inferiority. The nation also suffers a loss of manpower and is unable to marshal maximum strength at a moment when such strength is most needed.

3. The Right to Freedom of Conscience and Expression

In a free society there is faith in the ability of the people to make sound, rational judgments. But such judgments are possible only where the people have access to all relevant facts and to all prevailing interpretations of the facts. How can such judgments be formed on a sound basis if arguments, viewpoints, or opinions are arbitrarily suppressed? How can the concept of the marketplace of thought in which truth ultimately prevails retain its validity if the thought of certain individuals is denied the right of circulation? The Committee reaffirms our tradition that freedom of expression may be curbed by law only where the danger to the well-being of society is clear and present.

Our forefathers fought bloody wars and suffered torture and death for the right to worship God according to the varied dictates of conscience. Complete religious liberty has been accepted as an unquestioned personal freedom since our Bill of Rights was adopted. We have insisted only that religious freedom may not be pleaded as an excuse for criminal or clearly anti-social conduct.

4. The Right to Equality of Opportunity

It is not enough that full and equal membership in society entitles the individual to an equal voice in the control of his government; it must also give him the right to enjoy the benefits of society and to contribute to its progress. The opportunity of each individual to obtain useful employment, and to have access to services in the fields of education, housing, health, recreation and transportation, whether available free or at a price, must be provided with complete disregard for race, color, creed, and national origin. Without this equality of opportunity the individual is deprived of the chance to develop his potentialities and to share the fruits of society. The group also suffers through the loss of the contributions which might have been made by persons excluded from the main channels of social and economic activity.

THE HERITAGE AND THE REALITY

Our American heritage of freedom and equality has given us prestige among the nations of the world and a strong feeling of national pride at home. There is much reason for that pride. But pride is no substitute for steady and honest performance, and the record shows that at varying times in American history the gulf between ideals and practice has been wide. We have had human slavery. We have had religious persecution. We have had mob rule. We still have their ideological remnants in the unwarrantable "pride and prejudice" of some of our people and practices. From our work as a Committee, we have learned much that has shocked us, and much that has made us feel ashamed. But we have seen nothing to shake our conviction that the civil rights of the American people—all of them—can be strengthened quickly and effectively by the normal processes of democratic, constitutional government. That strengthening, we believe, will make our daily life more and more consonant with the spirit of the American heritage of freedom. But it will require as much courage, as much imagination, as much perseverance as anything which we have ever done together. The members of this Committee reaffirm their faith in the American heritage and in its promise.

II
The Record: Short of the Goal

The heritage which we have reviewed has been forged by many men through several centuries. In that time the face of our nation has changed almost beyond recognition. New lands, new peoples, new institutions have brought new problems. Again and again the promise of freedom and equality has found new forms of expression, new frameworks of meaning. The goal still remains clear although it is yet to be reached.

The record is neither as black as our detractors paint it, nor as white as people of good will would like it to be. To a large extent the light and dark shades in the picture are a reflection of the nature of our people. The phrase, "civil rights", is an abbreviation for a whole complex of relationships among individuals and among groups. We cannot properly understand the American civil rights record without giving attention to the composition of the American people.

OUR DIVERSE POPULATION

America has been populated by immigrants from many nations on four continents. Some of these people have disappeared in the larger population. Others, for various reasons, have persisted as "minorities." All have shaped with their hands, with their minds, and with their hearts the character of our national life. The cultural diversity of the United States has flavored the whole political, economic, and social development of the nation. Our science, our industry, our art, our music, our philosophy have been formed and enriched by peoples from throughout the world.

Our diversity, however, has had one disadvantage. The fact that the forebears of some of us arrived in America later than those of others, the fact that some of us have lived in separate groups, and the fact that some of us have different customs and religious beliefs, or different

55

skin colors, have too often been seized upon as justification for discrimination.

A minority, broadly defined, is a group which is treated or which regards itself as a people apart. It is distinguishable by cultural or physical characteristics, or both. The extent to which it can be distinguished usually indicates its degree of apartness. On the other hand, minority lines in the United States often cut across one another. For example, south European immigrant groups are minority groups in relation to older, English-speaking immigrants. But they are part of the white majority in relation to the Negro minority. Members of religious minorities may belong either to minorities or majorities, based on race or national origin.

The dominant majority in the United States is Caucasian, English-speaking, Protestant, and of comparatively distant Anglo-Saxon or European background. This majority outnumbers any particular minority group, although its dominant position is less apparent when the minorities are added together.

Since the colonial period, two great streams of European immigration have peopled the country. The first was from northern and western Europe, and the second, lasting from the end of the Civil War to the end of World War I, from southern and eastern Europe. Immigrants are no longer allowed to come in the vast numbers of the past. However, one out of every four Americans is still either a foreign-born white or the child of foreign-born white parents. One out of every five white Americans speaks some language other than English in his home.

Religious differences among Americans have in the past been closely allied with national origin. The bulk of the early population was Protestant, although there were some Catholics and small numbers of Jews among the settlers. The second great stream of southern and eastern Europeans included large numbers of Catholics and Jews.

Of those people in the United States who are church members, a majority are Protestants. In certain sections of the country, however, the majority becomes the minority. For example, in Boston the great majority are Catholics, and Protestants are a minority. The largest religious minorities in the country as a whole are the Catholics and the Jews. Identification of people as Catholics tends to rest on their affiliation with the Church, just as it does with Protestants. Jews, however, are usually identified as being Jewish if it is known that some of their ancestors belonged to that religious tradition. There are a myriad of

Protestant denominations and other religions, any one of which may be considered a minority.

Groups whose colors makes them more easily identified are set apart from the "dominant majority" much more than are the Caucasian minorities. The Negroes are by far the largest of these groups. They were brought here from almost the very beginning of our history, in small numbers as indentured servants and in larger numbers as slaves. Many were freed before the Civil War, but most of them were emancipated at that time. Today, one in every ten Americans is a Negro. Our other racial minorities are all much smaller than the thirteen million Negroes. But these groups, identified by physical appearance, unique culture traits, or both, are often geographically concentrated. As a result, irrespective of their small number in the total population, theirs are the predominant civil rights problems in particular localities.

The great majority of immigrants to the United States from other American countries have been Mexicans, who began entering this country around the turn of the century. Although Mexicans and persons of Mexican descent, numbering over a million and a quarter, have found their way to all sections of the country, more than three-fourths of them have settled in Texas and California.

Two of the oldest minority groups in the country are the Indians and the Hispanos. The great majority, but by no means all, of the 400,000 Indians live on reservations. The diversity of their original native cultures is reflected in the present groups. From reservation to reservation Indian life varies. The Hispanos of New Mexico and southern Colorado are descendants of the first Spanish settlers in the Rio Grande Valley, and still live in many ways as the early settlers did. There are about 250,000 of them, and they form a majority of the population in some parts of New Mexico.

At the time of the second stream of European immigration, we were also drawing immigrants from the Far East, mainly from China and Japan. All of them faced the same problems as did the European immigrants, greatly intensified by physical characteristics which no amount of acceptance of western ways could change. The Chinese came, mostly from Canton, in the middle of the nineteenth century. They were followed by the Japanese in the last decade of that century, and the first two of the present one. The Filipinos came still later. In 1940 there were about 127,000 persons of Japanese descent in the United States, 77,000 of Chinese descent, 45,000 of Filipino origin, and small groups from India and Korea. Before the war the largest of these groups was concentrated on the West Coast, where the bulk of Chinese Americans and Filipino Americans still live. Over a third of the Japanese Americans who had lived on the West Coast before they were evacuated during the war have chosen to make their homes in the East and Midwest.

Our diverse population also includes the inhabitants of areas administered by the United States: Hawaii, Alaska, Puerto Rico, the Virgin Islands, Guam, American Samoa, the Trust Territory of the Pacific and the Panama Canal Zone. More than 2,500,000 people live in these dependent areas. They include Caucasians, Negroes, Asians, Eskimos, Indians, Polynesians and Micronesians. Of these peoples, only the Puerto Ricans have immigrated in substantial numbers to the mainland. By 1940, 150,000 had entered the country, and since then the rate of immigration has increased tremendously. Most of them have settled in New York City.

The varied nature of our population has resulted in differing relationships among groups and individuals. In many cases persons of different races or cultures have shown a high respect for each other, thereby reflecting our belief in equality. But other relationships have been characterized by prejudice and hostility and have reflected our failure to live up to that belief. In this report we are not concerned with the civil rights of particular minority groups as such. We are concerned with the civil rights of Americans no matter who they are. The record shows, however, that the civil rights of certain minority groups have been in particular danger. After noting some signs of recent progress, we shall turn to a lengthier analysis of the condition of our rights.

SIGNS OF RECENT PROGRESS

Since the assignment of this Committee is to recommend ways of strengthening the civil rights of all of the people, we have naturally made it our business to consider the ways in which they are weak. We repeat that it would be a grievous mistake to misread this as meaning that there is nothing in our record of which to be proud. There is a great deal; enough, we believe, to warrant our conviction that no nation in history has ever offered more hope of the final realization of the ultimate ideal of freedom and equality than has ours. In no other nation have so many people come as close to this ideal as in America.

There are many signs of progress and portents of still more to come. Some of these signs will now be noted; others will be referred to as the condition of our rights is examined.

The Committee believes that the greatest hope for the future is the increasing awareness by more and more Americans of the gulf between our civil rights principles and our practices. Only a free people can continually question and appraise the adequacy of its institutions.

Over the past years, leaders of opinion—in public life, in our press, radio, and motion pictures, in the churches, in the schools and colleges, in business, in trade unions, and in the professions—have recognized their responsibility to act effectively in their own lives and to work to strengthen civil rights. The Committee has been much impressed by the number and work of private organizations whose chief aim is the furtherance of freedom. They have accomplished much and are entitled to a great deal of credit for their work. The existence of several groups in the South which are working for the advancement of civil rights is particularly heartening. Their courageous, unceasing efforts have already produced impressive results which surely foreshadow still further progress. We are also encouraged by the number of communities which have established official bodies to better the relations among their people and to protect the rights of their minorities.

The existence of these private agencies is a sign of the fundamental vigor of our democracy, and of our resourcefulness in devising techniques for self-help. These private agencies have rendered invaluable service to this Committee. Almost without exception, however, all of these groups have indicated to us a belief that their own educational efforts are not enough, and that increased federal protection of civil rights is needed. They see no conflict between leadership by the national government and private local enterprise in the safeguarding of civil rights.

The past decade—particularly the war years—gives us much reason for confidence in the ability of our nation to better its civil rights record even in the midst of crisis. Equality of opportunity came closer to reality for many members of minority groups during this recent period. A few forward-looking state and local governments have acted to conserve these gains and even move ahead. New York State, in particular, has an impressive variety of civil rights laws on its statute books. A few other states and cities have followed suit, especially in the fair employment practice field. The voluntary elimination of racial bans or differentials in employment practices by many business concerns, and the employment of Negro baseball players by teams in both major leagues, deserve high praise.

Similarly, one recent survey of Negro progress, made by Charles S. Johnson, and appropriately entitled "Into the Main Stream," reports that ". . . the biggest single forward surge of Negroes into the main stream of American life in the past ten years has been their movement into the ranks of organized labor." Mention should also be made of the ending of segregated schools in cities like Trenton and Gary; the lifting of restrictions against Negro doctors by hospitals in St. Louis and Gary; the establishment of interracial churches in many communities; and the employment of more than three-score Negro teachers by twenty-five white or predominantly white colleges.

A dramatic, and far from unimportant recent incident was the handling of a threatened rebellion against the presence of a Negro player on the Brooklyn Dodgers by members of another team. It is reported that the president of the National League dealt with the recalcitrant players firmly and with dispatch. He is reported to have said:

> If you do this you will be suspended from the league. You will find that the friends you think you have in the press box will not support you, that you will be outcasts. I do not care if half the league strikes. Those who do it will encounter quick retribution. All will be suspended and I don't care if it wrecks the National League for 5 years. This is the United States of America and one citizen has as much right to play as another.

Some officers high in the ranks of the armed forces have shown a heartening recognition of the need to make the Army, Navy, Air Forces, and the Coast Guard more representative of the democracy whose defense they are. We must not lose sight of the fact that compared with the situation in previous wars, this one reflected sharp improvement in the utilization of minority groups.

The freedom of most of our people to seek the truth and express themselves freely is a vigorous, healthy reality. No press has ever been freer of government control than is ours. Freedom of religion, aside from discrimination against the members of one or two sects, is today remarkably secure.

With respect to freedom of expression, it is particularly noteworthy that we were able to pass through four years of total warfare without serious inroads on this right. This was done in spite of the prediction of many that our free society would not be able to stand the strain of another war.

In the political arena, members of minority groups are increasingly taking advantage of the protection of their right to the ballot by the courts and the national government. Particularly encouraging are reports of increased voting by Negroes in many southern states, both in primary and general elections.

Efforts to professionalize state and local police forces are also encouraging. California and North Carolina among the states, and Chicago among the cities especially deserve mention in this connection, as does the FBI's National Police Academy. Mention should also be made of the employment of Negroes as police officers in some two-score southern cities, and of a growing tendency of southern courts to see that the law is enforced impartially and equal justice done to all.

Finally, the Committee wishes to call attention to the very substantial and steady decline in the number of lynchings which has occurred in the last two decades. From a high point of 64 lynchings in 1921, the figure fell during the 1920's to a low of 10 in 1928. During the decade of the 1930's the total climbed again to a high of 28 in 1933, although the decade ended with a low of 3 in 1939. Since 1940, the annual figure has never exceeded 6; on the other hand, there has not yet been a year in which America has been completely free of the crime of lynching. The Committee believes that the striking improvement in the record is a thing to be devoutly thankful for; but it also believes that a single lynching is one too many!

THE CONDITION OF OUR RIGHTS

1. The Right to Safety and Security of the Person

Vital to the integrity of the individual and to the stability of a democratic society is the right of each individual to physical freedom, to security against illegal violence, and to fair, orderly legal process. Most Americans enjoy this right, but it is not yet secure for all. Too many of our people still live under the harrowing fear of violence or death at the hands of a mob or of brutal treatment by police officers. Many fear entanglement with the law because of the knowledge that the justice rendered in some courts is not equal for all persons. In a few areas the freedom to move about and choose one's job is endangered by attempts to hold workers in peonage or other forms of involuntary servitude.

THE CRIME OF LYNCHING

In 1946 at least six persons in the United States were lynched by mobs. Three of them had not been charged, either by the police or anyone else, with an offense. Of the three that had been charged, one had been accused of stealing a saddle. (The real thieves were discovered after the lynching.) Another was said to have broken into a house. A third was charged with stabbing a man. All were Negroes. During the same year, mobs were prevented from lynching 22 persons, of whom 21 were Negroes, 1 white.

On July 20, 1946, a white farmer, Loy Harrison, posted bond for the release of Roger Malcolm from the jail at Monroe, Georgia. Malcolm, a young Negro, had been involved in a fight with his white employer during the course of which the latter had been stabbed. It is reported that there was talk of lynching Malcolm at the time of the incident and while he was in jail. Upon Malcolm's release, Harrison started to drive Malcolm, Malcolm's wife, and a Negro overseas veteran, George Dorsey, and his wife, out of Monroe. At a bridge along the way a large group of unmasked white men, armed with pistols and shotguns, was waiting. They stopped Harrison's car and removed Malcolm and Dorsey. As they were leading the two men away, Harrison later stated, one of the women called out the name of a member of the mob. Thereupon the lynchers returned and removed the two women from the car. Three volleys of shots were fired as if by a squad of professional executioners. The coroner's report said that at least 60 bullets were found in the scarcely recognizable bodies. Harrison consistently denied that he could identify any of the unmasked murderers. State and federal grand juries reviewed the evidence in the case, but no person has yet been indicted for the crime.

Later that summer, in Minden, Louisiana, a young Negro named John Jones was arrested on suspicion of housebreaking. Another Negro youth, Albert Harris, was arrested at about the same time, and beaten in an effort to implicate Jones. He was then released, only to be rearrested after a few days. On August 6th, early in the evening, and before there had been any trial of the charges against them, Jones and Harris were released by a deputy sheriff. Waiting in the jail yard was a group of white men. There was evidence that, with the aid of the deputy sheriff, the young men were put into a car. They were then driven into the country. Jones was beaten to death. Harris, left for

ALTHOUGH LYNCHING HAS DECLINED SHARPLY...
NO YEAR SINCE 1882 HAS BEEN FREE OF IT!

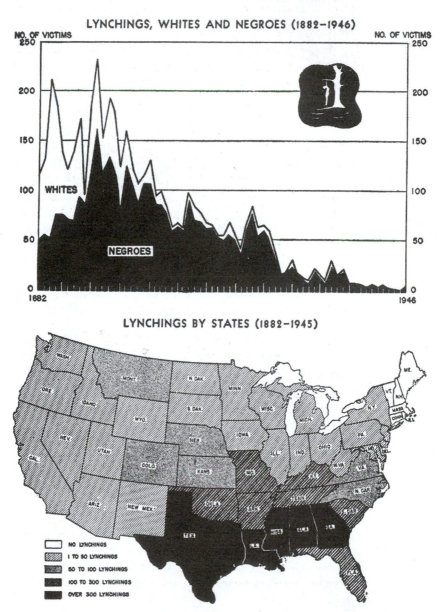

LYNCHINGS, WHITES AND NEGROES (1882–1946)

NO. OF VICTIMS

WHITES

NEGROES

1882

1946

LYNCHINGS BY STATES (1882–1945)

NO LYNCHINGS
1 TO 50 LYNCHINGS
50 TO 100 LYNCHINGS
100 TO 300 LYNCHINGS
OVER 300 LYNCHINGS

dead, revived and escaped. Five persons, including two deputy sheriffs, were indicted and brought to trial in a federal court for this crime. All were acquitted.

These are two of the less brutal lynchings of the past years. The victims in these cases were not mutilated or burned.

The record for 1947 is incomplete. There has been one lynching, one case in which the victim escaped, and other instances where mobs have been unable to accomplish their purpose. On February 17, 1947, a Negro youth named Willie Earle, accused of fatally stabbing a taxi driver in the small city of Greenville, South Carolina, was removed from jail by a mob, viciously beaten and finally shot to death. In an unusual and impressive instance of state prosecution, 31 men were tried for this crime. All were acquitted on the evening of May 21, 1947. Early the next morning, in Jackson, North Carolina, another Negro youth, Godwin Bush, arrested on a charge of approaching a white woman, was removed from a local jail by a mob, after having been exhibited through the town by the sheriff. Bush succeeded in escaping from his abductors, and, after hiding for two days in nearby woods, was able to surrender himself safely into the custody of FBI agents and officers of the state. The Committee finds it encouraging to note that the Governor of North Carolina has made vigorous efforts to bring to justice those responsible for this attempted lynching.

While available statistics show that, decade by decade, lynchings have decreased, this Committee has found that in the year 1947 lynching remains one of the most serious threats to the civil rights of Americans. It is still possible for a mob to abduct and murder a person in some sections of the country with almost certain assurance of escaping punishment for the crime. The decade from 1936 through 1946 saw at least 43 lynchings. No person received the death penalty, and the majority of the guilty persons were not even prosecuted.

The communities in which lynchings occur tend to condone the crime. Punishment of lynchers is not accepted as the responsibility of state or local governments in these communities. Frequently, state officials participate in the crime, actively or passively. Federal efforts to punish the crime are resisted. Condonation of lynching is indicated by the failure of some local law enforcement officials to make adequate efforts to break up a mob. It is further shown by failure in most cases to make any real effort to apprehend or try those guilty. If the federal government enters a case, local officials sometimes actively resist the federal investigation. Local citizens often combine to impede the effort to apprehend the criminals by convenient "loss of memory";

grand juries refuse to indict; trial juries acquit in the face of over-whelming proof of guilt.

The large number of attempted lynchings highlights, even more than those which have succeeded, the widespread readiness of many communities to resort to mob violence. Thus, for seven of the years from 1937 to 1946 for which statistics are reported, the conservative estimates of the Tuskegee Institute show that 226 persons were res-cued from threatened lynching. Over 200 of these were Negroes.

Most rescues from lynchings are made by local officials. There is heartening evidence that an ever-increasing number of these officers have the will and the courage to defend their prisoners against mob action. But this reflects only partial progress toward adequate law enforcement. In some instances lynchers are dissuaded by promises that the desired result will be accomplished "legally" and the machin-ery of justice is sometimes sensitive to the demands of such implied bargains. In some communities there is more official zeal to avoid mob violence which will injure the reputation of the community than there is to protect innocent persons.

The devastating consequences of lynchings go far beyond what is shown by counting the victims. When a person is lynched and the lynchers go unpunished, thousands wonder where the evil will appear again and what mischance may produce another victim. And every time lynchers go unpunished, Negroes have learned to expect other forms of violence at the hands of private citizens or public officials. In describing the thwarted efforts of the Department of Justice to identify those responsible for one lynching, J. Edgar Hoover stated to the Committee: "The arrogance of most of the white population of that county was unbelievable, and the fear of the Negroes was almost unbelievable."

The almost complete immunity from punishment enjoyed by lynch-ers is merely a striking form of the broad and general immunity from punishment enjoyed by whites in many communities for less extreme offenses against Negroes. Moreover, lynching is the ultimate threat by which his inferior status is driven home to the Negro. As a terrorist device, it reinforces all the other disabilities placed upon him. The threat of lynching always hangs over the head of the southern Negro; the knowledge that a misinterpreted word or action can lead to his death is a dreadful burden.

POLICE BRUTALITY

We have reported the failure of some public officials to fulfill their most elementary duty—the protection of persons against mob violence.

We must also report more widespread and varied forms of official misconduct. These include violent physical attacks by police officers on members of minority groups, the use of third degree methods to extort confessions, and brutality against prisoners. Civil rights violations of this kind are by no means universal and many law enforcement agencies have gone far in recent years toward stamping out these evils.

In various localities, scattered throughout the country, unprofessional or undisciplined police, while avoiding brutality, fail to recognize and to safeguard the civil rights of the citizenry. Insensitive to the necessary limits of police authority, untrained officers frequently overstep the bounds of their proper duties. At times this appears in unwarranted arrests, unduly prolonged detention before arraignment, and abuse of the search and seizure power. Cases involving these breaches of civil rights constantly come before the courts. The frequency with which such cases arise is proof that improper police conduct is still widespread, for it must be assumed that there are many instances of the abuse of police power which do not reach the courts. Most of the victims of such abuses are ignorant, friendless persons, unaware of their rights, and without the means of challenging those who have violated those rights.

Where lawless police forces exist, their activities may impair the civil rights of any citizen. In one place the brunt of illegal police activity may fall on suspected vagrants, in another on union organizers, and in another on unpopular racial or religious minorities, such as Negroes, Mexicans, or Jehovah's Witnesses. But wherever unfettered police lawlessness exists, civil rights may be vulnerable to the prejudices of the region or of dominant local groups, and to the caprice of individual policemen. Unpopular, weak, or defenseless groups are most apt to suffer.

Considerable evidence in the files of the Department of Justice supports this assertion. For example, in one case in 1945 a group of white juvenile offenders made an abortive effort to escape from a midwestern prison. The attempt was quickly and fairly easily subdued. In the course of the attempt a trusty was injured. The prison officials, after rounding up the boys, allowed other trusties to vent their anger at the injury to their comrade by physically attacking the defenseless prisoners. After this had occurred the boys were then severely beaten, one by one, by the prison officials.

Much of the illegal official action which has been brought to the attention of the Committee is centered in the South. There is evidence of lawless police action against whites and Negroes alike, but the dominant pattern is that of race prejudice. J. Edgar Hoover referred, in his testimony before the Committee, to a particular jail where "it was seldom that a Negro man or women was incarcerated who was not given a severe beating, which started off with a pistol whipping and ended with a rubber hose."

The files of the Department abound with evidence of illegal official action in southern states. In one case, the victim was arrested on a charge of stealing a tire, taken to the courthouse, beaten by three officers with a blackjack until his head was a bloody pulp, and then dragged unconscious through the streets to the jail where he was thrown, dying, onto the floor. In another case, a constable arrested a Negro, against whom he bore a personal grudge, beat him brutally with a bullwhip and then forced his victim, in spite of his protestations of being unable to swim, to jump into a river where he drowned. In a third case, there was evidence that officers arrested a Negro maid on a charge of stealing jewelry from her employer, took her to jail and severely beat and whipped her in an unsuccessful effort to extort a confession. All of these cases occurred within the last five years.

There are other cases in the files of the Department of Justice of officers who seem to be "trigger-happy" where weak or poor persons are concerned. In a number of instances, Negroes have been shot, supposedly in self-defense, under circumstances indicating, at best, unsatisfactory police work in the handling of criminals, and, at worst, a callous willingness to kill.

Toward the end of the work of this Committee a particularly shocking instance of this occurred. On July 11, 1947, eight Negro prisoners in the State highway prison camp in Glynn County, Georgia, were killed by their white guards as they allegedly attempted to escape. The Glynn County grand jury exonerated the warden of the camp and four guards of all charges. At later hearings on the highway prison camp system held by the State Board of Corrections, conflicting evidence was presented. But one witness testified that there was no evidence that the prisoners were trying to escape. In any case, he said it was not necessary to use guns on them in the circumstances. "There was no justification for the killing. I saw the Negroes where they fell. Two were killed where they crawled under the bunkhouse and two others as they ran under their cells. The only thing they were trying to escape was death. Only one tried to get over the fence." The warden and four guards were indicted by a federal grand jury on October 1, 1947.

It is difficult to accept at face value police claims in cases of this type that action has been taken against prisoners in "self defense" or to "prevent escape." Even if these protestations are accepted, the incidence of shooting in the ordinary course of law enforcement in some sections of the country is a serious reflection on these police forces. Other officers in other places seem able to enforce the law and to guard prisoners without resort to violent means.

The total picture—adding the connivance of some police officials in lynchings to their record of brutality against Negroes in other situations—is, in the opinion of this Committee, a serious reflection on American justice. We know that Americans everywhere deplore this violence. We recognize further that there are many law enforcement officers in the South and the North who do not commit violent acts against Negroes or other friendless culprits. We are convinced, however, that the incidence of police brutality against Negroes is disturbingly high.

ADMINISTRATION OF JUSTICE

In addition to the treatment experienced by the weak and friendless person at the hands of police officers, he sometimes finds that the judicial process itself does not give him full and equal justice. This may appear in unfair and perfunctory trials, or in fines and prison sentences that are heavier than those imposed on other members of the community guilty of the same offenses.

In part, the inability of the Negro, Mexican, or Indian to obtain equal justice may be attributed to extrajudicial factors. The low income of a member of any one of these minorities may prevent him from securing competent counsel to defend his rights. It may prevent him from posting bail or bond to secure his release from jail during trial. It may predetermine his choice, upon conviction, of paying a fine or going to jail. But these facts should not obscure or condone the extent to which the judicial system itself is responsible for the less-than-equal justice meted out to members of certain minority groups.

The United States Supreme Court in a number of recent decisions has censured state courts for accepting evidence procured by third-degree methods, for failing to provide accused persons with adequate legal counsel, and for excluding Negroes from jury lists. For example, in one of these cases, *Chambers v. Florida,* the Supreme Court, in 1940, set aside the conviction by the state court of four young Negroes on the ground that it should have rejected confessions extorted from

the accused by the use of third degree methods. The Court referred
to the basic principle that "all people must stand on an equality before
the bar of justice in each American court." It added:

> Today, as in ages past, we are not without tragic proof that the
> exalted power of some governments to punish manufactured crime
> dictatorially is the handmaid of tyranny. Under our constitutional
> system, courts stand against any winds that blow as havens of
> refuge for those who might otherwise suffer because they are help-
> less, weak, outnumbered, or because they are nonconforming vic-
> tims of prejudice and public excitement. Due process of law,
> preserved for all by our Constitution, commands that no such prac-
> tice as that disclosed by this record shall send any accused to his
> death. No higher duty, no more solemn responsibility, rests upon
> this Court, than that of translating into living law and maintaining
> this constitutional shield deliberately planned and inscribed for the
> benefit of every human being subject to our Constitution—of what-
> ever race, creed, or persuasion.

It is particularly unfortunate that the jury system has not always
served to protect the right of the minority member to a fair trial. All
too frequently trial by a jury of one's peers has no meaning for these
persons because of the complete absence of people of their own kind
from jury lists. While the Supreme Court and other appellate tribunals
have reversed convictions made by juries selected from lists from
which whole minority groups have been excluded, techniques of
exclusion continue to be employed. For example, Pauline Kibbe, in
her 1946 study of Latin Americans in Texas, states:

> In an estimated 50 counties where the Latin American population
> ranges from 15 to 40 percent, persons of Mexican descent have
> never been known to be called for jury service, even in the trial of
> civil suits.

The use of the fee system in many communities—where court officials are paid in whole or in part from the fines levied—also sometimes stimulates arbitrary arrests and encourages unjust convictions.
It is the unpopular minorities again that suffer most from this system,
since it is relatively easy for unscrupulous, fee-seeking officers to "railroad" such persons to jail. The existence of the fee system and the
frontier conditions in certain areas of Alaska contribute to discrimination against Indians and Eskimos in the administration of justice there.
The situation is such that federal officials are seriously considering a

proposal made by the Governor of Alaska to appoint a public defender for those groups.

The different standards of justice which we have allowed to exist in our country have had further repercussions. In certain states, the white population can threaten and do violence to the minority member with little or no fear of legal reprisal. Minority groups are sometimes convinced that they cannot expect fair treatment from the legal machinery. Because of this belief they may harbor and protect any of their members accused of crime. Their experience does not lead them to look upon the courts as "havens of refuge" for the victims of prejudice and public excitement.

INVOLUNTARY SERVITUDE

Slavery was abolished in this country nearly a century ago, and in its traditional form has disappeared. But the temptation to force poor and defenseless persons, by one device or another, into a condition of virtual slavery, still exists. As recently as 1944, in the case of *Pollock v. Williams,* the Supreme Court struck down as a violation of the Thirteenth Amendment to the Constitution an Alabama statute which enabled employers to force employees, in debt on account of advanced wage payments, to continue to work for them under threat of criminal punishment. This is one of the more subtle devices for securing forced labor. More direct is the practice whereby sheriffs in some areas free prisoners into the custody of local enterpreneurs who pay fines or post bonds. The prisoners then work for their "benefactors" under threat of returning to jail. Sometimes the original charge against the prisoners is trumped up for the purpose of securing labor by this means. In still other instances persons have been held in peonage by sheer force or by threats of prosecution for debt.

Since the Civil Rights Section was established in 1939, a widespread decline in peonage and involuntary servitude has occurred. However, the threat has not entirely disappeared. In 1945, the Department of Justice prosecuted a case in which a Negro woman and her ten year old son had been held in captivity by a Mississippi farmer. Forced to work on a farm by day, they were locked in a crude, windowless, chimneyless cabin by night. The mother had made three unsuccessful efforts to escape before federal authorities were informed of the situation. And as recently as 1947, an involuntary servitude case was successfully prosecuted by the federal government in California.

Where large numbers of people are frightened, uneducated, and underprivileged, the dangers of involuntary servitude remain. If economic conditions deteriorate, a more general recurrence of peonage may be anticipated.

THE WARTIME EVACUATION OF JAPANESE AMERICANS

The most striking mass interference since slavery with the right to physical freedom was the evacuation and exclusion of persons of Japanese descent from the West Coast during the past war. The evacuation of 110,000 men, women and children, two-thirds of whom were United States citizens, was made without a trial or any sort of hearing, at a time when the courts were functioning. These people were ordered out of a large section of the country and detained in "relocation centers." This evacuation program was carried out at the direction of the Commanding General of the West Coast Command, who acted under an Executive Order authorizing the Secretary of War and the military commanders to prescribe military areas from which any person or group could be excluded.

The ground given for the evacuation was that the military security of the nation demanded the exclusion of potentially disloyal people from the West Coast. We have not felt that it would be proper or feasible for this Committee to try to review all of the facts of the evacuation program. We remember well the doubts and fears of the early months of the war and we recognize that the evacuation policy seemed a necessary precaution to many at the time. But we are disturbed by the implications of this episode so far as the future of American civil rights is concerned. Fundamental to our whole system of law is the belief that guilt is personal and not a matter of heredity or association. Yet in this instance no specific evacuees were charged with disloyalty, espionage or sedition. The evacuation, in short, was not a criminal proceeding involving individuals, but a sort of mass quarantine measure. This Committee believes that further study should be given to this problem. Admittedly in time of modern total warfare much discretion must be given to the military to act in situations where civilian rights are concerned. Yet the Committee believes that ways and means can be found of safeguarding people against mass accusations and discriminatory treatment.

Finally it should be noted that hundreds of evacuees suffered serious property and business losses because of governmental action and through no fault of their own. The War Relocation Authority, charged with the administration of the evacuation program, recommended in its final report that some provision be made in federal law that claims for evacuation-caused property losses be "considered promptly and settled with a minimum of delay and inconvenience." Over a year has passed since then.

Also disturbing, though less spectacular, was the issuance by military authority during the recent war of individual orders of exclusion against citizens scattered widely throughout the "defense zones" established by the Army. These orders rested on the same Executive Order as did the mass evacuation of Japanese Americans. In the case of these individual orders a citizen living perhaps in Philadelphia, Boston, or San Francisco was ordered by the Army to move. He was not imprisoned, for he could go to any inland area. He was not accused of criminal or subversive conduct. He was merely held to be an "unsafe" person to have around. Fortunately these violations of civil rights were not very numerous. Moreover, the Army lost confidence in the exclusion orders as effective security measures and abandoned them—but not until more than 200 citizens had moved under military compulsion.

2. The Right to Citizenship and its Privileges

The status of citizenship is basic to the enjoyment of many of the rights discussed in this report. First of all one must be a citizen in order to participate fully in the political process of the United States. Only *citizens* of the United States are accorded the right to vote. Only *citizens* may hold public office. Only *citizens,* for these reasons, have an effective voice in our nation's affairs. Second, those barred from citizenship are thereby barred from many avenues of economic and social advancement open to American citizens.

All persons born in the United States, and subject to the jurisdiction thereof, are citizens of the United States and of the State wherein they reside. These are the words of the Constitution. They set an ideal of native citizenship by which all persons born in this country are citizens without regard to race, color, creed, or ancestry. They also describe our practice, for we have in fact followed the ideal very closely. American-born children of aliens have encountered no barriers to citizenship.

In granting citizenship by naturalization, a democracy may establish reasonable tests of the individual alien's eligibility for citizenship. But some of the standards of eligibility in our naturalization laws have nothing to do with a person's fitness to become a citizen. These standards are based solely on race or national origin, and penalize some residents who may otherwise have all the attributes necessary for

American citizenship. The largest group of American residents presently subject to this discrimination are those born in Japan. Residents of Korean origin, as well as persons born in certain other Asiatic countries and Pacific Island areas, are also denied citizenship status. Although many of these people have lived in this country for decades, will probably remain here until they die, have raised families of native-born American citizens, and are devoted to American principles, they are forbidden an opportunity to attain the citizenship status to which their children are born.

We have recently removed many of these citizenship barriers. Until World War II, the Chinese had been specifically barred from immigration and from naturalization by the Chinese exclusion laws. Other groups, such as the Filipinos, Western Hemisphere Indians, and people indigenous to India, were denied citizenship through interpretation of the naturalization laws which limited eligibility to "whites" or "persons of African nativity or descent." We have made eligible for naturalization the "races of the Western Hemisphere;" we have made special provision to permit the naturalization of Chinese, Filipinos, and persons indigenous to India.

In addition to the disabilities suffered by ineligible aliens at the hands of private persons—in employment, housing, etc.—they are singled out for additional discrimination under the law. Arizona, California, Idaho, Kansas, Louisiana, Montana, New Mexico, and Oregon forbid or severely restrict land ownership by ineligible aliens. California also forbids ineligible aliens to engage in commercial fishing and excludes them from equal benefits of old age pensions and other state relief. Many states admit only citizens to the bar and to the medical, teaching, and other professions, which means that the ineligible alien is permanently barred from these fields.

The bar to land holding—the "alien land law"—most seriously impairs the alien's economic opportunities. The first of the alien land laws, enacted by California in 1913, made it illegal for aliens ineligible for citizenship either to buy agricultural land or to lease it for a period exceeding three years. Other western states passed similar laws. However, the alien land laws were not rigidly enforced, partly because it was often advantageous to lease or sell land to the Japanese and partly because of loopholes in the laws. During the second World War the California laws were made much more stringent.

California is now vigorously enforcing its amended alien land law. This law goes much further than to forbid ineligible aliens to own land. In effect, it forbids American citizens of Japanese ancestry to support their ineligible alien parents with money derived from the beneficial use of land. It has put in jeopardy the legal title of land purchased for American-born children by alien Japanese parents. Two examples of the effects of this law were cited before the Committee by a Japanese American veteran. In one instance, Japanese American soldiers killed overseas made battlefield wills deeding their land to their parents. The parents could not, under the law, receive the land. Accordingly, it escheated to the state. The other involved two Japanese American brothers who returned from overseas service to find that California had attacked the validity of the title of land purchased for them as children by their parents, and which they had cultivated as their own before entering the service.

These land laws and other manifestations of discrimination against ineligible aliens have been made possible by the discriminatory provisions of our naturalization laws. The moral impact of this situation is indicated by the words of the Japanese American veteran already referred to:

> ... I would like to say that I believe most of us fought as we did because we felt that, in spite of the way we had been kicked around, America was still the land of opportunity for all of us. I know my mother sent five of her sons. Every one volunteered for combat. One was killed. The rest of us were wounded. We have over thirty individual decorations and medals among us. Well, my mother wants to become a citizen. It is for people like my mother and for a lot of Americans of good will throughout the United States who have a lot of confidence in us and our loyalty that we did the job we did.

THE SPECIAL PROBLEM OF CITIZENSHIP
IN GUAM AND AMERICAN SAMOA

The peoples of Hawaii, Alaska, Puerto Rico, and the Virgin Islands are American citizens, either by birth or by naturalization, as are people in the 48 states. But the 35,000 inhabitants of Guam and American Samoa are in the anomalous position of being neither citizens nor aliens, but nationals of the United States. They have none of the rights of citizenship, yet owe allegiance to the United States. They do not have an organic act establishing a local government and guaranteeing civil liberties, but are ruled by naval administrators who issue decrees, administer the laws, and sit as judges. At the request of the President, the present Congress is considering legislation giving citizenship to these people, providing them with a local government guaranteeing basic civil rights, and transferring the administration of the islands from the Navy to a civilian agency.

THE RIGHT TO VOTE

The right of all qualified citizens to vote is today considered axiomatic by most Americans. To achieve universal adult suffrage we have carried on vigorous political crusades since the earliest days of the Republic. In theory the aim has been achieved, but in fact there are many backwaters in our political life where the right to vote is not assured to every qualified citizen. The franchise is barred to some citizens because of race; to others by institutions or procedures which impede free access to the polls. Still other Americans are in substance disfranchised whenever electoral irregularities or corrupt practices dissipate their votes or distort their intended purpose. Some citizens—permanent residents of the District of Columbia—are excluded from political representation and the right to vote as a result of outmoded national traditions. As a result of such restrictions, all of these citizens are limited, in varying degrees, in their opportunities to seek office and to influence the conduct of government on an equal plane with other American citizens.

The denial of the suffrage on account of race is the most serious present interference with the right to vote. Until very recently, American Negro citizens in most southern states found it difficult to vote. Some Negroes have voted in parts of the upper South for the last twenty years. In recent years the situation in the deep South has changed to the point where it can be said that Negroes are beginning to exercise the political rights of free Americans. In the light of history, this represents progress, limited and precarious, but nevertheless progress.

This report cannot adequately describe the history of Negro disfranchisement. At different times, different methods have been employed. As legal devices for disfranchising the Negro have been held unconstitutional, new methods have been improvised to take their places. Intimidation and the threat of intimidation have always loomed behind these legal devices to make sure that the desired result is achieved.

Until 1944, the white primary, by which participation in the Democratic primary is limited to white citizens, was used in Texas, Alabama, Arkansas, Georgia, Louisiana, and Mississippi as the most effective modern "legal" device for disfranchising Negroes. While some southern

Negroes succeeded in spite of various obstacles in voting in general elections, almost none voted in the Democratic primaries. Since the Democratic primary is the only election of any significance, the device of the white primary resulted in exclusion of Negroes from government in these states. Over a period of time, advocates of white supremacy had refined this device to the point where it seemed to be constitutionally foolproof. The command of the Fifteenth Amendment, prohibiting states from abridging suffrage because of race or color, was circumvented by purporting to vest the power to exclude Negroes in the political party rather than in the state.

But in 1944, the United States Supreme Court in the case of *Smith v. Allwright* overruled an earlier decision and held the Texas white primary illegal. It declared that the exclusion rules of the Texas Democratic Party were in effect the rules of the state and were therefore forbidden by the Fifteenth Amendment.

Some states adapted their primary laws to the Supreme Court ruling, others resisted, first, by refusing to open white primaries to Negroes until further litigation made the Texas ruling applicable to them, then, by devising other methods of depriving Negroes of the ballot. Today the effort to preserve the pure white electoral system in these states is continuing.

Two states, Louisiana and Texas, repealed white primary provisions immediately after the Supreme Court decision; Florida, Alabama, and Georgia were forced to do so by further court rulings. South Carolina called a special session of the state legislature at which all state laws in any way regulating primaries were repealed. The theory governing this action was that by placing the primaries entirely outside the law and the structure of government the ruling in *Smith v. Allwright* would be rendered inapplicable. In a message to the special session of the general assembly, the Governor of the State said:

> After these statutes are repealed, in my opinion, we will have done everything within our power to guarantee white supremacy in our primaries of our State insofar as legislation is concerned. Should this prove inadequate, we South Carolinians will use the necessary methods to retain white supremacy in our primaries and to safeguard the homes and happiness of our people.
>
> White supremacy will be maintained in our primaries; let the chips fall where they may.

In 1947 the white primary in South Carolina, resting on its new foundation, was held invalid by the United States District Court for the

Eastern District of South Carolina in the case of *Elmore v. Harris.* In its opinion the Court said:

> Racial distinctions cannot exist in the machinery that selects the officers and lawmakers of the United States; and all citizens of this State and Country are entitled to cast a free and untrammelled ballot in our elections, and if the only material and realistic elections are clothed with the name "primary", they are equally entitled to vote there.

The case will undoubtedly be carried to the Supreme Court for a final decision.

Alabama took a different course from South Carolina. Instead of repealing the primary laws it sought to continue disfranchisement by establishing "qualifications" standards under which Negroes could be barred by administrative action. The "Boswell amendment" adopted by this state in November, 1946, set up a provision under which voters would be required "to understand and explain" provisions of the state constitution. Exclusion by this kind of device is a familiar southern phenomenon. The tradition is to ignore such tests with respect to white voters but to apply them to Negroes—literally, where there is any possibility of eliminating them under the test; fraudulently, where they meet the test.

In a recent case in the Department of Justice files, a Negro school teacher was disqualified under a North Carolina provision requiring an ability to read and interpret the Constitution. The registrar refused to register him on the ground that he had not read the federal Constitution in a satisfactory manner. However, in a statement to the FBI the registrar declared, "my decision not to register him was based solely on the disfranchisement of the colored people in this country rather than on his ability to read, to write and to explain the Constitution." This case was subsequently prosecuted by the Department of Justice and resulted in the conviction of the registrar.

The poll tax—another important legal obstacle to full suffrage in some southern states—limits white as well as Negro suffrage. The poll tax has frequently had an unequal racial effect, since, like the "understand and explain" clauses, it has been administered in a discriminatory manner. It has been very effective as an anti-Negro device. A poll tax simply places the payment of a fee between the voter and the ballot box. In some states it is cumulative; taxes not paid in years when the voter does not go to the polls pile up and he must pay more than one year's tax before he can vote. The poll tax has curtailed

SUFFRAGE IN POLL TAX STATES

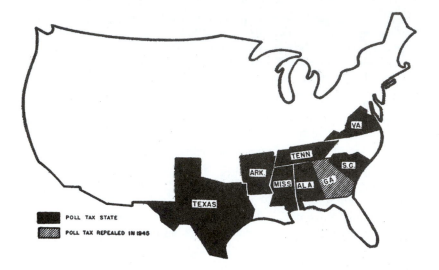

VA

TENN

ARK.

S.C.

MISS ALA GA

TEXAS

■ POLL TAX STATE

▨ POLL TAX REPEALED IN 1945

POTENTIAL VOTERS WHO VOTED IN
THE 1944 PRESIDENTIAL ELECTIONS

8 POLL TAX
 STATES*---- 18.31%

40 NON-POLL
 TAX STATES-- 68.74%

*INCLUDING GEORGIA.

the size of the entire electorate, white and Negro. Seven states—
Alabama, Arkansas, Mississippi, South Carolina, Tennessee, Texas,
and Virginia—still maintain this tax as a prerequisite to voting. Since
1921 four other states have abandoned the poll tax. These are North
Carolina, Louisiana, Florida, and Georgia.

It was estimated on the floor of the House of Representatives on
July 21, 1947, that:

> In the Presidential elections of 1944, 10 percent of the potential vot-
> ers voted in the seven poll-tax states, as against 49 percent in the
> free-vote states. In the congressional elections of 1946, the figures
> are 5 percent for the poll-tax states as compared with 33 percent for
> the free-voting states.

It has frequently been pointed out that the congressional representation of poll tax states is based on proportionately fewer voters than the
representation of other jurisdictions. It has also been urged that the
poll tax is in reality a tax levied by the state upon the citizen's federal
right to vote for members of Congress. In recent years there has been
a strong drive for federal legislation forbidding the requirement of a
poll tax as a prerequisite to voting in federal elections. The House of
Representatives passed an anti-poll tax bill for the fourth time in July
of 1947. The three previous bills passed by the House were killed in
the Senate.

In addition to formal, legal methods of disfranchisement, there are
the long-standing techniques of terror and intimidation, in the face of
which great courage is required of the Negro who tries to vote. In the
regions most characterized by generalized violence against Negroes,
little more than "advice" is often necessary to frighten them away
from the polls. They have learned, through the years, to discover
threats in mood and atmosphere. In one case in a deep southern state,
a middle-class Negro who had courageously attempted to vote and to
complain to the Department of Justice when he was refused access to
the polls, subsequently became so afraid of reprisal that he indicated
uncertainty whether he would be willing to testify in court. He asked,
if he should decide to testify, to be given ample notice of the date so
that he could first move his family out of the region.

In past years, American Indians have also been denied the right to
vote and other political rights in a number of states. Most of these
restrictions have been abandoned, but in two states, New Mexico and
Arizona, Indians continue to be disfranchised. The constitution of New
Mexico withholds suffrage from "Indians not taxed." In Arizona the

state constitution has been interpreted to deny the vote to Indians as being "persons under guardianship." Protests against these legal bans on Indian suffrage in the Southwest have gained force with the return of Indian veterans to those states.

The constitutionality of these laws is presently being tested. It has been pointed out that the concept of "Indians not taxed" is no longer meaningful; it is a vestige of the days when most Indians were not citizens and had not become part of the community of people of the United States. Indians are now citizens and subject to federal taxation. They are also subject to state taxes, except for lands held in trust for them by the United States government. There is therefore little justification for denying them the franchise on the assumption that they are excused from the burdens of other citizens.

THE RIGHT TO BEAR ARMS

Underlying the theory of compulsory wartime military service in a democratic state is the principle that every citizen, regardless of his station in life, must assist in the defense of the nation when its security is threatened. Despite the discrimination which they encounter in so many fields, minority group members have time and again met this responsibility. Moreover, since equality in military service assumes great importance as a symbol of democratic goals, minorities have regarded it not only as a duty but as a right.

Yet the record shows that the members of several minorities, fighting and dying for the survival of the nation in which they met bitter prejudice, found that there was discrimination against them even as they fell in battle. Prejudice in any area is an ugly, undemocratic phenomenon; in the armed services, where all men run the risk of death, it is particularly repugnant.

All of the armed forces have recently adopted policies which set as explicit objectives the achievement of equality of opportunity. The War Department has declared that it "intends to continue its efforts to make the best possible use of available personnel resources in the post-war Army and in any future emergency, without distinction as to race, religion, color or other non-military considerations." The Navy Department, speaking for both the Navy and the Marine Corps, has stated that "No distinction is made between individuals wearing a naval uniform because of race or color. The Navy accepts no theory of racial differences in inborn ability, but expects that every man wearing its uniform be trained and used in accordance with his maximum individual capacity determined on the basis of individual performance."

The Coast Guard has stressed "the importance of selecting men for what they are, for what they are capable of doing, and insisting on good conduct, good behavior, and good qualities of leadership for all hands . . . As a matter of policy Negro recruits receive the same consideration as all others."

However, despite the lessons of the war and the recent announcement of these policies, the records of the military forces disclose many areas in which there is a great need for further remedial action. Although generally speaking, the basis of recruitment has been somewhat broadened, Negroes, for example, are faced by an absolute bar against enlistment in any branch of the Marine Corps other than the steward's branch, and the Army cleaves to a ceiling for Negro personnel of about ten percent of the total strength of the service.

There are no official discriminatory requirements for entrance into the Navy and the Coast Guard, but the fact that Negroes constitute a disproportionately small part of the total strength of each of these branches of service (4.4 and 4.2 percent, respectively) may indicate the existence of discrimination in recruiting practices.

Within the services, studies made within the last year disclose that actual experience has been out of keeping with the declarations of policy on discrimination. In the Army, less than one Negro in 70 is commissioned, while there is one white officer for approximately every seven white enlisted men. In the Navy, there are only two Negro officers in a ratio of less than one to 10,000 Negro enlisted men; there are 58,571 white officers, or one for every seven enlisted whites. The Marine Corps has 7,798 officers, none of whom is a Negro, though there are 2,190 Negro enlisted men. Out of 2,981 Coast Guard officers, one is a Negro; there are 910 Negro enlisted men. The ratio of white Coast Guard commissioned to enlisted personnel is approximately one to six.

Similarly, in the enlisted grades, there is an exceedingly high concentration of Negroes in the lowest ratings, particularly in the Navy, Marine Corps, and Coast Guard. Almost 80 percent of the Negro sailors are serving as cooks, stewards, and steward's mates; less than two percent of the whites are assigned to duty in the same capacity. Almost 15 percent of all white enlisted marines are in the three highest grades; less than 2-1/2 percent of the Negro marines fall in the same category. The disparities in the Coast Guard are similarly great. The difference in the Army is somewhat smaller, but still significant: Less than nine percent of the Negro personnel are in the first three grades, while almost 16 percent of the whites hold these ranks.

Many factors other than discrimination contribute to this result. However, it is clear that discrimination is one of the major elements which keeps the services from attaining the objectives which they have set for themselves.

The admission of minorities to the service academies and other service schools is another area in which the armed forces have enjoyed relatively little success in their efforts to eliminate discrimination. With regard to schools within the services, the disparities indicate that selection for advanced training is doubtless often made on a color basis. As for the service academies, in the course of the last seventy-five years the Military Academy at West Point admitted a total of only thirty-seven Negro cadets, while the Naval Academy at Annapolis admitted only six. The Coast Guard Academy, while it selects applicants on the basis of open, competitive examinations without regard to color, has no knowledge of any Negro ever having been accepted. The absence of Negroes from the service academies is unfortunate because it means that our officers are trained in an undemocratic environment and are denied the opportunity to learn at an early stage in their service careers that men of different races can work and fight together harmoniously.

State authorities promulgate the regulations concerning enlistment of Negroes and the formation of Negro units in the National Guard. Most states do not have Negro units; of those that do, all but three require segregation by regulation. Of thirty-four states answering an inquiry made by the President's Advisory Commission on Universal Training, only two permit the integration of Negroes with white units. The Commission, commenting on discrimination, observed that it "considers harmful the policies of the states that exclude Negroes from their National Guard units. The civilian components should be expanded to include all segments of our population without segregation or discrimination. Total defense requires the participation of all citizens in our defense forces."

Looking to the future, the Commission also found that some of the present practices of the armed forces would negate many of the benefits of the proposed universal training program. Speaking of this program, it said:

> ... it must provide equality of privilege and opportunity for all those upon whom this obligation rests. Neither in the training itself, nor in the organization of any phase of this program, should there be discrimination for or against any person or group because of his race,

class, national origin, or religion. Segregation or special privilege in any form should have no place in the program. To permit them would nullify the important living lesson in citizenship which such training can give. Nothing could be more tragic for the future attitude of our people, and for the unity of our nation, than a program in which our Federal Government forced our young manhood to live for a period of time in an atmosphere which emphasized or bred class or racial differences.

When an individual enters the service of the country, he necessarily surrenders some of the rights and privileges which inhere in American citizenship. The government in return undertakes to protect his integrity as an individual and the dignity of his profession. He is entitled to enjoy the respect which should be shown the uniform of the armed services of the United States by all persons. Unfortunately, however, the uniform is not always accorded the esteem it warrants. Some of our servicemen are all too often treated with rudeness and discourtesy by civil authorities and the public. There are numerous instances in which they have been forced to move to segregated cars on public carriers. They have been denied access to places of public accommodation and recreation. When they attempt to assert their rights, they are sometimes met with threats and even outright attack. Federal officials find they have no present authority to intervene directly to protect men in uniform against such abuses.

The record is not without its brighter side. A start has been made toward eliminating differentials in opportunity and treatment of minorities in the armed forces. The Army is making experimental use of small all-Negro units as organic parts of large white organizations. Significantly, of the thirty-seven Negroes admitted to the Academy at West Point since 1870, twenty-one were accepted in the last ten years. In 1947, five Negroes were accepted, the largest enrollment of Negro cadets for a single year in the last seventy-five years. The Navy has adopted a policy of nonsegregation and has officially opened all branches to all personnel. The Coast Guard has abandoned, as a matter of policy, the restriction of Negro guardsmen to duty as cooks, stewards, and bakers. Training courses, indoctrination programs, pamphlets, and films have been provided for officers and enlisted men in the Army and Navy to promote understanding between groups and to facilitate the use of minority personnel.

But the evidence leaves no doubt that we have a long way to go. The armed forces, in actual practice, still maintain many barriers to equal treatment for all their members. In many cases, state and local agencies and private persons disregard the dignity of the uniform. There is much that remains to be done, much that can be done at once. Morally, the failure to act is indefensible. Practically, it costs lives and money in the inefficient use of human resources. Perhaps most important of all, we are not making use of one of the most effective techniques for educating the public to the practicability of American ideals as a way of life. During the last war we and our allies, with varying but undeniable success, found that the military services can be used to educate citizens on a broad range of social and political problems. The war experience brought to our attention a laboratory in which we may prove that the majority and minorities of our population can train and work and fight side by side in cooperation and harmony. We should not hesitate to take full advantage of this opportunity.

3. The Right to Freedom of Conscience and Expression

This right is an expression of confidence in the ability of freemen to learn the truth through the unhampered interplay of competing ideas. Where the right is generally exercised, the public benefits from the selective process of winnowing truth from falsehood, desirable ideas from evil ones. If the people are to govern themselves their only hope of doing so wisely lies in the collective wisdom derived from the fullest possible information, and in the fair presentation of differing opinions. The right is also necessary to permit each man to find his way to the religious and political beliefs which suit his private needs.

This Committee has made no extensive study of our record under the great freedoms which comprise this right: religion, speech, press, and assembly. To have done so would have meant making this vast field the dominant part of our inquiry. We were not prepared to do this, partly because it has been and is being well studied by others. What finally determined us was the conviction that this right is relatively secure. Americans worship as they choose. Our press is freer from government restraints than any the world has seen. Our citizens are normally free to exercise their right to speak without fear of retribution, and to assemble for unlimited public discussions. There still are, however, communities in which sporadic interferences with the rights of unpopular religious, political, and economic groups take place. The steady flow of federal court cases in recent years involving groups like the Jehovah's Witnesses proves that.

At the present time, in our opinion, the most immediate threat to the right to freedom of opinion and expression is indirect. It comes from efforts to deal with those few people in our midst who would destroy democracy. There are two groups whose refusal to accept and abide by the democratic process is all too clear. The first are the Communists whose counterparts in many countries have proved, by their treatment of those with whom they disagree, that their ideology does not include a belief in universal civil rights. The second are the native Fascists. Their statements and their actions—as well as those of their foreign counterparts—prove them to be equally hostile to the American heritage of freedom and equality.

It is natural and proper for good citizens to worry about the activities of these groups. Every member of this Committee shares that concern. Communists and Fascists may assert different objectives. This does not obscure the identity of the means which both are willing to use to further themselves. Both often use the words and symbols of democracy to mask their totalitarian tactics. But their concern for civil rights is always limited to themselves. Both are willing to lie about their political views when it is convenient. They feel no obligation to come before the public openly and say who they are and what they really want.

This Committee unqualifiedly opposes any attempt to impose *special* limitations on the rights of these people to speak and assemble. Our national past offers us two great touchstones to resolve the dilemma of maintaining the right to free expression and yet protecting our democracy against its enemies. One was offered by Jefferson in his first inaugural address: "If there be any among us who wish to dissolve the Union, or to change its republican form, let them stand undisturbed as monuments of the safety with which error of opinion may be tolerated where reason is left free to combat it." The second is the doctrine of "clear and present danger." This was laid down as a working principle by the Supreme Court in 1919 in *Schenck v. United States* in an opinion written by Justice Holmes. It says that no limitation of freedom of expression shall be made unless "the words are used in such circumstances and are of such a nature as to create a clear and present danger that they will bring about the substantive evils that Congress has a right to prevent." The next year in a dissenting opinion in *Schaefer v. United States* Justice Brandeis added this invaluable word of advice about the application of the doctrine: "Like many other rules for human conduct, it can be applied correctly only by the exercise of good judgment, and in the exercise of good judgment, calmness is, in time of deep feeling and on subjects which excite passion, as essential as fearlessness and honesty."

It is our feeling that the present threat to freedom of opinion grows out of the failure of some private and public persons to apply these standards. Specifically, public excitement about "Communists" has gone far beyond the dictates of the "good judgment" and "calmness" of which Holmes and Brandeis spoke. A state of near-hysteria now threatens to inhibit the freedom of genuine democrats.

At the same time we are afraid that the "reason" upon which Jefferson relied to combat error is hampered by the successful effort of some totalitarians to conceal their true nature. To expect people to reject totalitarians, when we do not provide mechanisms to guarantee that essential information is available, is foolhardy. These two concerns go together. If we fall back upon hysteria and repression as our weapons against totalitarians, we will defeat ourselves. Communists want nothing more than to be lumped with freedom-loving non-Communists. This simply makes it easier for them to conceal their true nature and to allege that the term "Communist" is "meaningless." Irresponsible opportunists who make it a practice to attack every person or group with whom they disagree as "Communists" have thereby actually aided their supposed "enemies." At the same time we cannot let these abuses deter us from the legitimate exposing of real Communists and real Fascists. Moreover, the same zeal must be shown in defending our democracy against one group as against the other.

CIVIL SERVANTS

Efforts to protect the government against disloyal employees may lead to dangerous "Red hunting". We firmly believe that the government has the obligation to have in its employ only citizens of unquestioned loyalty. We are, moreover, aware of the disclosures made in the Canadian espionage trials which reveal concerted attempts by Communists to procure secret government information either directly or through dupes. We also know that Communists feel no obligation to identify themselves as members of their party, and have completely divided loyalties, which make them dangerous in posts of government responsibility. We are further aware that there are certain governmental agencies which because of the confidential and highly secret character of their work must have absolute assurance of the complete loyalty of all their employees.

All of these factors make it difficult to maintain effective security. Several statutes now on the books make it possible to prosecute any federal employee who reveals restricted information. Those dissatisfied with these safeguards argue that the concealment by Communists and other subversives of their affiliations makes it impossible to weed them out until they have done serious damage. Therefore, they contend, it is necessary to have the loyalty of all federal employees checked by security police agencies. This Committee recognizes the need for some such protective measures. Yet our whole civil liberties history provides us with a clear warning against the possible misuse of loyalty checks to inhibit freedom of opinion and expression.

There are two possible dangers. In the first place, the standards by which the loyalty of an individual or an organization is to be determined may not be clearly defined. This is particularly true of any standard which permits condemnation of persons or groups because of "association." The character, the policies and the leadership of many organizations change. Individuals, too, change their opinions. The greatest care must be taken to avoid the misinterpretation of affiliation. Individuals may be members of suspect organizations out of ignorance. Before such affiliations may even be considered as relevant, the motive of the individual should be clearly established. The determination of the suspect character of organizations is complex and must be handled with the greatest care. For the individual the ultimate test must always be his own trustworthiness. Affiliation with a dubious organization is, by itself, not necessarily proof of untrustworthiness.

A second danger is that the procedure by which the loyalty of accused federal employees is determined may not accord with our traditions of due process of law. An employee whose loyalty is questioned is not charged with a crime. But loss of job and inability to obtain another one is a severe punishment to impose on any man. Accordingly, provision should be made for such traditional procedural safeguards as the right to a bill of particular accusations, the right to subpoena witnesses and documents where genuine security considerations permit, the right to be represented by counsel, the right to a stenographic report of proceedings, the right to a written decision, and the right of appeal.

More than the civil rights of our two million federal workers— important as they are—is involved here. All Americans are bound to be affected by what is done. The federal government must maintain a loyalty program which adequately protects the civil rights of its employees. Otherwise private employers and state and local governments may not protect the rights of *their* personnel, and in fact they may actually be encouraged to infringe these rights. It is a severe punishment to be discharged from the government for disloyalty, as the Supreme Court pointed out in 1946 in *United States v. Lovett*. Our system of democratic justice has proved again and again its ability to protect us in peace and in war. To make a conspicuous departure from it against government workers would surely weaken the safeguards of the right of all citizens to speak freely and to organize in furtherance of their opinions. Here as elsewhere, the federal government must set an example for the rest of the country by being uncommonly scrupulous in its respect for the civil rights of all citizens.

ENEMIES OF DEMOCRACY

As we have said, one of the things which totalitarians of both left and right have in common is a reluctance to come before the people honestly and say who they are, what they work for and who supports them. Those persons in our own country who try to stir up religious and racial hatreds are no exception. They understand that the vicious doctrines which they advocate have been morally outlawed in America for more than a century and a half. This Committee is as eager to guarantee their civil rights as those of the people they attack. But we do not believe in a definition of civil rights which includes freedom to avoid all responsibility for one's opinions. This would be an unwise and disastrous weakening of the democratic process. If these people wish to influence the public in our national forum of opinion they should be free to do so, regardless of how distasteful their views are to us. But the public must be able to evaluate these views. Exactly how much anonymous, hate-mongering or other subversive literature there is we do not know. The amount of such matter fluctuates greatly from time to time. At the present, according to several witnesses who appeared before the Committee, many of those who spread racial and religious prejudices have "gone underground." As recently as 1940, however, a study by the staff of the Senate Committee on Campaign Expenditures revealed that one-third of the election propaganda in the campaign of that year was completely anonymous and that one-half was partially and inadequately identified as to source and sponsorship. Moreover, the Committee reported that the anonymous material included "the most virulent, dishonest and defamatory propaganda." Congress has already taken the first step to remedy this inadequacy by amending the election laws to forbid the distribution of anonymous campaign literature.

The principle of disclosure is, we believe, the appropriate way to deal with those who would subvert our democracy by revolution or by encouraging disunity and destroying the civil rights of some groups. We have considered and rejected proposals which have been made to us for censoring or prohibiting material which defames religious or racial minority groups. Our purpose is not to constrict anyone's freedom to speak; it is rather to enable the people better to judge the true motives of those who try to sway them.

Congress has already made use of the principle of disclosure in both the economic and political spheres. The Securities and Exchange Commission, the Federal Trade Commission and the Pure Food and Drug Administration make available to the public information about sponsors of economic wares. In the political realm, the Federal Communications Commission, the Post Office Department, the Clerk of the House of Representatives, and the Secretary of the Senate—all of these under various statutes—are required to collect information about those who attempt to influence public opinion. Thousands of statements disclosing the ownership and control of newspapers using the second-class mailing privilege are filed annually with the Post Office Department. Hundreds of statements disclosing the ownership and control of radio stations are filed with the Federal Communications Commission. Hundreds of lobbyists are now required to disclose their efforts to influence Congress under the Congressional Reorganization Act. In 1938, Congress found it necessary to pass the Foreign Agents Registration Act which forced certain citizens and aliens alike to register with the Department of Justice the facts about their sponsorship and activities. The effectiveness of these efforts has varied. We believe, however, that they have been sufficiently successful to warrant their further extension to all of those who attempt to influence public opinion.

The ultimate responsibility for countering totalitarians of all kinds rests, as always, with the mass of good, democratic Americans, their organizations and their leaders. The federal government must set an example of careful adherence to the highest standards in guaranteeing freedom of opinion and expression to its employees. Beyond that it ought to provide a source of reference where private citizens and groups may find accurate information about the activities, sponsorship, and background of those who are active in the market place of public opinion.

4. The Right to Equality of Opportunity

THE RIGHT TO EMPLOYMENT

A man's right to an equal chance to utilize fully his skills and knowledge is essential. The meaning of a job goes far beyond the paycheck.

Good workers have a pride in the organization for which they work and feel satisfaction in the jobs they are doing. A witness before a congressional committee has recently said:

> Discrimination in employment damages lives, both the bodies and the minds, of those discriminated against and those who discriminate. It blights and perverts that healthy ambition to improve one's standard of living which we like to say is peculiarly American. It generates insecurity, fear, resentment, division and tension in our society.

In private business, in government, and in labor unions, the war years saw a marked advance both in hiring policies and in the removal of on-the-job discriminatory practices. Several factors contributed to this progress. The short labor market, the sense of unity among the people, and the leadership provided by the government all helped bring about a lessening of unfair employment practices. Yet we did not eliminate discrimination in employment. The Final Report of the federal Fair Employment Practice Committee, established in 1941 by President Roosevelt to eliminate discrimination in both government and private employment related to the war effort, makes this clear.

Four out of five cases which arose during the life of the Committee, concerned Negroes. However, many other minorities have suffered from discriminatory employment practices. The FEPC reports show that eight percent of the Committee's docket involved complaints of discrimination because of creed, and 70 percent of these concerned Jews. It should be noted that FEPC jurisdiction did not extend to financial institutions and the professions, where discrimination against Jews is especially prevalent. Witnesses before this Committee, representing still other minority groups, testified as follows:

The Japanese Americans: "We know, too, what discrimination in employment is. We know what it means to be unacceptable to union membership; what it means to be the last hired and first fired; what it means to have to work harder and longer for less wages. We know these things because we have been forced to experience them."

The Mexican Americans: "We opened an employment bureau (to help Mexican Americans) in our office last year for San Antonio. We wrote to business firms throughout the city, most of whom didn't answer. We would call certain firms and say that we heard they had an opening for a person in a stock room or some other type of work; or I would go myself. But thinking I was the same in prejudice as they, they would say, 'You know we never hire Mexicans'."

The
BASES OF JOB DISCRIMINATION
(COMPLAINTS TO FEPC, FISCAL YEAR 1943–44)

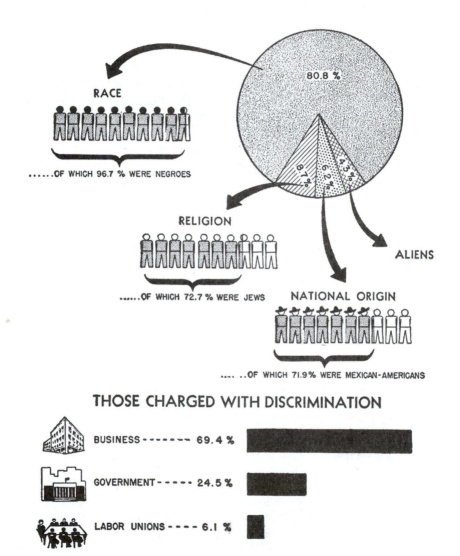

RACE

.......OF WHICH 96.7 % WERE NEGROES

80.8 %

8.7%

6.2%

4.3%

RELIGION

......OF WHICH 72.7 % WERE JEWS

ALIENS

NATIONAL ORIGIN

....OF WHICH 71.9% WERE MEXICAN-AMERICANS

THOSE CHARGED WITH DISCRIMINATION

BUSINESS ------- 69.4 %

GOVERNMENT ----- 24.5 %

LABOR UNIONS ---- 6.1 %

The American Indians: "As with the Negroes, Indians are employed readily when there is a shortage of labor and they can't get anyone else. When times get better, they are the first ones to be released."

Discriminatory hiring practices. — Discrimination is most acutely felt by minority group members in their inability to get a job suited to their qualifications. Exclusions of Negroes, Jews, or Mexicans in the process of hiring is effected in various ways — by newspaper advertisements requesting only whites or gentiles to apply, by registration or application blanks on which a space is reserved for "race" or "religion," by discriminatory job orders placed with employment agencies, or by the arbitrary policy of a company official in charge of hiring.

A survey conducted by the United States Employment Service and contained in the Final Report of the Fair Employment Practice Committee reveals that of the total job orders received by USES offices in 11 selected areas during the period of February 1–15, 1946, 24 percent of the orders were discriminatory. Of 38,195 orders received, 9,171 included specifications with regard to race, citizenship, religion, or some combination of these factors.

The National Community Relations Advisory Council has studied hiring practices since V-J Day. A 1946 survey of the practices of 134 private employment agencies in 10 cities (Boston, Chicago, Cincinnati, Cleveland, Detroit, Kansas City, Milwaukee, Philadelphia, St. Louis, and San Francisco) disclosed that 89 percent of these agencies included questions covering religion on their registration forms. In Chicago, a statistical count of discriminatory job orders was made by one of the largest commercial agencies in the city. This revealed that 60 percent of the executive jobs, 50 percent of the sales executive jobs, and 41 percent of the male clerical openings, and 24 percent of the female clerical openings were closed to Jews. Fully 83 percent of all orders placed with the agency carried discriminatory specifications. A companion study of help-wanted ads conducted in eight major cities during corresponding weeks in 1945 and 1946 showed that while the total volume of help-wanted advertising had declined, there was an over-all increase of 195 percent in discriminatory ads for 1946 over 1945.

The minority job seeker often finds that there are fields of employment where application is futile no matter how able or well-trained he is. Many northern business concerns have an unwritten rule against appointing Jews to executive positions; railroad management and unions discourage the employment of Negroes as engineers or conductors.

In some of our territories which are fairly free from other discrimination, unfair employment practices occur. Some of the larger business firms in Hawaii will not hire clerical or stenographic workers of Japanese ancestry where the public can see the worker. In Puerto Rico, with its large Negro population, generally only white people or very light colored persons are employed by banks, sugar corporations, airlines, shipping companies, and large department stores in clerical and executive positions.

Discrimination in hiring has forced many minority workers into low-paying and often menial jobs such as common laborer and domestic servant. This has done much to bring about the situation reported by the Bureau of the Census in 1940—

> Striking differences between the occupations of whites and Negroes were shown in 1940 census statistics. Farmers, farm laborers, and other laborers constituted 62.2 percent of all employed Negro men and only 28.5 percent of all employed white men. Only about 5 percent of all employed Negro men, compared with approximately 30 percent of employed white men, were engaged in professional, semi-professional, proprietary, managerial, and clerical or sales occupations. Skilled craftsmen represented 15.6 percent of employed white men and only 4.4 percent of employed Negro men. More than half of the Negro craftsmen were mechanics, carpenters, painters, plasterers and cement finishers, and masons.

On-the-job discrimination.—If he can get himself hired, the minority worker often finds that he is being paid less than other workers. This wage discrimination is sharply evident in studies made of individual cities and is especially exaggerated in the South. A survey, conducted by the Research and Information Department of the American Federation of Labor shows that the average weekly income of white veterans ranges from 30 to 78 percent above the average income of Negro veterans in 26 communities, 25 of them in the South. In Houston, for example, 36,000 white veterans had a weekly income of $49 and 4,000 Negro veterans had average incomes of $30—a difference of 63 percent. These differences are not caused solely by the relegation of the Negroes to lower types of work, but reflect wage discriminations between whites and Negroes for the same type of work. The Final Report of the FEPC states that the hourly wage rates for Negro common laborers averaged 47.4 cents in July, 1942, as compared with 65.3 cents for white laborers.

Nor can the disparity be blamed entirely on differences in education and training. The 1940 census reveals that the median annual income of Negro high school graduates was only $775 as compared with $1,454 for the white high school graduate; that the median Negro college graduate received $1,074 while his white counterpart was earning $2,046; that while 23.3 percent of white high school graduates had wage or salary incomes over $2,000, but four percent of Negro graduates achieved that level.

In presenting this evidence, the Committee is not ignoring the fact that an individual Negro worker may be less efficient than an individual white worker or vice versa. Nor does it suggest that wage differences which reflect actual differences in the competence of workers are unjustifiable. What is indefensible is a wage discrimination based, not on the worker's ability, but on his race.

While private business provided almost 70 percent of all cases docketed by the FEPC for the fiscal year 1943–44, about a fourth of the complaints were against the federal government itself. This at once calls to question the effectiveness of the Civil Service Commission rules against such discrimination, and the various departments' directives and executive orders that have restated this policy of nondiscrimination from time to time.

A case study, conducted in one government agency by the National Committee on Segregation in the Nation's Capital, demonstrates a pattern of discrimination existing in government service. Samples of Negro and white workers in this agency were matched for the variables of age, sex, marital status, educational level, length of service, division in which inducted, and job title and grade at which inducted. Out of 503 whites and 292 Negroes inducted into the agency in the fiscal year 1946, 40 pairs were perfectly matched for these variables. A few more Negroes than whites had veteran status, but the average efficiency ratings for the two groups were exactly the same.

A check on promotion and resignation for the sample was made in April, 1947. It was found that the whites had received 12 grade promotions in a total service of 22 years. This was an average of one promotion for each two man-years of service. The Negroes had received two grade promotions in a total service of 28 man-years. This was one promotion for each 14 man-years. In other words, it took the average Negro seven times as long as the average white to get a promotion, in spite of the fact that almost all of the variables which could affect promotion were exactly the same.

Finally, labor unions are guilty of discriminatory labor practices. Six percent of the complaints received by the FEPC were made against unions, and the FEPC states that when challenged, private industry eliminated discrimination much more readily than did unions. On the other hand, it should be noted that great strides have been made in the admission of minorities to unions. Both the American Federation of Labor and the Congress of Industrial Organizations have repeatedly condemned discriminatory union practices. But the national organizations have not yet fully attained their goals. Some railway unions have "Jim Crow" auxiliaries into which Negroes, Mexicans, or Orientals are shunted, with little or no voice in union affairs. Furthermore, there is a rigid upper limit on the type of job on which these members can be employed.

There is a danger that some of our wartime gains in the elimination of unfair employment practices will be lost unless prompt action is taken to preserve them. In the federal government, the employment of Negroes jumped from 40,000 before the war to 300,000 in 1944. And while only 10 percent of all Negroes employed in government held jobs other than custodial in 1938, 60 percent of the Negroes in 1944 were employed in clerical and professional categories. The chief danger at present looms in the form of discriminatory cut-backs of Negro personnel who were hired very largely by wartime agencies, and in the refusal by other agencies in the government to hire these "displaced employees."

In private industry, minority workers were heavily concentrated in war industries, which since the end of the war have suffered drastic cut-backs. In other industries the termination of manpower controls has encouraged some employers to resume prewar policies of exclusion or discriminatory treatment of minority workers. The first sentence in the summary of the FEPC Final Report bluntly observes that "the wartime gains of Negro, Mexican American, and Jewish workers are being lost through an unchecked revival of discriminatory practices."

Such postwar economic retrenchment as has occurred has disproportionally hit the minority groups. A United States Census Bureau survey, bearing out the adage that minority workers are "the last hired, first fired," discloses that from July, 1945, to April, 1946, unemployment among whites increased about one and one-half times while unemployment among nonwhites more than tripled. The situation has of course been aggravated by the accelerated migration of Negroes from the South to northern industrial areas during the war.

Efforts to improve the situation. — Reference has already been made to the Fair Employment Practice Committee. This Committee was established by President Roosevelt in an Executive Order dated June 25, 1941. Its mandate was to eliminate discriminatory employment practices within the federal government and in companies and unions which had contracts with the government or which were engaged in the production of materials necessary to the war effort. The FEPC, as a practical matter, served as a clearing house for complaints alleging various types of employment discrimination. It had no enforcement powers of its own; and no recourse to the courts.

The effectiveness of the FEPC was due almost entirely to its success as a mediation body in persuading a union or employer to revise the particular policy or practice complained of. During its most active two years, FEPC closed an average of 250 cases a month, about 100 of which were satisfactorily adjusted. The Committee's work ended in June, 1946, when Congress failed to appropriate funds for the ensuing fiscal year. In a letter of June 28, 1946, to the Committee accepting the resignation of its members, President Truman said:

> The degree of effectiveness which the Fair Employment Practice Committee was able to attain has shown once and for all that it is possible to equalize job opportunity by governmental action, and thus eventually to eliminate the influence of prejudice in the field of employment.

There are six states which have laws directed against discrimination in private employment. The New York, New Jersey, Massachusetts, and Connecticut statutes have strong enforcement provisions. In general, the statutes in these four states make it unlawful for employers to discriminate in hiring, firing, or conditions of employment, or for labor unions to exclude, expel, or discriminate, because of race, color, creed, or national origin. They also prohibit the use of discriminatory help-wanted ads and job applications by employers and employment agencies. State commissions are empowered to investigate complaints, to hold hearings, to attempt to conciliate, to issue cease-and-desist orders, and finally, to seek court enforcement of these orders. Indiana and Wisconsin have antidiscrimination statutes without enforcement provisions. The commissions in these two states serve therefore as educational and advisory agencies.

The progress that has been made in New York State under its fair employment practice act is suggested by the first annual report (for the year 1946) of the State Commission Against Discrimination. In its introduction the Report states: "The operation of the law has definitely resulted in progress in the elimination of illegal discriminatory practices. The testimony of people actually engaged in job-placement activities reveals that fields of opportunity previously closed to certain groups are now open to all, regardless of race, creed, color, or national origin. Resistance to the law has lessened as demonstrated by the fact that employees of all groups are being hired and upgraded into new occupational categories. Preemployment discriminatory inquiries are now the rarity, rather than the rule."

A few scattered cities, among them Chicago, Minneapolis, New York, and Cincinnati, have enacted ordinances designed to prevent discrimination in employment practices. These vary greatly in scope. Some are directed solely at municipal employment; others apply to private employers having contracts with the city; and at least one covers labor unions in addition to public and private employers. Some carry fines and imprisonment for violators, while others, with no sanctions or enforcement provisions, are little more than policy statements.

THE RIGHT TO EDUCATION

The United States has made remarkable progress toward the goal of universal education for its people. The number and variety of its schools and colleges are greater than ever before. Student bodies have become increasingly representative of all the different peoples who make up our population. Yet we have not finally eliminated prejudice and discrimination from the operation of either our public or our private schools and colleges. Two inadequacies are extremely serious. We have failed to provide Negroes and, to a lesser extent, other minority group members with equality of educational opportunities in our public institutions, particularly at the elementary and secondary school levels. We have allowed discrimination in the operation of many of our private institutions of higher education, particularly in the North with respect to Jewish students.

Discrimination in public schools. —The failure to give Negroes equal educational opportunities is naturally most acute in the South, where approximately 10 million Negroes live. The South is one of the poorer sections of the country and has at best only limited funds to spend on its schools. With 34.5 percent of the country's population, 17 southern states and the District of Columbia have 39.4 percent of our school children. Yet the South has only one-fifth of the taxpaying wealth of the nation. Actually, on a percentage basis, the South spends a greater share of its income on education than do the wealthier states in other parts of the country. For example, Mississippi, which has the lowest expenditure per school child of any state, is ninth in percentage of income devoted to education. A recent study showed Mississippi spending 3.41 percent of its income for education as against New York's figure of only 2.61 percent. But this meant $400 per classroom unit in Mississippi, and $4,100 in New York. Negro and white school children both suffer because of the South's basic inability to match the level of educational opportunity provided in other sections of the nation.

But it is the South's segregated school system which most directly discriminates against the Negro. This segregation is found today in 17 southern states and the District of Columbia. Poverty-stricken though it was after the close of the Civil War, the South chose to maintain two sets of public schools, one for whites and one for Negroes. With respect to education, as well as to other public services, the Committee believes that the "separate but equal" rule has not been obeyed in practice. There is a marked difference in quality between the educational opportunities offered white children and Negro children in the separate schools. Whatever test is used—expenditure per pupil, teachers' salaries, the number of pupils per teacher, transportation of students, adequacy of school buildings and educational equipment, length of school term, extent of curriculum—Negro students are invariably at a disadvantage. Opportunities for Negroes in public institutions of higher education in the South—particularly at the professional graduate school level—are severely limited.

Statistics in support of these conclusions are available. Figures provided by the United States Office of Education for the school year, 1943–44, show that the average length of the school term in the areas having separate schools was 173.5 days for whites, and 164 for Negroes; the number of pupils per teacher was 28 for white and 34 for Negroes; and the average annual salary for Negro teachers was lower than that for white teachers in all but three of the 18 areas. Salary figures are as follows:

STATE OR DISTRICT OF COLUMBIA	AVERAGE ANNUAL SALARY OF PRINCIPALS, SUPERVISORS, AND TEACHERS IN SCHOOLS FOR—	
	WHITES	NEGROES
Alabama	$1,158	$661
Arkansas	924	555
Delaware	1,953	1,814
Florida	1,530	970
Georgia	1,123	515
Louisiana	1,683	828
Maryland	2,085	2,002
Mississippi	1,107	342
Missouri	1,397	¹1,590
North Carolina	1,380	1,249
Oklahoma	1,428	1,438
South Carolina	1,203	615
Tennessee	1,071	1,010
Texas	1,395	946
Virginia	1,364	1,129
District of Columbia	2,610	2,610

¹Higher salaries due to the fact that most Negro schools are located in cities where all salaries are higher.

The South has made considerable progress in the last decade in narrowing the gap between educational opportunities afforded the white children and that afforded Negro children. For example, the gap between the length of the school year for whites and the shorter one for Negroes has been narrowed from 14.8 days in 1939–40 to 9.5 days in 1943–44. Similarly, the gap in student load per teacher in white and Negro schools has dropped from 8.5 students in 1939–40 to six students in 1943–44.

In spite of the improvement which is undoubtedly taking place, the Committee is convinced that the gap between white and Negro schools can never be completely eliminated by means of state funds alone. The cost of maintaining separate, but truly equal, school systems would seem to be utterly prohibitive in many of the southern states. It seems probable that the only means by which such a goal can finally be won will be through federal financial assistance. The extension of the federal grant-in-aid for educational purposes, already available to the land-grant colleges and, for vocational education, to the secondary school field, seems both imminent and desirable.

Whether the federal grant-in-aid should be used to support the maintenance of separate schools is an issue that the country must soon face.

In the North, segregation in education is not formal, and in some states is prohibited. Nevertheless, the existence of residential restrictions in many northern cities has had discriminatory effects on Negro education. In Chicago, for example, the schools which are most crowded and employ double shift schedules are practically all in Negro neighborhoods.

Other minorities encounter discrimination. Occasionally Indian children attending public schools in the western states are assigned to separate classrooms. Many Texas schools segregate Mexican American children in separate schools. In California segregation of Mexican American children was also practiced until recently. The combined effect of a federal court ruling, and legislative action repealing the statute under which school boards claimed authority to segregate, seems to have ended this pattern of discrimination in California schools.

Discrimination in private schools. —The second inadequacy in our present educational practices in America is the religious and racial discrimination that exists in the operation of some private educational institutions, both with respect to the admission of students and the treatment of them after admission.

The Committee is absolutely convinced of the importance of the private educational institution to a free society. It does not question the right of groups of private citizens to establish such institutions, determine their character and policies, and operate them. But it does believe that such schools immediately acquire a public character and importance. Invariably they enjoy government support, if only in the form of exemption from taxation and in the privilege of income-tax deduction extended to their benefactors. Inevitably, they render public service by training our young people for life in a democratic society. Consequently, they are possessed of a public responsibility from which there is no escape.

Leading educators assert that a careful selection in admissions practices may be necessary to insure a representative and diversified student body. Liberal arts colleges, in particular, have used this reasoning to limit the number of students enrolled from any one race or religion, as well as from any geographical section, preparatory school, or socioeconomic background.

Nevertheless it is clear that there is much discrimination, based on prejudice, in admission of students to private colleges, vocational schools, and graduate schools. Since accurate statistical data is almost impossible to obtain this is difficult to prove. But competent observers are agreed that existence of this condition is widespread. Application blanks of many American colleges and universities include questions pertaining to the candidate's racial origin, religious preference, parents' birthplace, etc. In many of our northern educational institutions enrollment of Jewish students seems never to exceed certain fixed points and there is never more than a token enrollment of Negroes.

The impact of discriminatory practices in private education is illustrated by the situation in New York City. The students of the city colleges of New York are predominantly Jewish, resulting in part from the discrimination practiced by some local private institutions. These colleges have high academic standards, but graduates from them with excellent records have been repeatedly denied admission to private and nonsectarian professional schools. A Special Investigating Committee of the Council of the City of New York, recently established to examine this situation, found convincing evidence of discrimination against graduates of the city colleges by the medical schools in the city in violation of the Civil Rights Act of New York. The Investigating Committee, after questioning witnesses and examining application blanks, concluded that various professional schools tried to get information about applicants which would indicate their race, religion, or national origin for "a purpose other than judging their qualifications for admission." Jews are not alone in being affected by these practices. One witness, a member of a medical school's admission committee, admitted to a prejudice against Irish Catholics which affected his judgment. The number of Negroes attending these medical schools has been extremely low; less than 50 have been graduated from them in 25 years.

Certainly the public cannot long tolerate practices by private educational institutions which are in serious conflict with patterns of democratic life, sanctioned by the overwhelming majority of our people. By the closing of the door through bigotry and prejudice to equality of educational opportunity, the public is denied the manifold social and economic benefits that the talented individual might otherwise contribute to our society.

THE RIGHT TO HOUSING

Equality of opportunity to rent or buy a home should exist for every American. Today, many of our citizens face a double barrier when they try to satisfy their housing needs. They first encounter a general housing shortage which makes it difficult for any family without a home to find one. They then encounter prejudice and discrimination based upon race, color, religion or national origin, which places them at a disadvantage in competing for the limited housing that is available. The fact that many of those who face this double barrier are war veterans only underlines the inadequacy of our housing record.

Discrimination in housing results primarily from business practices. These practices may arise from special interests of business groups, such as the profits to be derived from confining minorities to slum areas, or they may reflect community prejudice. One of the most common practices is the policy of landlords and real estate agents to prevent Negroes from renting outside of designated areas. Again, it is "good business" to develop exclusive "restricted" suburban developments which are barred to all but white gentiles. When Negro veterans seek "GI" loans in order to build homes, they are likely to find that credit from private banks, without whose services there is no possibility of taking advantage of the GI Bill of Rights, is less freely available to members of their race. Private builders show a tendency not to construct new homes except for white occupancy. These interlocking business customs and devices form the core of our discriminatory policy. But community prejudice also finds expression in open public agitation against construction of public housing projects for Negroes, and by violence against Negroes who seek to occupy public housing projects or to build in "white" sections.

The restrictive covenant. — Under rulings of the Supreme Court, it is legally impossible to segregate housing on a racial or religious basis by zoning ordinance. Accordingly, the restrictive covenant has become the most effective modern method of accomplishing such segregation. Restrictive covenants generally take the form of agreements written into deeds of sale by which property owners mutually bind themselves not to sell or lease to an "undesirable." These agreements have thus far been enforceable by court action. Through these covenants large areas of land are barred against use by various classes of American citizens. Some are directed against only one minority group, others against a list of minorities. These have included Armenians, Jews, Negroes, Mexicans, Syrians, Japanese, Chinese and Indians.

While we do not know how much land in the country is subject to such restrictions, we do know that many areas, particularly large cities in the North and West, such as Chicago, Cleveland, Washington, D.C., and Los Angeles, are widely affected. The amount of land covered by racial restrictions in Chicago has been estimated at 80 percent. Students of the subject state that virtually all new subdivisions are blanketed by these covenants. Land immediately surrounding ghetto areas is frequently restricted in order to prevent any expansion in the ghetto. Thus, where old ghettos are surrounded by restrictions, and new subdivisions are also encumbered by them, there is practically no place for the people against whom the restrictions are directed to go. Since minorities have been forced into crowded slum areas, and must ultimately have access to larger living areas, the restrictive covenant is providing our democratic society with one of its most challenging problems.

The constitutional and legal validity of this device has been tested in few states. Where there has been litigation, the appellate courts have up to this time uniformly upheld restrictions against use by barred groups and in most instances have also upheld restriction against ownership. While a case in the United States Supreme Court in 1926 was long believed to uphold the constitutional validity of restrictive covenants under the federal Constitution, this case has recently been challenged as a binding authority. Litigation is now pending testing the validity of restrictive covenants directed against Jews, American Indians and Negroes. The Supreme Court, apparently willing to reexamine the issue, has currently accepted two restrictive covenant cases for review and a more definite ruling may be expected shortly.

The purpose of the restrictive covenant can only effectively be achieved in the final analysis by obtaining court orders putting the power of the state behind the enforcement of the private agreement. While our American courts thus far have permitted judicial power to be utilized for these ends, the Supreme Court of Ontario has recently refused to follow this course. The Ontario judge, calling attention to the policy of the United Nations against racial or religious discrimination, said:

> In my opinion, nothing could be more calculated to create or deepen divisions between existing religious and ethnic groups in this province . . . than the sanction of a method of land transfer which would permit the segregation and confinement of particular groups to particular business or residential areas, or conversely, would exclude particular groups from particular business or residential areas.

There is eminent judicial and professional opinion in this country that our courts cannot constitutionally enforce racial restrictive covenants. In a recent California case a lower court judge held that the courts could not enforce such an agreement. And in a strong dissenting opinion in a recent covenant case Justice Edgerton, of the United States Court of Appeals for the District of Columbia, said:

> Suits like these, and the ghetto system they enforce are among our conspicuous failures to live together in peace. . . . The question in these cases is not whether law should punish racial discrimination, or even whether law should try to prevent racial discrimination, or even whether law should interfere with it in any way. The question is whether law should affirmatively support and enforce racial discrimination.

Public housing. —The federal government has been closely concerned with minority housing problems in recent years through its aid to local public housing authorities, through its insurance of loans to private builders and through its war and veterans' programs. Much of the improvement in the housing conditions of minorities in recent years has resulted from public building. The Federal Public Housing Authority has tried to allocate public housing fairly, and to make certain that equal standards are maintained. Many housing projects with mixed racial occupancy have been operated with great success.

The Committee is glad to note that the Federal Housing Agency, which guarantees loans for certain types of private building, has recently abandoned the policy by which it encouraged the placing of racial restrictive covenants on projects supported by government guarantees.

It must be noted, however, that even if government, local or federal, does not encourage racial restrictions, private interests may put discriminatory practices into effect if proper safeguards are not devised. The experience of Stuyvesant Town in New York City is a case in point. There the city made great financial concessions to a private corporation, the Metropolitan Life Insurance Company, to induce construction of a large housing project, which was to be subject to a variety of restrictions designed to make it serve community housing needs. But, in the absence of any direct requirement of equitable distribution of the benefits of the project the Company barred Negroes from occupancy in Stuyvesant Town. Yet New York is a city in which mixed public housing projects have been maintained for many years.

THE RIGHT TO HEALTH SERVICE

Increased attention is being given throughout the United States to the health needs of our people. Minority groups are sharing in the improvements which are taking place. But there is serious discrimination in the availability of medical care, and many segments of our population do not measure up to the standards of health which have been attained by our people as a whole.

For example, the death rate from all causes for the entire country in 1945 was 10.5 per thousand of estimated population. The Chinese, however, had a rate of 12.8; the Negroes, 12.0; the Indians, 12.0; and the Japanese, 11.5. Similarly, many diseases strike minorities much harder than the majority groups. Tuberculosis accounts for the death of more than twice as many Negroes as whites. Among Indians in rural United States, the death rate from tuberculosis is more than 10 times as high as that for whites; in Alaska, the native deaths from this cause are over 30 times greater. In Texas, seven Latin Americans died of tuberculosis for every Anglo American. Infant deaths furnish another example of this pattern. On a nation-wide basis, the infant mortality rate was more than half again as high for Negroes as for whites. In Texas, it was almost three times as high for Latin as for Anglo infants. Maternal deaths show like disproportions. In New York City, where the vast majority of the Puerto Ricans in this country are located, reports from social workers and city health authorities indicate that the frequency of illness among the Puerto Ricans is much higher than among other groups.

There are many factors which contribute to the discrepancies between the health of the majority and the minorities. As has already been noted, our minorities are seriously handicapped by their economic status. Frequently, because of poverty, they are unable to afford even the minimum of medical care or a diet adequate to build up resistance to disease. The depressed economic status of many of our minorities combined with restrictive covenants in housing prevents them from living in a sanitary, health-giving environment. Children who are not admitted to clean, healthful playgrounds must find their fun in the crowded, dirty areas in which they are allowed. Discrimination in education withholds from many people the basic information and knowledge so essential to good health.

A more direct cause of unequal opportunity in the field of health is the discriminatory pattern that prevails with respect to medical facilities and personnel. Many hospitals will not admit Negro patients. The United States Public Health Service estimates on the basis of a preliminary survey that only approximately 15,000 hospital beds out of a total of one and one-half million beds are presently available to Negroes. Thus, though Negroes constitute about ten percent of the population, only one percent of the hospital beds are open to them. In Chicago, a study by the Mayor's Commission on Human Relations in 1946 disclosed that "although most hospital officials denied the existence of a discriminatory admission policy, Negroes represented a negligible percentage of patients admitted."

The situation is further complicated by the shortage of medical personnel available for the treatment of patients from minority groups. This is particularly evident among the Negroes; in 1937, only 35 percent of southern Negro babies were delivered by doctors, as compared to 90 percent of northern babies of both races. There were in 1940 only 3,530 Negro physicians and surgeons; 7,192 trained and student Negro nurses; and 1,471 Negro dentists in a total Negro population of 13,000,000. The ratio of Negro physicians to the total Negro population was about one to 3,377, while that of the total number of physicians to the general population of the country was one to 750. Moreover, a high proportion of these were employed in the North. In the South, with a Negro population of almost 10,000,000, there were in 1940 about 2,000 Negro doctors, or only one to every 4,900 colored persons.

One important reason for this acute shortage of skilled medical men is the discriminatory policy of our medical schools in admitting minority students. Medical schools graduate approximately 5,000 students a year, but only about 145 of these are Negro. And of these 145, 130 are from two Negro schools; thus, only about fifteen Negroes are graduated from all the other medical schools of the country each year.

To these handicaps must be added the refusal of some medical societies and many hospitals to admit Negro physicians and internes for practice. Denied the facilities and training which are available to other doctors, Negro members of the profession are often unable to keep abreast of developments in medicine and to qualify as specialists. This discrimination contributes to the state of Negro health.

Though the expectation of life at birth is still lower for nonwhites than whites, the relative increase in life expectancy between 1930 and 1940 was nearly twice as great for nonwhites as whites. The life expectancy of Negro males in this period increased 9.9 percent; of Negro females, 11.5 per cent; of white males and females, 6.0 per cent and 7.0 percent respectively. However, the figure for white persons is still appreciably higher than for nonwhite persons; white males can expect to live sixty-three years as compared with fifty-two for Negro males, and white females sixty-seven years compared with fifty-five years for Negro females.

Progress has been made in reducing Negro deaths due to tuberculosis, diphtheria, whooping cough, diarrhea, enteritis, and syphilis. Among the Mexicans in Texas, vigorous programs have been undertaken by federal and local officials. Baby clinics, home nursing classes, family life courses, maternity clinics and other measures have been established. The Indian Service now operates 69 hospitals and sanitoria in the United States, 7 in Alaska; 14 school health centers; and 100 field dispensaries. Special efforts are being made to combat tuberculosis, a leading cause of illness and death among Indians. Another sign of progress is the decision of the American Nurses Association, in 1946, to accept all qualified applicants as members of the national organization, even when they cannot, for local reasons, enter county societies.

THE RIGHT TO PUBLIC SERVICES AND ACCOMMODATIONS

Services supplied by the government should be distributed in a nondiscriminatory way. Activities financed by the public treasury should serve the whole people; they cannot, in consonance with the democratic principle, be used to advance the welfare of a portion of the population only. Moreover, many privately-owned and operated enterprises should recognize a responsibility to sell to all who wish to buy their services. They cannot be permitted to confine their benefits to a selected clientele. This is particularly true of those private businesses which hold franchises from the state or enjoy a monopoly status. Even when no franchise has been granted, and competition exists, certain private businesses because of the essential character of the services they render should serve all comers. It has been made clear to the Committee that unfortunately, many public services, supplied by both government and private business, do not reach all persons on an equality of access basis.

Discrimination in federal services. — Discrimination in public services supplied by the federal government is never directly authorized by legislation. It sometimes results inadvertently from the limited coverage of social service legislation. Thus, the old age and survivors' insurance and unemployment compensation systems do not cover agriculture, domestic service, and self-employed persons. Sixty-five percent of all Negro workers fall into these categories compared with 40 percent of all white workers. Large numbers of Mexican American, Hispano, and Japanese American workers also fail to benefit by this legislation because of their concentration in farm work.

Discrimination is sometimes evident in the admission of individuals to the benefits of the program by local administrators. The aims of some of our broadest social legislation are negated to the extent that this discrimination occurs. Evidence indicating the existence of such discrimination against Indians in certain localities has been brought to the attention of the Committee. It would appear that much of this discrimination is based on the mistaken belief that the Office of Indian Affairs provides the Indians with all needed public services. Actually, the Office furnishes very limited services which by no means replace those supplied the general public by government agencies. The Committee believes the extent of this misunderstanding and of resulting inequalities in services rendered Indians should be promptly ascertained by appropriate agencies, and steps taken to bring an end to those which are found to exist.

Negroes are sometimes not admitted locally to the benefits of certain services, or are given unequal service. This is shown by a study of public assistance made by Dr. Richard Sterner in 1942 in the investigation of the American Negro, sponsored by the Carnegie Corporation. Because of a higher proportion of dependency, Negroes have a greater need for old age assistance than whites, but average grants in the old age assistance program were found to be lower for Negroes than for whites. Sterner also found that certain Farm Security benefits were less for Negroes than for whites. More recently, the Farmers Home Administration has been making valiant efforts toward assuring that Negro farmers receive their share. Discrepancies of coverage and benefits can be cited also for the care of delinquent, destitute, and handicapped children and aid to the blind.

Discrimination in state and local services.—Where state or local facilities are allocated to Negroes, either because of segregation or as a result of geographical concentration of the colored population, the services are almost always inferior to those provided whites. For example, in 1940, in thirteen southern states providing 774 public libraries, ninety-nine, or less than one seventh, served Negroes. The streets in Negro districts in the North as well as in the South are often not kept up to the standards maintained in white areas. Public parks, beaches and playgrounds are generally closed to Negroes in the South, and on the rare occasion when substitutes are offered they are inferior. Furthermore, since the Negro schools are usually unsatisfactory, they are not suitable for community centers; thus, in 1937, about half of all the cities having Negro community centers were located in the North and West, despite the heavy concentration of Negro population in the South.

Discrimination in places of public accommodation. —When we turn
from public services supplied by government to those supplied by private enterprise, discrimination against minorities becomes more pronounced. Our social conscience has brought about an elimination of
some of the most flagrant inequalities in the distribution of government services. But it is often blind to the serious effect upon the individual which results from the discriminatory rendering of service by
private agencies.

Most Americans patronize restaurants, theaters, shops, and other
places offering service to the public according to their individual preferences and their ability to pay. They take their right to enter such
places and to be served for granted. This is not the case with other
Americans. Because of their race or their color or their creed, they are
barred from access to some places and given unequal service in others. In many sections of this country, some people must pause and
give thought before they enter places serving the public if they wish
to avoid embarrassment, arrest, or even possible violence.

As interpreted by the Supreme Court the Constitution does not
guarantee equal access to places of public accommodation and amusement. A Civil Rights Act was passed by Congress in 1875 which
declared that no distinction should be made because of race or color
in the accommodations offered by inns, public conveyances, theaters,
and similar places. This act was declared unconstitutional by the
Supreme Court in 1883, in the *Civil Rights Cases.* Thereafter legislation on the matter was left entirely to the states. They may, and do,
either compel segregation, or outlaw it, or they may leave it to the
managers of private establishments to make whatever distinction they
wish in selecting their patrons.

Eighteen states have statutes prohibiting discrimination in places of
public accommodation. These states prohibit discrimination in restaurants, and usually in other eating places. Most of them prohibit discrimination in public conveyances of all types, and over half of them,
in theaters and barber shops. All include some general phrase, such
as "and all other places of public accommodation." The courts, however, have tended to limit this general phrasing by the list of specific
places. The statutes can be enforced by criminal action or by a civil
suit for damages.

At the other extreme, 20 states by law compel segregation in one
way or another. The remaining 10 states have no laws on the subject.
In the states with compulsory segregation laws Negroes are usually
separated from whites in all forms of public transportation, and in

hotels, restaurants, and places of amusement. Fourteen states require railroads to separate the races, and two authorize railroads to provide such separation. Train conductors are given power to enforce these laws. Under the Supreme Court decision in *Morgan v. Virginia,* such laws do not apply to passengers in interstate transportation. However, this decision does not prevent carriers from voluntarily enforcing segregation. Eight states require separate waiting rooms, 11 require separation in buses, 10 in street cars and three in steamships and ferries. In instances where completely separate facilities are provided, as in railroad coaches and waiting rooms, those set aside for the Negro are usually inferior in quality.

In the states which do legally secure the right of access, practice does not necessarily conform to the law. One prominent Negro has stated that it is difficult to find a meal or a hotel room in the downtown areas of most northern cities. The display of "whites only" signs may sometimes go unchallenged. When laws guaranteeing equal access to places of public accommodation are enforced, the penalty is usually small and the chance of being prosecuted or sued a second time is slight.

Devices to get around the law are more common than direct violation of the law. Unwanted customers are discouraged from patronizing places by letting them wait indefinitely for service, charging higher prices, giving poor service, and publicly embarrassing them in various ways. In a recent campaign to compel enforcement of a civil rights statute in Cincinnati, many restaurants closed their doors to make repairs. Nevertheless, these campaigns are often successful, and without the statutes would be impossible. In Chicago in 1946, the Mayor's Commission on Human Relations invoked the State Civil Rights Statute to break down the bars against Negroes in the roller-skating rinks of the city.

Sometimes the pattern of segregation in public-service facilities spreads from the states having compulsory separation of the races to states which are free from such laws. For example, the Pennsylvania Railroad in its terminal in New York City segregates Negroes in coaches on through trains bound for the South, even though it does not do so on its own trains operating as far as Washington.

In the Southwest, Mexicans are barred from certain places of recreation. In some rural and semi-rural communities, operators of cafes, beer parlors, barber shops, and theaters are adamant in refusing service to all Latin Americans. Jews are discriminated against principally in recreational and resort areas in the North where beaches, hotels, and similar facilities are closed to them. Often this is indicated by "Gentiles only" or "restricted" labels. Japanese Americans have also frequently faced "No Japs Wanted" signs in store windows, and poor service in other places. Indians sometimes have difficulty getting service and hotel accommodations in different parts of the country. They meet a more serious problem, however, in areas surrounding reservations. The Assistant Commissioner of Indian Affairs described the scene in one town:

> I have recently been in a community in New Mexico, more than half of whose non-Indian citizens survive only because of the trade and business which the town's proximity to the reservation affords them, and yet the hundreds of Indians who frequent the town for marketing and other purposes are denied access to all but the most unsanitary and undesirable eating, lodging, and rest-room facilities.

SEGREGATION RECONSIDERED

The "Separate But Equal" Failure

Mention has already been made of the "separate but equal" policy of the southern states by which Negroes are said to be entitled to the same public service as whites but on a strictly segregated basis. The theory behind this policy is complex. On one hand, it recognizes Negroes as citizens and as intelligent human beings entitled to enjoy the status accorded the individual in our American heritage of freedom. It theoretically gives them access to all the rights, privileges, and services of a civilized, democratic society. On the other hand, it brands the Negro with the mark of inferiority and asserts that he is not fit to associate with white people.

Legally enforced segregation has been followed throughout the South since the close of the Reconstruction era. In these states it is generally illegal for Negroes to attend the same schools as whites; attend theaters patronized by whites; visit parks where whites relax; eat, sleep or meet in hotels, restaurants, or public halls frequented by whites. This is only a partial enumeration—legally imposed separation of races has become highly refined. In the eyes of the law, it is also an offense for whites to attend "Negro" schools, theaters and similar places. The result has been the familiar system of racial segregation in both public and private institutions which cuts across the daily lives of southern citizens from the cradle to the grave.

Legally-enforced segregation has been largely limited to the South. But segregation is also widely prevalent in the North, particularly in housing, and in hotel and restaurant accommodations. Segregation has not been enforced by states alone. The federal goverment has tolerated it even where it has full authority to eliminate it. We have already examined the situation in the armed forces. Another prominent example is the record in the Panama Canal Zone.

Although the federal government has exclusive jurisdiction over the Panama Canal Zone, a segregated way of life for Negroes and for whites exists. The latter are United States citizens who are employed in the Zone. Most of the Negroes are from Caribbean countries, and are British subjects. Although some of them have lived in the Zone for many years, and their children know no other country, they cannot become citizens because United States naturalization laws do not apply. Professional, skilled, and supervisory workers (gold) are supposed to be segregated from unskilled labor (silver). In a recent report, the Governor of the Zone described the situation:

> The force employed by the Panama Canal and the Panama Railroad Company is composed of two classes which for local convenience have been designated "gold" and "silver" employees. The terms . . . originated during the construction period of the Canal from the practice of paying in silver coin common laborers and other unskilled or semi-skilled workers employed in the Tropic while skilled craftsmen and those occupying executive, professional, and similar positions were paid in gold coin, the latter group being recruited largely from the United States. Although all employees are now paid in United States currency, *the original terms used to designate the two classes of employees have been retained for convenience. The terms "gold" and "silver" are applied also to quarters, commissaries, clubhouses, and other public facilities.* [Italics committee's.]

This system of "convenience" has operated to the serious detriment of the Negro workers. There are separate and lower standards for them in occupation and wages, education, housing, and recreation. The Zone government is at present engaged in a concerted effort to improve facilities and services for the Negro workers. The "gold" and "silver" signs labeling separate drinking fountain and rest-room facilities have recently been taken down. Nevertheless, Zone public institutions, all under government control, still segregate the gold and silver workers. This includes housing, government commissaries, and recreational establishments.

The Supreme Court and Segregation

The Fourteenth Amendment forbids a state to deny "to any person within its jurisdiction the equal protection of the laws." Moreover, the general spirit of the three Civil War Amendments seems to guarantee to all persons a full and equal status in American society.

Yet the Supreme Court, beginning with its decision in *Plessy v. Ferguson,* in 1896, has approved state legislation requiring segregation between Negroes and whites on the theory that segregation, as such, is not discriminatory. The Court dismissed the contention that "the enforced separation of the two races stamps the colored race with a badge of inferiority," and observed, "if this be so, it is not by reason of anything found in the act, but solely because the colored race chooses to put that construction upon it." So long as laws requiring segregation do not establish unequal facilities, the legal doctrine holds, there is no unreasonable discrimination and therefore no denial of equal protection under the law.

This judicial legalization of segregation was not accomplished without protest. Justice Harlan, a Kentuckian, in one of the most vigorous and forthright dissenting opinions in Supreme Court history, denounced his colleagues for the manner in which they interpreted away the substance of the Thirteenth and Fourteenth Amendments. In his dissent in the *Plessy* case, he said:

> Our Constitution is color blind, and neither knows nor tolerates classes among citizens. . . .
> We boast of the freedom enjoyed by our people above all other peoples. But it is difficult to reconcile that boast with a state of the law which, practically, puts the brand of servitude and degradation upon a large class of our fellow citizens, our equals before the law. The thin disguise of "equal" accommodations . . . will not mislead anyone, or atone for the wrong this day done.

If evidence beyond that of dispassionate reason was needed to justify Justice Harlan's statement, history has provided it. Segregation has become the cornerstone of the elaborate structure of discrimination against some American citizens. Theoretically this system simply duplicates educational, recreational and other public services, according facilities to the two races which are "separate but equal." In the Committee's opinion this is one of the outstanding myths of American history for it is almost always true that while indeed separate, these facilities are far from equal. Throughout the segregated public institutions, Negroes have been denied an equal share of tax-supported services and facilities. So far as private institutions are concerned, there is no specific legal disability on the right of Negroes to develop equal institutions of their own. However, the economic, social, and indirect legal obstacles to this course are staggering.

Following the *Plessy* decision, the Supreme Court for many years enforced with a degree of leniency the rule that segregated facilities must be equal. Gradually, however, the Court became stricter about requiring a showing of equality. During the last decade, in line with its vigorous defense of civil rights generally, the Court has been particularly insistent upon adherence to the "equal" part of the separate but equal rule. In 1938, in *Missouri ex rel. Gaines v. Canada,* it held that Missouri might not fulfill its obligation under the rule by offering to pay the tuition of a Negro resident of Missouri at an out-of-state law school in lieu of permitting him to attend the law school at the University of Missouri. The Court laid down the plain rule that if a state chooses to provide within its borders specialized educational facilities for citizens of one race, it must make similar provision, also within its borders, for citizens of other races.

This insistence upon equal facilities is encouraging. Experience requires the prediction, however, that the degree of equality will never be complete, and never certain. In any event we believe that not even the most mathematically precise equality of segregated institutions can properly be considered equality under the law. No argument or rationalization can alter this basic fact: a law which forbids a group of American citizens to associate with other citizens in the ordinary course of daily living creates inequality by imposing a caste status on the minority group.

Experience Versus Segregation

If reason and history were not enough to substantiate the argument against segregation, recent experiences further strengthen it. For these experiences demonstrate that segregation is an obstacle to establishing harmonious relationships among groups. They prove that where the artificial barriers which divide people and groups from one another are broken, tension and conflict begin to be replaced by cooperative effort and an environment in which civil rights can thrive.

One of these experiences is recorded in Report No. ETO–82 of the Research Branch, Information and Education Division, in the European Theater of Operations of the Army. In 1945, during the fighting in France, the Army was faced with a shortage of combat ground troops. The Theater Command decided to make use of Negro service troops in the area. A substantial number of Negro enlisted men accepted the invitation to volunteer for combat training and service. Many of these volunteers gave up their rank as noncommissioned officers for what they considered to be the privilege of combat. They were not very different from the run of Negro troops in the Army.

The Negro soldiers were trained and organized into platoons, which were placed in regiments in eleven white combat divisions. For months the Negro and white men in these divisions worked and fought side by side. Then, white officers, noncommissioned officers, and enlisted men in seven of the eleven divisions were interviewed. At least two of the divisions were composed of men who were predominantly southern in background. It is surprising how little the response of these southern men varied from that of men from other parts of the country.

Two out of every three white men admitted that at first they had been unfavorable to the idea of serving alongside colored platoons. Three out of every four said that their feelings toward the Negro soldiers had changed after serving with them in combat. These are some representative comments:

A platoon sergeant from South Carolina:

> When I heard about it I said I'd be damned if I'd wear the same shoulder patch they did. After that first day when we saw how they fought I changed my mind. They're just like any of the other boys to us.

A platoon sergeant from New Jersey:

> Didn't mind it myself. I'll tell you though, I came to think a lot more of them since.

A platoon leader from Texas:

> We all expected trouble. Haven't had any. One reason may be that we briefed the white boys in advance—told them these men were volunteers coming up here to fight and that we wouldn't stand for any foolishness.

A regimental commander:

> I'm from the South—most of us here are—and I was pretty dubious as to how it would work out. But I'll have to admit we haven't had a bit of trouble. I selected the best company commander I had to put over them.

A first sergeant from Alabama:

> I didn't want them myself at first. Now I have more trust in them. I used to think they would be yellow in combat, but I have seen them work.

The great majority of white officers and enlisted men agreed that the Negro soldiers who had fought alongside them had performed excellently in combat. Eight out of ten white men said they had done very well and almost all of the rest that they had done fairly well. Only two percent of the enlisted men and none of the officers felt that they had done "not so well" or were "undecided." No white officer or enlisted man said that they had done "not very well."

But the findings which have the greatest significance for the elimination of prejudices are in the answers to this question:

> Some Army divisions have companies which include Negro platoons and white platoons. How would you feel about it if your outfit was set up something like this?

The question was asked of four sample groups of white servicemen. The first had had direct, immediate and personal contact with Negroes as fellow solders; the second had been close to the situation and had had an opportunity to see how it worked; the third had been further away and the fourth had had no experience whatsoever.

The conclusion can be stated simply: the closer white infantrymen had been to the actual experience of working with Negroes in combat units the more willing they were to accept integrated Negro platoons in white companies as a good idea for the future. Moreover, the sharpest break was between groups which had even the slightest contact with the experience of integration, and those which had none at all.

The Merchant Marine presents a very different situation with respect to the relations between Negroes and whites than the Armed Forces. Negroes have served aboard ship for many years. There have been constant campaigns on the part of some of the seamen's unions to gain equality for them, as well as efforts to overcome prejudice among the white members. More than 400 merchant seamen were asked a series of indirect questions which were then built into an "Index of Prejudice Against Negroes." The results reported by Ira N. Brophy in the Public Opinion Quarterly, Winter, 1945–46, were surprising. They demonstrated that whether a man had been born in the North or the South was not important in determining whether he was prejudiced against Negroes. The extent of his education and the jobs he had held before he went to sea were not important. What was important was whether the men were members of unions with tolerant policies toward Negroes; how many trips to sea a man had made; how many times he had been under enemy fire; and how many times he had been to sea with Negroes. Here again what determined whether a white man was prejudiced against Negroes was the kind and amount of experience he had had with them. Where there was contact with Negroes on an equal footing in a situation of mutual dependence and common effort prejudice declined.

A study of two housing communities reinforces still further the pattern revealed in the Army and the Merchant Marine instances. The study was done under the direction of Professor Robert K. Merton of Columbia University for the Lavanburg Foundation and reported to this Committee by Professor Paul F. Lazarsfeld. An interracial housing community was set up in a northern city. Before they moved into the project only one out of every 25 whites thought that race relations would turn out well, while five times as many felt that there would be nothing but conflict between the people of the two races. After a few years, one out of every five whites said that race relations were better than they had thought they would be, while only about one-fourth as many thought that they were worse than they had expected. But of the people who had anticipated really serious race conflicts, three out of every four were willing to say that their fears had been proved groundless. Moreover, people who had worked with Negroes were considerably more willing to live in the same community with them. While 40 percent of them expressed such willingness, only 28 percent of the whites who had never worked with Negroes did. Other data collected in these studies of intergroup relations in housing communities indicate that the more institutions there are in any community in which Negroes and whites may meet together normally, the less prejudice will be found. Roughly the same patterns seem to be true of religious groups.

These three studies were done under widely varying circumstances by different scientists, with different people as subjects. The results add up to an indictment of segregation.

The separate but equal doctrine stands convicted on three grounds. It contravenes the equalitarian spirit of the American heritage. It has failed to operate, for history shows that inequality of service has been the omnipresent consequence of separation. It has institutionalized segregation and kept groups apart despite indisputable evidence that normal contacts among these groups tend to promote social harmony.

The Committee is not convinced that an end to segregation in education or in the enjoyment of public services essential to people in a modern society would mean an intrusion upon the private life of the individual. In a democracy, each individual must have freedom to choose his friends and to control the pattern of his personal and family life. But we see nothing inconsistent between this freedom and a recognition of the truth that democracy also means that in going to school, working, participating in the political process, serving in the armed forces, enjoying government services in such fields as health and recreation, making use of transportation and other public accommodation facilities, and living in specific communities and neighborhoods, distinctions of race, color, and creed have no place.

CIVIL RIGHTS IN THE NATION'S CAPITAL

We have seen how, throughout the country, our practice lags behind the American tradition of freedom and equality. A single community — the nation's capital — illustrates dramatically the shortcomings in our record and the need for change. The District of Columbia should symbolize to our own citizens and to the people of all countries our great tradition of civil liberty. Instead, it is a graphic illustration of a failure of democracy. As the seat of our federal government under the authority of Congress, the failure of the District is a failure of all of the people.

For Negro Americans, Washington is not just the nation's capital. It is the point at which all public transportation into the South becomes "Jim Crow." If he stops in Washington, a Negro may dine like other men in the Union Station, but as soon as he steps out into the capital, he leaves such democratic practices behind. With very few exceptions, he is refused service at downtown restaurants, he may not attend a downtown movie or play, and he has to go into the poorer section of the city to find a night's lodging. The Negro who decides to settle in the District must often find a home in an overcrowded, substandard area. He must often take a job below the level of his ability. He must send his children to the inferior public schools set aside for Negroes and entrust his family's health to medical agencies which give inferior service. In addition, he must endure the countless daily humiliations that the system of segregation imposes upon the one-third of Washington that is Negro.

The origin of the pattern of discrimination in Washington is partly explained by its location in a border area where many southern

THE NATION'S CAPITAL
A SYMBOL OF FREEDOM AND EQUALITY?

A NEGRO TRAVELING FROM NORTH TO SOUTH — MUST CHANGE TO JIM CROW TRAINS IN WASHINGTON, D.C.

NORTH

WASHINGTON, D.C.

SOUTH

IF HE DECIDES TO REMAIN IN D. C. OVERNIGHT HE WILL FIND THAT:

HE CANNOT EAT IN A DOWNTOWN RESTAURANT

HE CANNOT ATTEND A DOWNTOWN MOVIE OR PLAY.

HE CANNOT SLEEP IN A DOWNTOWN HOTEL.

IF HE DECIDES TO STAY IN D. C.

HE USUALLY MUST FIND A HOME IN AN OVERCROWDED, SUB-STANDARD, SEGREGATED AREA:

NEGRO–OCCUPIED DWELLINGS

40% SUBSTANDARD

WHITE–OCCUPIED DWELLINGS

12% SUBSTANDARD

HE MUST SEND HIS CHILDREN TO INFERIOR JIM CROW SCHOOLS:

WHITES
CAPACITY EXCEEDS ENROLLMENT BY 27%

NEGROES
ENROLLMENT EXCEEDS CAPACITY BY 8%

HE MUST ENTRUST HIS FAMILY'S HEALTH TO MEDICAL AGENCIES WHICH GIVE THEM INFERIOR SERVICES:

WHITE   NEGRO

 HOSPITALS IN THE DISTRICT OF COLUMBIA EITHER DO NOT ADMIT NEGROES OR ADMIT THEM ON A SEGREGATED BASIS

customs prevail. Certain political and local pressure groups, and the administrative decisions of municipal officials contribute to its persistence. Attempts to guarantee equal rights on a segregated basis have failed. In recent years the "separate and unequal" pattern has been extended to areas where it had not previously existed. Except where the federal government has made a few independent advances, as in federal employment and the use of federal recreational facilities, racial segregation is rigid. It extends to ludicrous extremes. Inconsistencies are evident: Constitution Hall, owned by the Daughters of the American Revolution, seats concert audiences without distinctions of color, but allows no Negroes on its stage to give regular commercial concerts. On the other hand, the commercial legitimate theater has had Negro actors on its stage, but stubbornly refuses to admit Negro patrons.

Discrimination in education.—The core of Washington's segregated society is its dual system of public education. It operates under Congressional legislation which assumes the fact of segregation but nowhere makes it mandatory. The Board of Education and a white Superintendent of Schools administer two wholly separate school systems. The desire of Congress to insure equal facilities is implemented by a requirement that appropriations be allocated to white and Negro education in proportion to the numbers of children of school age. But this has not been successful. Negro schools are inferior to white schools in almost every respect. The white school buildings have a capacity which is 27 percent greater than actual enrollment. In the colored schools, enrollment exceeds building capacity by eight percent. Classes in the Negro schools are considerably larger and the teaching load of the Negro teachers considerably heavier. Less than one percent of all white school children, but over 15 percent of colored children, receive only part-time instruction. Similar inequalities exist in school buildings, equipment, textbook supplies, kindergarten classes, athletic, and recreational facilities.

The District Superintendent of Schools recently answered charges of inequality in school facilities with the statement that "Absolute equality of educational opportunity is impossible. Reasonable equality . . . is the goal." The conditions described above eloquently document the extent to which even "reasonable equality" is impossible in a segregated school system.

Official freezing of the segregated school system is complete. The Board of Education frowns on visits by whites to Negro schools and by Negroes to white schools. Intercultural education programs are stillborn because they are considered a threat to the prevailing pattern. Interracial athletic and forensic competition is forbidden. Two cases illustrate the lengths to which the District's officialdom goes to prevent interracial contact. During the war, the Office of Price Administration asked permission to use a school building at night for in-service training of its clerks. The request was denied solely because the class would have included both white and colored employees. In the other case a white girl was ordered to withdraw from a Negro vocational school where she had enrolled for a course not offered by any other public school in Washington.

Private universities in the District have followed the lead of the public schools. Two of the large universities and most of the smaller schools admit no colored students. American University admits them to its School of Social Science and Public Affairs, but not to the College of Arts and Sciences. Catholic University, on the other hand, presents an outstanding example of successful interracial education. In the last few years, Negroes have been admitted, and there is no color distinction in classes. Last year a Negro was elected a class officer. The presence of Howard University in Washington alleviates somewhat the problem of higher education for the District's Negroes. While Howard University is primarily a Negro institution, it also admits white students.

Discrimination in housing. — In the past, many of Washington's Negroes and whites have lived close together in many parts of the city, and where mixed neighborhoods still exist, incidents of racial friction are rare. Now, however, Negroes are increasingly being forced into a few overcrowded slums.

Programs for the development of highways, parks, and public buildings have often played an unfortunate role in rooting out Negro neighborhoods. There has been a commendable desire to beautify the city of Washington. But there has been little concern for the fate of persons displaced by beautification projects.

The superior economic position of whites also contributes to the shrinkage of Negro neighborhoods. In areas like Georgetown and the old fort sites, white residents and realtors have been buying up Negro properties and converting them to choice residential use. Only occasionally does this process work in reverse: in deteriorating areas, white owners can sometimes get higher prices from Negroes, who have little from which to choose, than they can from white buyers.

The chief weapon in the effort to keep Negroes from moving out of overcrowded quarters into white neighborhoods is the restrictive covenant. New building sites and many older areas are now covenanted. Some covenants exclude all nonmembers of the Caucasian race; others bar only Negroes, or Negroes and members of "Semitic races." Even where covenants do not prevail, the powerful local real estate fraternity protects white areas from "invasion." The all-white Washington Real Estate Board has a "code of ethics" which prohibits its members from selling land in predominantly white areas to Negroes, and the realtors are supported in this practice by nonmember dealers, banks, and loan companies. Two of the city's newspapers will not accept ads offering property in white areas for sale to Negroes. Because the policy of the National Capital Housing Authority is to follow the "community pattern," all public housing projects are completely segregated and housing for Negroes is built only in established Negro neighborhoods. The Authority has spent most of its funds for permanent housing to build homes for Negroes, but its appropriations have been limited.

Housing conditions are poor for Washington residents in general, but largely because of the pressures just described, they are much worse for Negroes. According to a recent Board of Trade report on city planning, 70 percent of the inhabitants of the city's three worst slum areas are Negroes. The largest single slum in the District houses about seven percent of the white and 30 percent of the Negro population. In 1940, one-eighth of the white dwellings in Washington and 40 percent of those occupied by Negroes were substandard; 15 percent of white-occupied and 38 percent of Negro-occupied dwellings had more than one person per room.

Discrimination in employment. — More than one-third of the jobs in Washington are with the federal government. Therefore, discriminatory practices of government agencies, which have already been discussed, are important to District Negroes. The District government itself has only a small proportion of Negro employees, and most of these are confined to unskilled and menial jobs. Partial exceptions to this are the Metropolitan Police, the segregated Fire Service, and the school system with its segregated staff. A ranking District official during the war told an interviewer: "Negroes in the District of Columbia have no right to ask for jobs on the basis of merit," the rationalization being that whites own most of the property and pay the bulk of municipal taxes.

Negroes are confined to the lowest paid and least skilled jobs in private employment. In 1940, three-fourths of all Negro workers in Washington were domestics, service workers or laborers, while only

one-eighth of the white workers held jobs of that type. At the other
end of the scale, only one-eighth of all Negro workers were clerks,
salesmen, managers, proprietors or professionals, while two-thirds of
the white workers were in jobs of this kind. There are similar striking
racial differences in average income and length of workweek.

A few examples will illustrate the part discrimination has played in
causing these differences. During the war, Washington's public transportation system bogged down badly for lack of qualified street car
and bus operators. The Capital Transit Company advertised for workers hundreds of miles away and even recruited government employees on a part-time basis. In spite of this, the company would not
employ qualified Negroes as operators. In building construction, one
of Washington's largest industries, the various building trade unions
discriminate against colored craftsmen. They are either excluded completely, allowed to work only on projects to be occupied by Negroes,
admitted only as helpers to white journeymen, or not allowed to
become apprentices. The numerous large white hotels employ
Negroes only in such capacities as chambermaids, busboys, waiters,
and coal stokers. There are no colored salespeople in the large department stores. In laundries and cleaning plants where wages are low
and hours long, most of the workers are colored, but supervisors are
white; where whites and Negroes perform the same work, there is a
wage differential of from 20 to 30 percent. The District Bar Association and the Medical Society are for whites only.

Discrimination in health services. — The greatest inequalities are
evident in Washington's concern for the health of its residents. Freedmen's Hospital, federally supported and affiliated with Howard University, is for Negroes only, and three-fourths of the beds in the municipal
Gallinger Hospital are usually occupied by Negroes in segregated
wards. Four of the twelve private hospitals in the city do not admit
Negro in-patients, and the rest accept only a few in segregated wards.
It is peculiarly shocking to find church hospitals practicing discrimination. Far fewer hospital beds in proportion to population are available
to Negroes than to whites. Sickness rates are higher among Negroes
than whites, which aggravates this situation. All but the smallest clinics are segregated. Group Health Association, however, does not discriminate either in membership or services.

No Negro physician is allowed to practice in Gallinger Hospital,
although it is publicly supported and the majority of its patients are
colored. Nor are they allowed in St. Elizabeth's, a federal institution,
or any of the private hospitals. Only Freedmen's is open to them, and

then only for the care of assigned ward patients. Thus the Negro physician cannot follow his own patients into the hospital. Negro medical students are similarly discriminated against in the provision of training facilities.

Public and private agency welfare services are available to both colored and white residents, but institutional care is provided only on a segregated basis and the institutions for Negroes are far inferior in both number and quality to those for whites. Here again, the lower economic position of Negroes and their consequent need for care aggravates the problem.

Discrimination in recreational services.—In the field of public recreation, compulsory segregation has increased over the past 25 years. Various public authorities have closed to one race or the other numerous facilities where whites and Negroes once played together harmoniously. In 1942, the District of Columbia Board of Recreation was set up to centralize the control of public recreation facilities. Congress eliminated from the locally sponsored bill a provision that would have required the new Board to continue segregation. But it took no positive stand on the issue, and the Board has adopted regulations which enforce segregation in all the parks and playgrounds under its control.

Under this policy, facilities in seven out of 26 "natural areas" in the District have been turned over to Negroes. Because the Negro areas are disproportionately concentrated in the older, crowded parts of the city, white facilities are generally superior to those allotted to Negroes. Furthermore, whites and Negroes alike who live far from facilities open to their race have easy access to none. White residents who had shared with Negroes the use of the Rose Park Tennis Courts protested in vain against being barred from them.

On the other hand, recreation facilities under the jurisdiction of the Department of the Interior are open to all races, and serious friction is nonexistent. District officials have tried repeatedly to have these facilities turned over to the Recreation Board. The transfer has not been made because the Board will not agree to refrain from imposing segregation in their use.

Most private recreational groups follow the official policy of segregation, although occasional interracial competitions have been held successfully by some. The Washington Branch of the Amateur Athletic Union allows no interracial contests under its auspices. For example, no Negro may enter the local Golden Gloves Tournament, although they compete in the national tournament.

Discrimination in places of public accommodation. — Public transportation is provided without separation of the races, and the spectators at most professional sporting events are unsegregated. But other public accommodations are a focal point of Negro resentment, because rigorous segregation in practice means exclusion. No downtown theater except the burlesque house admits Negroes. They may see movies only in their neighborhood houses. Some department stores and many downtown shops exclude Negro patrons by ignoring them or refusing to show the stock they request or making them wait until all white customers have been served. A Negro is seldom accepted at the downtown hotels unless special arrangements are made. Although they may dine at the Union Station, the YWCA, and the cafeterias in government office buildings, the overwhelming majority of downtown restaurants are closed to them.

The shamefulness and absurdity of Washington's treatment of Negro Americans is highlighted by the presence of many dark-skinned foreign visitors. Capital custom not only humiliates colored citizens, but is a source of considerable embarrassment to these visitors. White residents, because they are the dominant group, share in both the humiliation and the embarrassment. Foreign officials are often mistaken for American Negroes and refused food, lodging and entertainment. However, once it is established that they are not Americans, they are accommodated.

This is the situation that exists in the District of Columbia. The Committee feels most deeply that it is intolerable.

III

Government's Responsibility: Securing the Rights

The National Government of the United States must take the lead in safeguarding the civil rights of all Americans. We believe that this is one of the most important observations that can be made about the civil rights problem in our country today. We agree with the words used by the President, in an address at the Lincoln Memorial in Washington in June, 1947:

> We must make the Federal Government a friendly, vigilant defender of the rights and equalities of all Americans. . . . Our National Government must show the way.

It is essential that our rights be preserved against the tyrannical actions of public officers. Our forefathers saw the need for such protection when they gave us the Bill of Rights as a safeguard against arbitrary government. But this is not enough today. We need more than protection of our rights against government; we need protection of our rights against private persons or groups, seeking to undermine them. In the words of the President:

> We cannot be content with a civil liberties program which emphasizes only the need of protection against the possibility of tyranny by the Government. . . . We must keep moving forward, with new concepts of civil rights to safeguard our heritage. The extension of civil rights today means not protection of the people against the Government, but protection of the people by the Government.

There are several reasons why we believe the federal government must play a leading role in our efforts as a nation to improve our civil rights record.

First, many of the most serious wrongs against individual rights are committed by private persons or by local public officers. In the most flagrant of all such wrongs—lynching—private individuals, aided upon occasion by state or local officials, are the ones who take the law

126

into their own hands and deprive the victim of his life. The very fact that these outrages continue to occur, coupled with the fact that the states have been unable to eliminate them, points clearly to a strong need for federal safeguards.

Second, it is a sound policy to use the idealism and prestige of our whole people to check the wayward tendencies of a part of them. It is true that the conscience of a nation is colored by the moral sense of its local communities. Still, the American people have traditionally shown high national regard for civil rights, even though the record in many a community has been far from good. We should not fail to make use of this in combating civil rights violations. The local community must be encouraged to set its own house in order. But the need for leadership is pressing. That leadership is available in the national government and it should be used. We cannot afford to delay action until the most backward community has learned to prize civil liberty and has taken adequate steps to safeguard the rights of every one of its citizens.

Third, our civil rights record has growing international implications. These cannot safely be disregarded by the government at the national level which is responsible for our relations with the world, and left entirely to government at the local level for proper recognition and action. Many of man's problems, we have been learning, are capable of ultimate solution only through international cooperation and action. The subject of human rights, itself, has been made a major concern of the United Nations. It would indeed be ironical if in our own country the argument should prevail that safeguarding the rights of the individual is the exclusive, or even the primary concern of local government.

A lynching in a rural American community is not a challenge to that community's conscience alone. The repercussions of such a crime are heard not only in the locality, or indeed only in our own nation. They echo from one end of the globe to the other, and the world looks to the American national government for both an explanation of how such a shocking event can occur in a civilized country and remedial action to prevent its recurrence.

Similarly, interference with the right of a qualified citizen to vote locally cannot today remain a local problem. An American diplomat cannot forcefully argue for free elections in foreign lands without meeting the challenge that in many sections of America qualified voters do not have free access to the polls. Can it be doubted that this is a right which the national government must make secure?

Fourth, the steadily growing tendency of the American people to look to the national government for the protection of their civil rights is highly significant. This popular demand does not by itself prove the case for national government action. But the persistent and deep-felt desire of the American citizen for federal action safeguarding his civil rights is neither a request for spoils by a selfish pressure group, nor is it a shortsighted and opportunistic attempt by a temporary majority to urge the government into a dubious or unwise course of action. It is a demand rooted in the folkways of the people, sound in instinct and reason, and impossible to ignore. The American people are loyal to the institutions of local self-government, and distrust highly central-ized power. But we have never hesitated to entrust power and respon-sibility to the national government when need for such a course of action has been demonstrated and the people themselves are con-vinced of that need.

Finally, the national government should assume leadership in our American civil rights program because there is much in the field of civil rights that it is squarely responsible for in its own direct dealings with millions of persons. It is the largest single employer of labor in the country. More than two million persons are on its payroll. The freedom of opinion and expression enjoyed by these people is in many ways dependent upon the attitudes and practices of the government. By not restricting this freedom beyond a point necessary to insure the efficiency and loyalty of its workers, the government, itself, can make a very large contribution to the effort to achieve true freedom of thought in America. By scrupulously following fair employment prac-tices, it not only sets a model for other employers to follow, but also directly protects the rights of more than two million workers to fair employment.

The same is true of the armed forces. Their policies are completely determined by the federal government. That government has the power, the opportunity and the duty to see that discrimination and prejudice are completely eliminated from the armed services, and that the American soldier or sailor enjoys as full a measure of civil liberty as is commensurate with military service.

The District of Columbia and our dependent areas are under the immediate authority of the national government. By safeguarding civil rights in these areas, it can protect several million people directly, and encourage the states and local communities throughout the coun-try to do likewise. Finally, through its extensive public services, the national government is the largest single agency in the land endeavoring to satisfy the wants and needs of the consumer. By making certain that these services are continuously available to all persons without regard to race, color, creed or national origin, a very important step toward the elimination of discrimination in American life will have been taken.

Leadership by the federal government in safeguarding civil rights does not mean exclusive action by that government. There is much that the states and local communities can do in this field, and much that they alone can do. The Committee believes that Justice Holmes' view of the states as 48 laboratories for social and economic experimentation is still valid. The very complexity of the civil rights problem calls for much experimental, remedial action which may be better undertaken by the states than by the national government. Parallel state and local action supporting the national program is highly desirable. It is obvious that even though the federal government should take steps to stamp out the crime of lynching, the states cannot escape the responsibility to employ all of the powers and resources available to them for the same end. Or again, the enactment of a federal fair employment practice act will not render similar state legislation unnecessary.

In certain areas the states must do far more than parallel federal action. Either for constitutional or administrative reasons, they must remain the primary protectors of civil rights. This is true of governmental efforts to control or outlaw racial or religious discrimination practiced by privately supported public-service institutions such as schools and hospitals, and of places of public accommodation such as hotels, restaurants, theaters, and stores.

Furthermore, government action alone, whether federal, state, local, or all combined, cannot provide complete protection of civil rights. Everything that government does stems from and is conditioned by the state of public opinion. Civil rights in this country will never be adequately protected until the intelligent will of the American people approves and demands that protection. Great responsibility, therefore, will always rest upon private organizations and private individuals who are in a position to educate and shape public opinion. The argument is sometimes made that because prejudice and intolerance cannot be eliminated through legislation and government control we should abandon that action in favor of the long, slow, evolutionary effects of education and voluntary private efforts. We believe that this argument misses the point and that the choice it poses between legislation and education as to the means of improving civil rights is an unnecessary one. In our opinion, both approaches to the goal are valid, and are, moreover, essential to each other.

It may be impossible to overcome prejudice by law, but many of the evil discriminatory practices which are the visible manifestations of prejudice can be brought to an end through proper government controls. At the same time, it is highly desirable that efforts be made to understand more fully the causes of prejudice and to stamp them out. These efforts will necessarily occupy much time and can in many instances best be made by private organizations and individuals. At the close of this section on government responsibility, further attention will be given to the problem of prejudice and its elimination.

The Committee rejects the argument that governmental controls are themselves necessarily threats to liberty. This statement overlooks the fact that freedom in a civilized society is always founded on law enforced by government. Freedom in the absence of law is anarchy.

Because it believes there is need for leadership by the national government, the Committee has not hesitated to recommend increased action by that government in support of our civil rights. At the same time, it has not overlooked the many possibilities for remedial action by the states, nor the benefits to be derived from private efforts in the never-ending struggle to make civil liberty more secure in America. Certain of the Committee's recommendations look in each of these directions.

CONSTITUTIONAL TRADITIONS AS TO GOVERNMENTAL PROTECTION OF CIVIL RIGHTS

The Committee believes that national leadership in this field is entirely consistent with our American constitutional traditions. It is true that the federal government does not possess broad, clearly defined delegated powers to protect civil rights which it may exercise at its discretion. A detailed examination of the constitutional aspects of the civil rights problem makes clear that very real difficulties lie in the way of federal action in certain areas. It also makes clear that effective federal power does exist under the Constitution.

The Constitution, as it came from the Philadelphia Convention in 1787, granted to Congress no express power to enact civil rights legislation of any kind. Moreover, the first ten Amendments, which make up our Bill of Rights, far from granting any positive powers to the federal government, serve as express limitations upon it. The Thirteenth,

Fourteenth, and Fifteenth Amendments added to the Constitution immediately following the close of the Civil War do expressly authorize Congress to pass laws in certain civil rights areas. But the areas are of limited extent and are not clearly defined. Thus, there is nothing in the Constitution which in so many words authorizes the national government to protect the civil rights of the American people on a comprehensive basis.

The Committee is aware of the fate of the civil rights program developed by Congress following the close of the Civil War. Between 1866 and 1875, Congress passed seven statutes which in a collective sense were designed to give more specific meaning and reality to the three Civil War Amendments. By these acts, Congress attempted on a broad basis to provide federal protection of the civil rights of individuals against interference either by public officers or private individuals.

This early program was largely a failure. But it is important to note that remnants of the legislation remained on the federal statute books in 1939. Furthermore, in that year they served as the basis for the creation of the Civil Rights Section in the Department of Justice. The rest of the legislation had disappeared as the result of a series of six adverse decisions by the Supreme Court between 1876 and 1906, and the passage of repeal acts by Congress in 1894 and 1909.

The Committee does not believe that the action of the Supreme Court in declaring parts of the nineteenth century civil rights legislation unconstitutional proves that a well-conceived present-day attempt to strengthen the federal civil rights program would meet a similar fate. Certain of these early decisions of the Court have long been criticized by eminent authorities on American constitutional law. In every one of the cases there was a dissenting opinion. That by Justice Harlan in the Civil Rights Cases of 1883 is a particularly powerful statement. The majority's concept of the extent of federal power to protect civil rights struck him as being entirely too narrow and artificial. He states that he "cannot resist the conclusion that the substance and spirit of the recent amendments of the Constitution have been sacrificed by a subtle and ingenious verbal criticism." So powerful a dissent remains a living force in constitutional law and is bound to be thoughtfully considered by any later Supreme Court when the validity of new civil rights laws comes before it for decision.

The adverse decisions of the Court in all of these cases depend upon the use of the Thirteenth, Fourteenth, and Fifteenth Amendments as a basis for civil rights legislation. The constitutional bases upon which Congress may enact civil rights laws of varying types are far broader, however, than the clauses of these three amendments. Furthermore, offsetting these six adverse decisions of the Supreme Court are others in which various federal civil rights laws have been upheld. Sections 51 and 52 of Title 18 of the United States Code have been upheld by the Court. Both are derived from the Reconstruction period legislation, and remain on the statute books today.

The Committee believes that a positive program of action by the national government falls well within the limits of governmental power established by our Constitution. Two strong considerations have led to this conclusion. One depends upon the broad character and principles of the Constitution, the other upon its more specific provisions.

Our Constitution has long been recognized by the Supreme Court itself as a flexible document, subject to varying interpretations and capable of being adapted to the different needs of changing times. Chief Justice Marshall in his great opinion in *McCulloch v. Maryland* called it ". . . a constitution intended to endure for ages to come, and consequently, to be adapted to the various crises of human affairs." The American people, by and large, have accepted John Marshall's view for more than a century and a quarter. Again and again, the Constitution and its clauses have been construed to authorize positive governmental programs designed to solve the nation's changing problems. Again and again, the Supreme Court of the United States has approved these programs as falling within the limits of the Constitution. Our nation has had to cope with problems growing out of wars, economic depressions, floods, soil erosion, strife between labor and management, and threats to a system of free enterprise. A basis for governmental action at the national level has been found within the Constitution for such policies as the control of prices; regulation of agricultural production; requirement of collective bargaining; social security benefits for millions of people; prohibition of industrial monopolies; drafting of millions of men into the armed services in peacetime as well as in time of war; regulation of the sale of stocks, bonds, and other securities; establishment of vast governmental flood-control and electric power projects; and an attack upon such crimes as white slavery, kidnaping, trade in narcotics, and the theft of automobiles.

The Supreme Court has held these legislative policies valid, not as exercises of new powers, but as the application of old-established powers to new problems and situations. The adequate protection of civil rights is not a new problem, but it is a pressing one, and we believe that the Supreme Court will be as statesmanlike in interpreting the powers of Congress to deal with this problem as it has been in its interpretation of the commerce power. No one wishes Congress to exceed its constitutional powers or wishes the Supreme Court to uphold invalid statutes. But when the clauses of the Constitution contain language from which substantial power to protect civil rights may reasonably be implied we believe the Supreme Court will be as ready to apply John Marshall's doctrine of liberal construction as it has been in dealing with laws in other fields.

There are several specific constitutional bases upon which a federal civil rights program can be built. Some have been recognized and approved by the courts. Others have the support of leading students of the American constitutional system. Some are beyond dispute; others are frankly controversial. Collectively, however, they provide an encouraging basis for action. The President and Congress must determine the wisdom of a broader civil rights program at the policy level. They should be advised that such a program, carefully framed, will meet the test of constitutionality.

The several specific constitutional bases for federal action in the civil rights field brought to our attention follow. Those numbered from one through eight have either been specifically approved by the Supreme Court or seem to be clearly valid. Those numbered from nine through eleven are more controversial and will be discussed at greater length.

1. *Power to protect the right to vote.* —The extent of federal power to protect the suffrage varies, depending on the type of election (state or national), the type of interference (whether it affects the voting procedure, or is based on race or sex) and the source of interference (state and local officers or private persons). Among the specific sources of federal power are: Article I, Section 4, which permits federal protection of the procedure for voting in federal elections against interference from any source; the Fourteenth Amendment which supports protection against state interference with equality of opportunity to vote in any election; the Fifteenth Amendment which supports action against state interference because of race or color with the right to vote in any election; and the Nineteenth Amendment, which supports action against state interference based on sex with the right to vote in any election.

2. *Power to protect the right to freedom from slavery and involuntary servitude.* —This power derives from the Thirteenth Amendment: "Neither slavery nor involuntary servitude, except as a punishment

for crime whereof the party shall have been duly convicted, shall exist within the United States, or any place subject to their jurisdiction." This permits legislation designed to protect against actions of private persons or state or local officials.

3. *Power to protect rights to fair legal process, to free speech and assembly, and to equal protection of the laws.* — This power, derived from the "due process," "equal protection" and "privileges or immunities" clauses of the Fourteenth Amendment, cannot be readily summarized, except for the fact that, under Supreme Court rulings, it protects only against interferences by agencies of state or local government. In a wide variety of specific situations — such as cases involving the validity of ordinances licensing the distribution of handbills, the adequacy of representation by counsel, or the validity of state laws or administrative action claimed to discriminate against minorities — the Supreme Court has delineated areas of activity protected by these constitutional provisions. Congress is expressly authorized to enact legislation to implement this power, and has passed some statutes for this purpose.

4. *The war power.* — Under Section 8 of Article I of the Constitution Congress has extensive power to regulate the armed forces and to legislate concerning the national defense and security. Congress may thus legislate with respect to treatment of minority groups in the services, with respect to interference with members of the services, and with respect to construction or operation of military and naval installations. Related is the congressional power to assure distribution of veterans' benefits on an equal basis.

5. *Power to regulate activities which relate to interstate commerce.* — Congress has exercised its broad power to regulate interstate commerce derived from Article I, Section 8 of the Constitution, to institute reforms in many fields. Outstanding examples are the Fair Labor Standards Act, which fixes maximum hours and minimum wages in work relating to interstate commerce, the National Labor Relations Act, which regulates labor-management relations affecting interstate commerce, and the Federal Safety Appliance Act, which specifies safety standards for interstate transportation. The commerce power could be the basis for fair employment legislation relating to activities affecting interstate commerce, and for laws prohibiting discriminatory practices by interstate carriers.

6. *The taxing and spending powers.* — Also derived from Article I, Section 8, these are among the most extensive congressional powers, and have been repeatedly used to effectuate federal programs. An out-

standing example is the Social Security program. Federal grants-in-aid have almost always been conditioned on compliance with congressionally declared standards, as have exemptions from taxation. Congress has power to impose similarly appropriate conditions in spending or taxing programs which affect civil rights problems. Another facet of these powers permits Congress to require persons who enter into contracts with the federal government, or supply the government with goods or services to conform with national policy. For example, in the Walsh-Healey Act, Congress has made compliance with minimum wage and maximum hour standards a condition of performance of federal supply contracts.

7. *The postal power.*—Under its plenary power over the postal system (stemming from Article I, Section 8) Congress has acted to protect use of the mails against certain undesirable purposes. This power is, of course, subject to the constitutional limits on congressional power to impair free speech. Within those limits, however, there may be room for certain types of legislation—such as the exclusion of anonymous hate group literature from the mails.

8. *Power over the District of Columbia and the Territories.*—Under Article I, Section 8 and Article IV, Section 3, Congress has full power of government over the District of Columbia and the various territories. It may thus pass any legislation proper for complete protection of the civil rights of all persons residing in those areas.

9. *Power derived from the Constitution as a whole to protect the rights essential to national citizens in a democratic nation.*

No such power is expressly granted to Congress in the Constitution. It has long been asserted that the basic rights falling into this category, such as freedom of speech and press or the right of assembly, exist at the state level and depend upon state action for their protection against interference by private persons. However, the Supreme Court long ago suggested that such rights have a national significance as exercised in connection with the national political process, and that they may be protected by national legislation. In 1876, in the case of *United States v. Cruikshank,* the issue of federal power to protect the right of assembly against interference by private persons was raised. In a dictum the court said:

> The right of the people peaceably to assemble for the purpose of petitioning Congress for a redress of grievances, or for anything else connected with the powers or the duties of the national government, is an attribute of national citizenship, and, as such, under the

protection of, and guaranteed by, the United States. The very idea of a government, republican in form, implies a right on the part of its citizens to meet peaceably for consultation in respect to public affairs and to petition for a redress of grievances.

As recently as 1940, the Fifth Circuit Court of Appeals in the case of *Powe v. United States,* likewise in a dictum said:

Because the federal government is a republican one in which the will of the people ought to prevail, and because that will ought to be expressive of an informed public opinion, the freedom of speaking and printing on subjects relating to that government, its elections, its laws, its operations and its officers is vital to it.

And the court said that Congress has power under the Constitution to protect freedom of discussion, so defined, against all threats.

Unfortunately, these dicta have not been directly tested in practice. It is impossible to say how far the courts may be willing to go in recognizing the existence of specific rights at the national level, or in approving the power of Congress to protect these rights as necessary to a democratic nation. But the basis seems to be a valid one and it might support national civil rights legislation of considerable significance.

10. *Power derived from the treaty clause in Article II, Section 2 of the Constitution, to protect civil rights which acquire a treaty status.*

In its decision in *Missouri v. Holland* in 1920, the Supreme Court ruled that Congress may enact statutes to carry out treaty obligations, even where, in the absence of a treaty, it has no other power to pass such a statute. This doctrine has an obvious importance as a possible basis for civil rights legislation.

The United Nations Charter, approved by the United States Senate as a treaty, makes several references to human rights. Articles 55 and 56 are of particular importance. They are:

ARTICLE 55

With a view to the creation of conditions of stability and well-being which are necessary for peaceful and friendly relations among nations based on respect for the principle of equal rights and self-determination of peoples, the United Nations shall promote:

a. Higher standards of living, full employment, and conditions of economic and social progress and development;

b. Solutions of international economic, social, health and related problems; and international cultural and educational cooperation; and *c.* Universal respect for, and observance of, human rights and fundamental freedoms for all without distinction as to race, sex, language, or religion.

ARTICLE 56

All members pledge themselves to take joint and separate action in cooperation with the Organization for the achievement of the purposes set forth in Article 55.

A strong argument can be made under the precedent of *Missouri v. Holland* that Congress can take "separate action" to achieve the purposes set forth in Article 55 by passing legislation designed to secure "respect for, and observance of, human rights and fundamental freedoms for all without distinction as to race, sex, language, or religion."

Some persons believe that Article 2 (7) of the United Nations Charter limits the argument of the last paragraph. This provision is:

Nothing contained in the present Charter shall authorize the United Nations to intervene in matters which are essentially within the domestic jurisdiction of any state or shall require the Members to submit such matters to settlement under the present charter. . . .

The Human Rights Commission of the United Nations is at present working on a detailed international bill of rights designed to give more specific meaning to the general principle announced in Article 55 of the Charter. If this document is accepted by the United States as a member state, an even stronger basis for congressional action under the treaty power may be established.

11. *Power derived from the "republican form of government" clause in Article IV, Section 4, of the Constitution, to protect rights essential to state and local citizens in a democracy.*

This clause reads "The United States shall guarantee to every State in this Union a republican form of government . . ." This phraseology is admittedly vague, and has had relatively little interpretation by the Supreme Court. But other vague clauses of the Constitution, such as the commerce clause or the due process of law clauses, have lent themselves to broad interpretation. It is possible that guaranteeing "a republican form of government" includes the power to protect essential civil rights against interference by public officers or private persons.

In view of this analysis of the Constitution, both as to its broad character and its more specific clauses, the Committee believes that federal legislation in support of civil liberty is legitimate and well within the scope of the Constitution.

We wish to emphasize that a program of action by the federal government where there is deprivation of civil rights will not be a new departure. In particular, two agencies of the federal government have had important responsibilities for protecting the liberties of the people. These are the Supreme Court and the Department of Justice.

THE ROLE OF THE SUPREME COURT AS A GUARDIAN OF CIVIL RIGHTS

Throughout its entire history, one of the great responsibilities of the Supreme Court has been to protect the civil rights of the American people against encroachment. However, during the first half of our history, its chief responsibility in this respect was to enforce the Bill of Rights against the federal government. Few violations of the Bill of Rights were brought to the attention of the Court and accordingly it rendered few decisions in civil rights cases before 1870. Thereafter, the three Civil War Amendments provided a further basis for judicial protection of civil rights, but the Court interpreted these Amendments narrowly and thereby greatly restricted its jurisdiction over civil rights matters. Nonetheless, the protection provided by the Court has gradually increased through the years. Since 1925, this protection has become extremely important as a result of new developments in the law of civil liberty.

One development is the rule now followed by the Court that the Fourteenth Amendment extends the basic guarantees of the Bill of Rights into the areas of state and local government. As has been seen, the original Bill of Rights has always afforded protection against wrongful actions by the federal government. There is evidence that the Fourteenth Amendment was intended by its framers to extend this protection against wrongful actions by the state and local governments. For 60 years following ratification of the Amendment, the Supreme Court refused to sanction this point of view. But in *Gitlow v. New York* in 1925, and in *Near v. Minnesota* in 1931, the Supreme Court reversed itself. In a long series of cases since 1931, it has safeguarded the rights of the individual by invalidating state laws and setting aside certain state judicial rulings.

A second development has stemmed from the challenging of certain statutes as to constitutionality on the ground that they interfere with civil rights. Through the years, the Supreme Court has followed the rule that any statute, federal, or state, which is challenged as to constitutionality, shall be presumed to be valid unless its violation of the Constitution is proved beyond all reasonable doubt. In the last decade, however, the Court has announced a new doctrine that when a law appears to encroach upon a civil right—in particular, freedom of speech, press, religion, and assembly—the presumption is that the law is invalid, unless its advocates can show that the interference is justified because of the existence of a "clear and present danger" to the public security.

These new developments have resulted in a striking increase in the number of civil rights cases heard by the Supreme Court. They have greatly increased the opportunity of the individual whose rights are encroached upon by a state or local government to seek the protection of the Court. For example, in more than 20 cases since 1938 the Court has dealt with charges that states or cities have violated the religious liberty of the Jehovah's Witnesses. In the great majority of these cases the Court held that the action complained of was invalid.

It is not too much to say that during the last 10 years, the disposition of cases of this kind has been as important as any work performed by the Court. As an agency of the federal government, it is now actively engaged in the broad effort to safeguard civil rights.

THE CIVIL RIGHTS SECTION EXPERIMENT

From the days of the civil rights legislation of the 1860's and 1870's, there remained on the federal statute books scattered provisions of civil rights law. Responsibility for the enforcement of these laws rested with the Department of Justice. From time to time, it took prosecutive action under them but no coordinated program was developed. However, in 1939, to encourage more vigorous use of these laws and to centralize responsibility for their enforcement, Attorney General Frank Murphy established a Civil Rights Section in the Criminal Division of the Department.

This agency has now had eight years of experience. The President's Committee on Civil Rights has regarded an examination of the Section's organization and achievements as one of its most important assignments. We wish to point out at once that we believe that the Section's record is a remarkable one. In many instances during these eight years, the Section, the FBI and the United States Attorneys in the field have done invaluable work. They deserve the highest praise for the imagination and courage they have often shown. Indeed, we have found that the total achievement of the Department of Justice in the civil rights field during the period of the Section's existence goes well beyond anything that had previously been accomplished. Yet the record is by no means a perfect one, and it seems clear that the time has come to evaluate the experiment, to note criticisms of the program, and to suggest ways of improving it.

As our recommendations will show, one of the most important objectives of this Committee is to strengthen the federal civil rights enforcement machinery. We believe that the achievements of these agencies offer great promise for the future. But only by remedying some of the imperfections in the machinery can this progress be assured. Some of these imperfections will now be discussed.

1. *Weak statutory tools.*—No new civil rights laws were passed by Congress at the time of the agency's creation. It was compelled to utilize the remnants of the post–Civil War legislation. The three laws which have been of major importance are Sections 51, 52 and 444 of Title 18 ("Criminal Code and Criminal Procedure") of the United States Code. All three statutes define federal crimes. Sections 51 and 52 are short, generally worded statutes which seek to protect undefined civil rights. Section 444 is also brief, but it protects one right only—the right to be free from peonage.

Section 51 is in form a conspiracy statute, making it a crime for two or more persons to conspire to "injure, oppress, threaten or intimidate any citizen in the free exercise or enjoyment of any right or privilege secured to him by the Constitution or laws of the United States." Persons convicted under the act can be fined up to $5,000, imprisoned up to 10 years, and are to be "thereafter ineligible to any office or place of honor, profit or trust created by the Constitution or laws of the United States."

Section 52, likewise, penalizes deprivation of "rights, privileges, or immunities" secured by the Constitution and laws of the United States, but it is directed only against those deprivations of rights which are "willful" and which occur "under color of any law." Section 52 is thus limited to the protection of rights against interferences by public officers, whereas Section 51 may be used to prosecute private persons as well as public officers. Section 52 is not a conspiracy statute and may be used to prosecute one person. It differs further from Section 51 in carrying much lighter penalties—a maximum fine of $1,000, and a maximum prison term of one year.

OUR FEDERAL CIVIL RIGHTS MACHINERY NEEDS STRENGTHENING

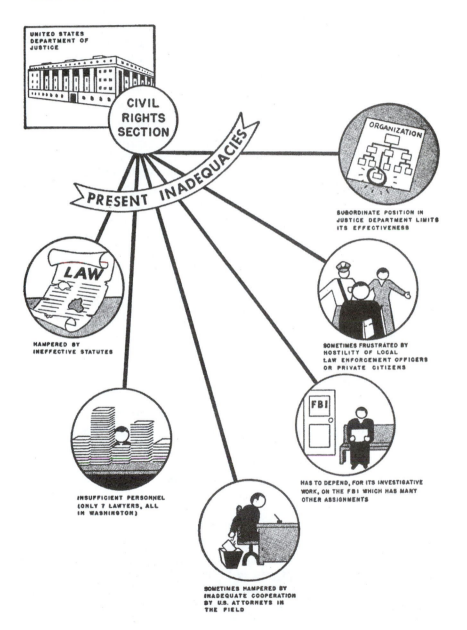

CIVIL RIGHTS SECTION

UNITED STATES DEPARTMENT OF JUSTICE

PRESENT INADEQUACIES

ORGANIZATION

SUBORDINATE POSITION IN JUSTICE DEPARTMENT LIMITS ITS EFFECTIVENESS

LAW

HAMPERED BY INEFFECTIVE STATUTES

SOMETIMES FRUSTRATED BY HOSTILITY OF LOCAL LAW ENFORCEMENT OFFICERS OR PRIVATE CITIZENS

FBI

INSUFFICIENT PERSONNEL (ONLY 7 LAWYERS, ALL IN WASHINGTON)

HAS TO DEPEND, FOR ITS INVESTIGATIVE WORK, ON THE FBI WHICH HAS MANY OTHER ASSIGNMENTS

SOMETIMES HAMPERED BY INADEQUATE COOPERATION BY U.S. ATTORNEYS IN THE FIELD

141

Section 444, often called the Antipeonage Act, provides that anyone who "holds, arrests, returns, or causes to be held, arrested or returned, or in any manner aids in the arrest or return of a person to a condition of peonage, shall be fined not more than $5,000, or imprisoned not more than five years or both."

Section 51 and Section 444 had had considerable use when the Civil Rights Section was created in 1939, and had been held constitutional by the Supreme Court. Moreover, Section 51 had been successfully used to protect several specific federal rights against invasion by private individuals. With one exception, however, these rights were all relatively minor ones, such as the right to inform federal officers of the commission of a federal crime; the right of a witness before a federal tribunal to enjoy protection; and the right to make entries and hold land under the homestead laws. The one really important right which had been protected by Section 51 before 1939 was the right of a qualified voter to participate in a federal election, and to have his ballot honestly counted.

Section 52, on the other hand, had had almost no use and had not been tested as to constitutionality. Since 1939, these laws have all been employed by the Civil Rights Section in the development of a more comprehensive civil rights program.

Sections 51 and 52, however, have presented serious difficulties as a basis for any extensive federal civil rights program. One difficulty is that both carry criminal sanctions only. The awkward results of this limitation are discussed at a later point. It is sufficient to say here that it has made the Civil Rights Section primarily a policeman prosecuting criminals.

The most serious difficulty which the Civil Rights Section has encountered in using these sections has been to determine the specific civil rights they protect. Presumably, the two laws protect any and all rights established by the Constitution or by federal statute. But the Constitution nowhere lists personal rights which may be protected by the government, nor does any federal statute enumerate them. In using Section 51 and 52 to protect specific rights, the Civil Rights Section has been compelled to employ an experimental technique and to endeavor to extend the list of these rights, case by case. Considerable success has been achieved in this undertaking, and action in the future may expand further the list of rights under Section 51 protected against interference by private individuals. The list of federal rights running against interference by state officers and protected by Section 52 is a somewhat more definite one. Decisions of the Supreme

Court in recent years have read many of the rights established by the first 10 Amendments into the Fourteenth Amendment. This has made them federal rights against state interference.

A further handicap under which the Section has worked has been the insistence of the courts that the use of these statutes should be governed by the traditional and wholly sound legal doctrine that criminal laws must adequately define the conduct which is forbidden. Because these statutes are vaguely worded, the courts have sometimes been reluctant to see them applied in specific situations. They have taken the position that the accused had not received sufficient warning from the vague terms of the statute that his conduct was forbidden.

Another handicap has been the further tendency of the courts to interpret these laws narrowly and to limit the list of rights which they are intended to protect. This follows from judicial doubts about legislative intent with respect to the Acts. The legislative history of civil rights laws in Congress since 1866 has been confusing. The repeal by Congress in 1894 and 1909 of much civil rights legislation has led the courts to question some of the uses to which Sections 51 and 52 have been put. On its face, each of these statutes has a potential usefulness of great breadth. In practice, each has proved to be an instrument of limited value. This is clearly illustrated by some of the cases in which the Sections have been invoked.

Screws v. United States, decided by the Supreme Court in 1945, illustrates an unsuccessful attempt to make Section 52 play the role of a federal antilynching act. In this case, a Georgia sheriff, aided by a deputy sheriff and a local police officer arrested a Negro on a warrant charging him with the theft of a tire. The three men then proceeded to beat the Negro to death. Ultimately, the Department of Justice prosecuted the three men. It charged them with having, under color of law, deprived their victim of his federal right under the Fourteenth Amendment to be tried by due process of law when charged with an offense against the state. They were convicted in the federal trial court. The Supreme Court set this conviction aside on the ground that the trial judge had failed to charge the jury properly. One of the components of the crime defined by Section 52 is willful action on the part of a lawbreaker to deprive his victim of a federal right. In the judgment of the Supreme Court, this requirement of the statute saved the law from the charge that its failure to enumerate the rights protected by it rendered it unconstitutional on grounds of vagueness. In other words, the Supreme Court held that a person cannot be prosecuted under Section

52 unless there is evidence that he knew of the existence of a specific federal right and willfully intended to deprive his victim of that right. The failure of the judge to analyze the law in this fashion in his charge to the jury entitled the defendant to a new trial. This clearly illustrates the technical difficulties under which the Civil Rights Section labors when it endeavors to use the ancient Section 52 as a basis for federal prosecution in lynching or police brutality cases. When the federal government brought Screws and his associates to trial a second time, they were acquitted.

That Section 52 has not, however, lost all of its usefulness in cases of this type is shown by the decision of the Fifth Circuit Court of Appeals in *Crews v. United States,* in 1947. Crews, a Florida county constable, arrested a Negro farm hand and alleged that he was drunk. He then proceeded to beat his prisoner with a bullwhip, and forced him to jump into the Suwannee River where the Negro was drowned. The Civil Rights Section prosecuted Crews on the charge that he had violated Section 52 by depriving his victim of the right to a fair trial by due process of law. The trial jury found Crews guilty. He appealed to the Circuit Court of Appeals, arguing that his "act was solely one of personal vengeance and entirely devoid of official character and authority. . . ." He claimed that he thus could not, under color of law, have willfully deprived his victim of a federal right. The Circuit Court rejected this argument and upheld the conviction. Distinguishing the case from the *Screws* case, it held that the jury had been properly instructed that the defendant had to act willfully in order to violate Section 52, and that there was sufficient evidence that Crews had so acted. The Circuit Court said further that evidence indicating that a police officer mistreated a prisoner out of personal malice or spite is not inconsistent with the conclusion that the officer also willfully intended to deprive this victim of his constitutional rights.

This review of the language of the three key statutes, and the way the courts have handled them, makes it clear that the Civil Rights Section has been working under definite and serious legal handicaps.

2. Insufficient personnel. — At the present time the Civil Rights Section has a complement of seven lawyers, all stationed in Washington. It depends on the FBI for all investigative work, and on the regional United States Attorneys for prosecution of specific cases. Enforcement of the civil rights statutes is not its only task. It also administers the criminal provision of the Fair Labor Standards Act, the Safety Appliance Act, the Hatch Act, and certain other statutes. It is responsible for processing most of the mail received by the federal government which in any way bears on civil rights. Although other resources of the Department of Justice are available to supplement the Civil Rights Section staff, the Section is the only agency in the Department with specialized experience in civil rights work. This small staff is inadequate either for maximum enforcement of existing civil rights statutes, or for enforcement of additional legislation such as that recommended by this Committee.

The Committee has found that relatively few cases have been prosecuted by the Section, and that in part this is the result of its insufficient personnel. The Section simply does not have an adequate staff for the careful, continuing study of civil rights violations, often highly elusive and technically difficult, which occur in many areas of human relations.

On the other hand, there is much misunderstanding about the discrepancy between the very large volume of mail received by the Section and the small number of cases it takes to court. An analysis has shown that approximately 22 percent of the agency's incoming mail contains complaints of civil rights violations and that these complaints number from 1,500 to 2,500 each year. The Civil Rights Section has prosecuted about 178 cases in eight years.

There are a number of possible explanations of the small number of cases prosecuted. In the beginning of its existence, the Civil Rights Section was required to move slowly in order to find cases which would be most useful in delineating the scope of the civil rights statutes. Although the period of legal experimentation is substantially over, the case law developed in this period in certain respects hampers forceful prosecution. In addition, it must be realized that investigation of many "complaints" shows that they do not present a basis for prosecution. With due regard to these points, however, it is our judgment that the number of cases prosecuted merits some criticism.

3. *Adequacy of cooperation by United States Attorneys.* — Whenever a complaint of a civil rights violation appears to merit prosecutive action it must, under the organization of the Department of Justice, be processed through the office of the United States Attorney in the district where the prosecution is to be brought.

The Civil Rights Section frequently seeks the advice of those Attorneys before deciding whether a complaint should be investigated. The opinion of these men will often determine whether the case will be prosecuted. Intelligent and sympathetic cooperation of the United States Attorneys is, therefore, crucial to effective federal enforcement of the civil rights laws. Many United States Attorneys extend such

146

cooperation. However, a staff survey of a random selection of the Section's case files disclosed serious shortcomings in the work of some United States Attorneys.

It should be remembered that these men are local lawyers appointed by the President, subject to confirmation by the Senate, for a term of four years. To them is entrusted the task of initiating proceedings where there has been a civil rights violation, and of prosecuting the actual cases. This often places the United States Attorney in the unenviable position of having to take a public stand in court against the ingrained prejudices and mores of his own community. There have been outstanding examples of United States Attorneys, whatever their personal beliefs, courageously and vigorously assuming this position; there are indications that others have been less willing to set themselves up against local public opinion.

In one case involving interference with the rights of Negroes to vote, the United States Attorney insisted that the evidence developed by the investigation did not make out a case under federal law and recommended that the file be closed. Noting the "clear admissions" of the public officers against whom the charge of interference had been filed, the Civil Rights Section promptly overruled the United States Attorney, who then wrote the Section:

> Assuming that you will direct prosecution, I wish to suggest that inasmuch as you have a unit set up within the Department for the prosecution of these cases that you assign an attorney for the trial of this case and for drawing the bill of indictment; in other words, take charge of the case with all the assistance our office can give. . . . The reason I am requesting this is because I have a deep conviction that I cannot win it. We have had several of these cases and have not yet had a true bill.

Similarly, in a case in which a local constable had brutally killed a Negro, the local United States Attorney was asked for his views, after an FBI investigation had been made. He expressed grave doubts as to the advisability of proceeding under Section 52. In the same letter, he expressed his personal belief that Section 52 was unconstitutional, quoting liberally from the arguments of the dissenting justices in the *Screws* case. The Civil Rights Section prosecuted anyway, and obtained a conviction.

In another case involving the killing of a Negro by a deputy sheriff, the Civil Rights Section sought the advice of the United States Attorney on July 30, and referred him to the FBI report of its investigation in the case. On September 13, the Section again asked for the advice of the United States Attorney. On October 10, it repeated its request for the third time. On October 14, the United States Attorney wrote that he had not received the FBI report, but would express his views to the Section as soon as he obtained it. On October 17, he advised that he had received the report and he thought the matter should be closed. He gave no reason for his opinion. The Civil Rights Section closed the case, apparently because the Civil Rights Section attorney in charge reported, according to a note in the file, that "X— will not go on anything."

These delays are very serious, for they may have a fatal effect upon the prosecution of cases. Public interest in the case dies and it becomes increasingly difficult to persuade a grand jury to indict. Witnesses scatter, evidence grows cold, and a conviction, always difficult to obtain in a civil rights case, may become impossible.

All too frequently, United States Attorneys are allowed to become the final arbiters in the disposition of civil rights cases. The Department of Justice should make more vigorous use of its authority to stimulate, educate, prod, and even overrule United States Attorneys in the handling of cases in this area.

4. *The Civil Rights Section's dependence upon the FBI for its investigative work.*

The FBI handles virtually all of the investigative work in federal civil rights cases. It is unnecessary to comment on the remarkably successful record of the FBI in the general field of law enforcement. In the civil rights field there are many cases where high caliber investigative work has been done by the Bureau. However, there are also indications that upon occasion investigations in this very difficult and highly specialized area have not measured up to the Bureau's high standard in the handling of other types of cases.

There is evidence in the civil rights case files in the Department of Justice that the Bureau has sometimes felt that it was burdensome and difficult to undertake as many specific civil rights investigations as are requested. Moreover, investigations have not always been as full as the needs of the situation would warrant. Such shortcomings should be remedied by streamlining the somewhat cumbersome administrative relationships among the Civil Rights Section, the Criminal Division of the Department of Justice, the Office of the Attorney General and the Federal Bureau of Investigation.

The tendency of FBI agents to work in close cooperation with local police officers has sometimes been detrimental to the handling of civil rights investigations. At times, these local officers are themselves under suspicion. Even where this is not so, the victims or witnesses in civil rights cases are apt to be weak and frightened people who are not encouraged to tell their stories freely to federal agents where the latter are working closely with local police officers. In ordinary crime detection work, it is highly desirable for the FBI to cooperate closely with the local police. Having in general established such a wholly sound relationship, it is sometimes difficult for the FBI agent to break this relationship and to work without, or even against, the local police when a civil rights case comes along.

A second difficulty which explains investigative shortcomings in some civil rights cases is the fact that the FBI agent must be trained broadly in law enforcement work and must be active on a wide front in enforcing the great variety of federal criminal statutes which now exist. Accordingly, the agent is not always prepared to cope with the elusive and difficult aspects of a civil rights case. More highly specialized training of agents in this field would overcome some of the occasional shortcomings which are now present in the Bureau's work in cases of this type.

5. *Hostility of local officers and local communities.* —The prejudices of communities where civil rights violations occur often defeat federal law enforcement. Evidence of this is found in the behavior of juries. A recent example was the 1946, Minden, Louisiana, lynching when two Negroes were released from the local jail into the hands of a mob and so unmercifully beaten that one, a veteran, died. Mr. Hoover called it "the best case we have ever made out; we had clear-cut, uncontroverted evidence of the conspiracy." Five of the mob members were indicted by the federal government and promptly acquitted by the jury.

The Minden case was at least partially successful. It survived the grand jury stage and went to trial. In other cases federal grand juries simply refuse to return indictments.

Similar local prejudice thwarts the efforts of the FBI to obtain information from local citizens—even including local law-enforcement officers. Speaking of the problems encountered by the FBI in civil rights cases, Mr. Hoover stated: "We are faced, usually, in these investigations, with what I would call an iron curtain, in practically every one of these cases in the communities in which the investigations have to be conducted. Now we are absolutely powerless, as investigators, unless the citizens of a community come forward with information. In other words, our function is to go out and get the evidence. We have to have sources of information, we have got to be able to go to citizens and have them talk freely and frankly to us, so that we may prepare the case for the prosecuting attorney."

A case in point is the 1946, Monroe, Georgia, lynching. Four Negroes had been killed. Twenty agents were assigned to the case; 2,790 individuals interviewed; and 106 witnesses presented to the grand jury—which failed to return an indictment.

Mr. Hoover also stated to the Committee:

> We have had cases involving civil rights where we have had no cooperation from local authorities. In one instance, the sheriff boasted that he intended to take no action. Another law enforcement agency made a perfunctory inquiry. We worked on the case by ourselves.

Local prejudice also interferes with the efforts of federal law enforcement officers because of the fear it instills and the silence it inspires in government witnesses. In 1945, an alleged police brutality case was reported to the Civil Rights Section. The affidavit of the complainant, a Negro minister, suggested a clear-cut case. The minister, who was an eye-witness to the incident, had fled from his southern home to Chicago because of threats by both the local police and citizenry. When interviewed by the FBI, he confirmed his allegations, but positively stated that he would not be willing to testify in the community where the offense occurred. The FBI, in the same investigation, met similar evidences of intimidation of Negro witnesses. Some of them flatly refused to sign statements, or, if called as witnesses, to testify in court.

6. *The position of the Civil Rights Section in the Department of Justice.* —The Civil Rights Section's name suggests to many citizens that it is a powerful arm of the government devoting its time and energy to the protection of all our valued civil liberties. This is, of course, incorrect. The Section is only one unit in the Criminal Division of the Department of Justice. As such, it lacks the prestige and authority which may be necessary to deal effectively with other parts of the Department and to secure the kind of cooperation necessary to a thorough-going enforcement of civil rights law. There have been instances where the Section has not asserted itself when United States Attorneys are uncooperative or investigative reports are inadequate. As the organization of the Department now stands, the Section is in a poor position to take a strong stand in such contingencies.

It may easily be a direct result of the Civil Rights Section's subordinate position that the total picture of work derived from the staff survey is that of a sincere, hardworking, but perhaps overcautious agency. Its relative lack of prestige in the Department of Justice, the legal and constitutional difficulties which confront it, the problems caused by its administrative relation to the FBI, the hostility of some United States Attorneys, the force of local prejudice, and the size of its staff all combine to make the Section less effective and less self-assured than the challenge of its assignment demands.

THE PROBLEM OF SANCTIONS

The difficulty of devising and employing adequate means to lead people to obey civil rights legislation cannot be evaded. The chief sanction that has been used to secure the enforcement of federal civil rights laws has been the criminal one. Admittedly this sanction has not been an adequate one. It has proved difficult to enforce in many situations. Whenever the criminal sanction is resorted to, the Constitution guarantees the right to a grand jury hearing, and the right to trial by jury to any person accused of crime under federal law. These jury proceedings must be held in the state and district where the offence was committed. Accordingly, a federal criminal prosecution is not an undertaking in which an outside, impartial power weighs in the scales of justice a wrongful act done in a local community. Instead, federal prosecutors must persuade local citizens both to indict and to convict their fellows, often their neighbors and friends, if federal criminal laws are to be enforced and violations punished.

The right of an accused person to be tried by a jury of his peers in his own locality has long been regarded as a cornerstone of our system of criminal justice, but it has not made easy the use of federal criminal sanctions in civil rights cases. Two factors are responsible. One is that the victim in a typical civil rights case, the person who has been lynched or otherwise mistreated, often enjoys little or no standing in his own community. People whose civil rights are most in danger are very often members of weak and unpopular minorities. Sometimes they are as individuals weak, unattractive, and troublesome. All too frequently, members of juries in civil rights cases are prejudiced against the victim, and sympathetic toward the accused. Where this atmosphere exists, it is not easy to persuade juries to apply criminal sanctions.

The second factor hampering federal officials is the cry of outside interference which is almost certain to be raised by the accused's counsel in civil rights cases. The record of federal prosecutions clearly shows that members of grand and trial juries again and again have shown a sensitivity to this cry.

The result is that many a federal civil rights case, seemingly airtight, is lost for want of an indictment or conviction where an attempt is made to invoke a criminal sanction. The case files in the Department of Justice indicate the frequency with which this result occurs. For example, a memorandum submitted to the Department of Justice by a government attorney, after a jury had failed to convict in an election case, says:

> The case ended in a verdict of not guilty for the defendants, which under the circumstances [local prejudice against the Negro victims] and considering the locale, is not surprising. The case is a perfect example of a situation where the Government succeeds in proving all the allegations of the indictment, but in spite of this a jury returns a verdict of not guilty.

The criminal sanction is useful nevertheless in civil rights cases. Convictions have been obtained by the federal government in a number of cases and these convictions have had a wholesome result. The Civil Rights Section points to a drastic decline in recent years in the number of peonage complaints received by it. Two or three successful prosecutions in peonage cases in the early years of this decade certainly contributed to this result. While other factors, such as the rise in employment opportunities during the war and postwar years have helped bring about the decline of peonage, the convictions unquestionably had a wholesome effect.

Even where the federal government has failed to win convictions, the mere attempt to invoke criminal penalties in civil rights cases where flagrant wrongs have been committed has often had a sobering influence upon local attitudes and practices. For example, after the acquittal of the accused in a police brutality case, the United States Attorney wrote the Attorney General as follows:

> The defendants are at liberty, but it is my humble opinion that the prosecution will do good for years to come. None of these state officers likes to be hauled into the Federal Court. Of course, I do not think any man should be indicted unless he is guilty; but such prosecutions as this do a lot of good in the case of a guilty defendant even though he is not convicted. It will also have its effect on other State officers.

Again, in a letter to the Attorney General written by an attorney who served as Special Assistant to the Attorney General and helped argue a federal lynching case which ended in the acquittal of the defendants, it is stated:

> I think the prosecution in Mississippi was beneficial. For a period of five years, no prisoner has been taken from an officer in Mississippi and lynched. The trial of the case impressed officers from the Governor down to the Constables with the importance of an officer according to a prisoner the highest degree of protection.

The failure of the government to win convictions in airtight criminal cases does not mean that this is a hopeless approach. If juries are unwilling to convict in civil rights cases, it is clear that in part, the answer lies elsewhere. It lies in educational efforts to remind the American people of the importance of preserving their civil rights traditions, and of the necessity and the validity of invoking criminal sanctions against civil rights violations.

Since the criminal sanction as a means of enforcing public policy with respect to civil rights has such obvious limitation, the Committee concludes that we should resort to a wide variety of sanctions—old and new. Some of these will be discussed at a later point in connection with the Committee's recommendations for action. Others may properly be discussed here.

The use of civil sanctions to supplement criminal penalties in securing the enforcement of civil rights legislation is desirable. The writ of injunction and the suit for damages have often been used in civil rights cases, but their use has depended upon the initiative of the individual victim, since he has the burden of invoking them.

Two federal statutes, derived from the civil rights legislation of the post–Civil War period, provide civil sanctions paralleling the criminal sanctions of Sections 51 and 52. These are Sections 43 and 47 of Title 8 of the United States Code. The former allows an injured party to bring an action against any person who, under color of law, has deprived him of a federal right. The latter allows an individual to bring a similar action against two or more persons who have conspired to interfere with his federal rights. These two statutes have been used in a few notable instances in recent years by imaginative attorneys to seek civil redress for persons whose civil rights have been encroached upon.

A legal remedy of fairly recent origin, the declaratory judgment, could be effectively used in cases in which civil rights are threatened. Like the injunction, it is a preventive remedy. It permits persons whose rights are threatened, but not yet invaded, to appeal to the courts to declare in advance what one's rights are. The declaratory judgment might be used to bring into court the issue of the validity of certain legal devices for disfranchising the Negro. Its virtue is that it would bring a settlement of that issue before any citizen had lost his right to vote. It stands thereby in contrast to the more traditional remedies which merely permit the voter who has not been allowed to vote to sue for damages those responsible for depriving him of the right.

The potential use of civil sanctions in civil rights cases is very great. In general, they are of little value in combating intermittent civil rights violations. They obviously could not prevent a lynching. But many violations of rights are of a persistent type; they take the form of longstanding denials of the right to vote, or refusal to give certain persons access to government services or to places of public accommodation. In these cases civil penalties can frequently be effectively invoked. In many instances a civil action will accomplish results when criminal prosecution will not, because a jury which might be reluctant to convict a defendant in a criminal prosecution for a violation of civil rights might not hesitate to afford relief in the form of a civil penalty. However, there is a need to give the government itself greater power to use civil sanctions.

Two or three government sanctions quite different in character, and of recent origin, seem to the Committee to have usefulness in the civil rights field. One of these takes the form of an order of an administrative commission which has power to receive complaints, hold hearings and settle issues that have been brought to its attention. This method has recently been employed by New York and other states to deal with a civil rights problem—namely the outlawing of employment practices involving discrimination against workers because of their race, color, creed, or national origin. The New York State Commission Against Discrimination (SCAD) has authority to receive and consider complaints and to issue cease-and-desist orders against those who are found to be violating the antidiscrimination statute. These orders are enforceable in the courts. This procedure might be followed in other fields, such as education, health, housing, and access to places of public accommodation to secure the elimination of any kind of discrimination. The procedure has many advantages. Members of such a commission are ordinarily chosen for their technical ability. They are able to acquire professional competence during their term of office. Through the complaint and hearing device they can often settle many cases, and put an end to civil rights violations without resort to cease-and-desist orders or more extreme penalties. After all, the goal of a sanction is to deter people from civil rights violations, rather than to punish for the sake of punishment.

Another useful sanction is the grant-in-aid. Today, public services provided by state and local government agencies and by private organizations are increasingly financed by federal grants-in-aid in part or wholly. The federal government is spending hundreds of millions of dollars annually for this kind of support. These grants-in-aid could be made contingent upon the elimination of various forms of discrimination or other violations of civil rights. The increasing use of such a sanction is desirable.

A similar possibility is the use of the taxing power to discipline individuals and organizations which are guilty of discriminatory practices. The right of nonprofit educational or welfare organizations to be exempt from property or income taxes and the right of individuals to deduct from their income tax contributions made to such organizations might be deliberately withheld. This device is controversial in principle and with respect to administrative feasibility. The Committee believes that further study is necessary before specific use of this kind of sanction can be recommended.

The question is often raised why Congress has never invoked the penalty clause of the Fourteenth Amendment. This clause permits Congress to reduce a state's basis of representation in the lower house of Congress in proportion to its denial of the right to vote to male citizens, 21 years of age and over. Aside from the political considerations which are bound to influence congressional action, the fact stands out that no one knows just how to go about enforcing this clause. How does one compute the number of Negroes who are denied the right to vote in a southern state? Are all the Negroes disfranchised who do not vote, or only those who go to the polls and are turned away? These are illustrative of the difficult questions involved. The Committee merely desires to call attention to this sanction and suggest that further study be made of its possible effectiveness in protecting the right of suffrage.

The Committee does believe that we must show both courage and imagination in devising and using new tools for the enforcement of civil rights policy. It believes that the national government has at its command varied powers and administrative machinery which are capable of being used with great profit in safeguarding civil rights. Experimentation in the use of these powers and this machinery for such a worthwhile purpose is eminently desirable and should be undertaken immediately.

In concluding this survey of what government is doing and can do to protect the civil rights of its citizens the Committee wishes to emphasize that the task must not be viewed as a narrow and technical assignment. It is a task which demands the intelligent and loyal cooperative action of all three of the major departments of our government.

It is the responsibility of Congress to plot our policy for the protection of civil rights. This should be done generously, courageously, and without evasion of responsibility made in deference to any group or geographical section. Our laws in this vitally important field can be clarified, strengthened, and broadened in scope.

Our civil rights will not be adequately protected, however, by good laws badly enforced. Executive and administrative officers must be fully familiar with the policies established by the legislature and must loyally and efficiently implement them by every device at their command. What is gained by passing a law that there shall be no racial or religious discrimination in the federal civil service if department heads and personnel officers are willing to countenance such discrimination in practice?

Finally, while we cannot ask our appellate courts to hold valid laws which they believe to be invalid, we may reasonably expect them to be sympathetic toward efforts to protect civil rights, and to interpret fairly and generously statutes designed for that purpose. We are entitled in addition to expect our lower courts, even in the areas in which prejudice and intolerance run strong, to apply courageously the established doctrines of law announced by the Supreme Court. Since the Missouri law school case, for example, there ought to be no indecision in the mind of any state or federal judge in insisting that states provide fully equal professional educational facilities for Negroes on demand.

The nation's program for the protection of civil rights, in short, should move forward on three fronts, legislative, executive, and judicial. Anything short of this full cooperative effort will jeopardize the success of the entire program.

THE CLIMATE OF OPINION

The adoption of specific legislation, the implementation of laws or the development of new administrative policies and procedures cannot alone bring us all the way to full civil rights. The strong arm of government can cope with individual acts of discrimination, injustice and violence. But in one sense, the actual infringements of civil rights by public or private persons are only symptoms. They reflect the imperfections of our social order, and the ignorance and moral weaknesses of some of our people.

There are social and psychological conditions which foster civil rights; there are others which imperil them. In a world forever tottering on the brink of war, civil rights will be precarious at best. In a nation wracked by depression and widespread economic insecurity, the inclination to consider civil rights a luxury will be more easily accepted. We need peace and prosperity for their own sake; we need them to secure our civil rights as well. We must make constructive efforts to create an appropriate national outlook—a climate of public opinion which will outlaw individual abridgements of personal freedom, a climate of opinion as free from prejudice as we can make it.

We do not have sufficient information to know all about the many variations of prejudice. We do know that most prejudice is learned. We know that it may result from actual experience, or propaganda, or both. It may derive from foolish generalizations about groups, from personal frustration, from economic or social competition, or from local environments that are built on discrimination. It ranges from the mild, secret feeling of the social snob to the violent, murderous impulses of the insanely prejudiced. It seems probable that no one can become a bigoted fanatic unless he has need for prejudice towards others to begin with. This may be a need for a feeling of superiority, for a feeling of being strong enough to exclude others from equality. The fear or insecurity which makes someone need prejudice is probably not enough to make a fanatic. There must also be ignorance to sustain the prejudice. Most prejudice can not survive real understanding of the great variations among people in any one group; or of the scientific findings which establish the equality of groups, and disprove racist nonsense; or of the fact that in a democratic commonwealth, prejudice is an immoral outlaw attitude.

The achievement of full civil rights in law may do as much to end prejudice as the end of prejudice may do to achieve full civil rights. The fewer the opportunities there are to use inequality in the law as a reinforcement of prejudice, the sooner prejudice will vanish. In addition, people must be taught about the evil effects of prejudice. They must be helped to understand why they have developed prejudices. It means trying to show them that it is unfair and stupid to condemn whole groups, that in every group they will find about the same proportion of people whom they will like or dislike; that each man must be judged by himself, on his own merits and faults.

We know from research studies that this can be done. We also know that we are not yet sufficiently skilled to have complete confidence in our educational methods. Since many bigots need their prejudices for reasons of their own, they do not like to give them up. Accordingly, they are very successful at avoiding written or spoken presentations which may disturb their prejudices.

One thing, however, which we can do, is to make certain that all Americans are familiar with the fundamental rights to which they are entitled and which they owe to one another. This is not the case at present. In October, 1946, the National Opinion Research Center at the University of Denver, asked a cross-section of our adult population a series of questions about the Bill of Rights. Only one out of five Americans had a reasonably accurate knowledge of what is in the first 10 Amendments to the Constitution. Completely confused and inaccurate descriptions were offered by 12 per cent. More than a third had heard of the Bill of Rights but could not identify it in any way. Another third had not even heard of it. The NORC also reported that "Even among the best informed people, however—the more privileged, educationally, economically, and occupationally—less than a majority can satisfactorily identify the Bill of Rights." There is no excuse for this kind of ignorance. It represents a dismal failure of our schools, our homes and our media of communication. Where efforts to overcome prejudice directly may boomerang, informing the people of the legally guaranteed rights to which all are entitled, almost certainly cannot. It is at least possible that this kind of information will ease the task of overcoming deep-rooted prejudice.

We are thus extremely sensitive to the general existence of lingering prejudices which must be overcome. It will take time. How much time will depend in a large measure on how quickly and aggressively we inaugurate a program of action under the leadership of the federal government. All of our governments, federal, state, and local, must be uncompromising enemies of discrimination, which is prejudice come to life. In turn, they must be reinforced by education—education through carefully planned experience, to break down the fears of groups; education through information to dispel ignorance about our heritage and our civil rights. There is no need to choose between these approaches. Neither one is adequate for the complete securing of our rights; both are indispensable to it.

IV
A Program of Action: The Committee's Recommendations

THE TIME IS NOW

Twice before in American history the nation has found it necessary to review the state of its civil rights. The first time was during the 15 years between 1776 and 1791, from the drafting of the Declaration of Independence through the Articles of Confederation experiment to the writing of the Constitution and the Bill of Rights. It was then that the distinctively American heritage was finally distilled from earlier views of liberty. The second time was when the Union was temporarily sundered over the question of whether it could exist "half-slave" and "half-free."

It is our profound conviction that we have come to a time for a third re-examination of the situation, and a sustained drive ahead. Our reasons for believing this are those of conscience, of self-interest, and of survival in a threatening world. Or to put it another way, we have a moral reason, an economic reason, and an international reason for believing that the time for action is now.

The Moral Reason

We have considered the American heritage of freedom at some length. We need no further justification for a broad and immediate program than the need to reaffirm our faith in the traditional American morality. The pervasive gap between our aims and what we actually do is creating a kind of moral dry rot which eats away at the emotional and rational bases of democratic beliefs. There are times when the difference between what we preach about civil rights and what we practice is shockingly illustrated by individual outrages. There are times when

158

the whole structure of our ideology is made ridiculous by individual instances. And there are certain continuing, quiet, omnipresent practices which do irreparable damage to our beliefs.

As examples of "moral erosion" there are the consequences of suffrage limitations in the South. The fact that Negroes and many whites have not been allowed to vote in some states has actually sapped the morality underlying universal suffrage. Many men in public and private life do not believe that those who have been kept from voting are capable of self rule. They finally convince themselves that disfranchised people do not really have the right to vote.

Wartime segregation in the armed forces is another instance of how a social pattern may wreak moral havoc. Practically all white officers and enlisted men in all branches of service saw Negro military personnel performing only the most menial functions. They saw Negroes recruited for the common defense treated as men apart and distinct from themselves. As a result, men who might otherwise have maintained the equalitarian morality of their forebears were given reason to look down on their fellow citizens. This has been sharply illustrated by the Army study discussed previously, in which white servicemen expressed great surprise at the excellent performance of Negroes who joined them in the firing line. Even now, very few people know of the successful experiment with integrated combat units. Yet it is important in explaining why some Negro troops did not do well; it is proof that equal treatment can produce equal performance.

Thousands upon thousands of small, unseen incidents reinforce the impact of headlined violations like lynchings, and broad social patterns like segregation and inequality of treatment. There is, for example, the matter of "fair play." As part of its training for democratic life, our youth is constantly told to "play fair," to abide by "the rules of the game," and to be "good sports." Yet, how many boys and girls in our country experience such things as Washington's annual marble tournament? Because of the prevailing pattern of segregation, established as a model for youth in the schools and recreation systems, separate tournaments are held for Negro and white boys. Parallel elimination contests are sponsored until only two victors remain. Without a contest between them, the white boy is automatically designated as the local champion and sent to the national tournament, while the Negro lad is relegated to the position of runner-up. What child can achieve any real understanding of fair play, or sportsmanship, of the rules of the game, after he has personally experienced such an example of inequality?

It is impossible to decide who suffers the greatest moral damage from our civil rights transgressions, because all of us are hurt. That is certainly true of those who are victimized. Their belief in the basic truth of the American promise is undermined. But they do have the realization, galling as it sometimes is, of being morally in the right. The damage to those who are responsible for these violations of our moral standards may well be greater. They, too, have been reared to honor the command of "free and equal." And all of us must share in the shame at the growth of hypocrisies like the "automatic" marble champion. All of us must endure the cynicism about democratic values which our failures breed.

The United States can no longer countenance these burdens on its common conscience, these inroads on its moral fiber.

The Economic Reason

One of the principal economic problems facing us and the rest of the world is achieving maximum production and continued prosperity. The loss of a huge, potential market for goods is a direct result of the economic discrimination which is practiced against many of our minority groups. A sort of vicious circle is produced. Discrimination depresses the wages and income of minority groups. As a result, their purchasing power is curtailed and markets are reduced. Reduced markets result in reduced production. This cuts down employment, which of course means lower wages and still fewer job opportunities. Rising fear, prejudice, and insecurity aggravate the very discrimination in employment which sets the vicious circle in motion.

Minority groups are not the sole victims of this economic waste; its impact is inevitably felt by the entire population. Eric Johnston, when President of the United States Chamber of Commerce, made this point with vividness and clarity:

> The withholding of jobs and business opportunities from some people does not make more jobs and business opportunities for others. Such a policy merely tends to drag down the whole economic level. You can't sell an electric refrigerator to a family that can't afford electricity. Perpetuating poverty for some merely guarantees stagnation for all. True economic progress demands that the whole nation move forward at the same time. It demands that all artificial barriers erected by ignorance and intolerance be removed. To put it in the simplest terms, we are all in business together. Intolerance is

a species of boycott and any business or job boycott is a cancer in the economic body of the nation. I repeat, intolerance is destructive; prejudice produces no wealth; discrimination is a fool's economy.

Economic discrimination prevents full use of all our resources. During the war, when we were called upon to make an all-out productive effort, we found that we lacked skilled laborers. This shortage might not have been so serious if minorities had not frequently been denied opportunities for training and experience. In the end, it cost large amounts of money and precious time to provide ourselves with trained persons.

Discrimination imposes a direct cost upon our economy through the wasteful duplication of many facilities and services required by the "separate but equal" policy. That the resources of the South are sorely strained by the burden of a double system of schools and other public services has already been indicated. Segregation is also economically wasteful for private business. Public transportation companies must often provide duplicate facilities to serve majority and minority groups separately. Places of public accommodation and recreation reject business when it comes in the form of unwanted persons. Stores reduce their sales by turning away minority customers. Factories must provide separate locker rooms, pay windows, drinking fountains, and washrooms for the different groups.

Discrimination in wage scales and hiring policies forces a higher proportion of some minority groups onto relief rolls than corresponding segments of the majority. A study by the Federal Emergency Relief Administration during the depression of the Thirties revealed that in every region the percentage of Negro families on relief was far greater than white families:

	PER CENT OF FAMILIES ON RELIEF MAY, 1934	
	NEGRO	WHITE
Northern cities	52.2	13.3
Border state cities	51.8	10.4
Southern cities	33.7	11.4

Similarly, the rates of disease, crime, and fires are disproportionately great in areas which are economically depressed as compared with wealthier areas. Many of the prominent American minorities are confined—by economic discrimination, by law, by restrictive covenants,

DISCRIMINATION IN EMPLOYMENT MEANS ...

INEFFICIENT USE
OF OUR LABOR FORCE....

LESS PURCHASING POWER

....AND A LOWER
LIVING STANDARD FOR <u>ALL</u>

LESS
CONSUMER DEMAND

LESS PRODUCTION

FAIR EMPLOYMENT PRACTICES WOULD HELP BRING ...

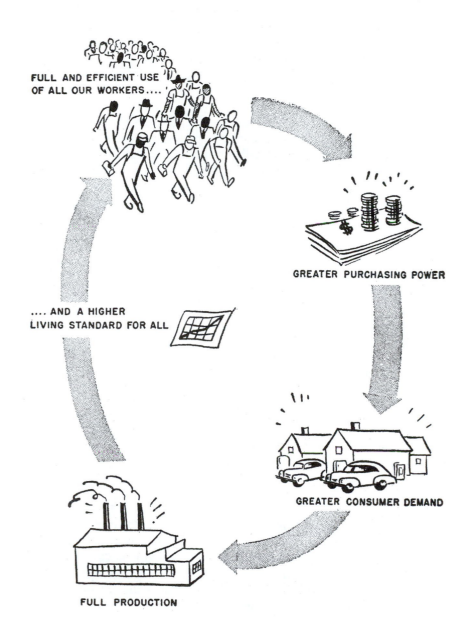

FULL AND EFFICIENT USE OF ALL OUR WORKERS....

GREATER PURCHASING POWER

.... AND A HIGHER LIVING STANDARD FOR ALL

GREATER CONSUMER DEMAND

FULL PRODUCTION

and by social pressure—to the most dilapidated, undesirable locations. Property in these locations yields a smaller return in taxes, which is seldom sufficient to meet the inordinately high cost of public services in depressed areas. The majority pays a high price in taxes for the low status of minorities.

To the costs of discrimination must be added the expensive investigations, trials, and property losses which result from civil rights violations. In the aggregate, these attain huge proportions. The 1943 Detroit riot alone resulted in the destruction of two million dollars in property.

Finally, the cost of prejudice cannot be computed in terms of markets, production, and expenditures. Perhaps the most expensive results are the least tangible ones. No nation can afford to have its component groups hostile toward one another without feeling the stress. People who live in a state of tension and suspicion cannot use their energy constructively. The frustrations of their restricted existence are translated into aggression against the dominant group. Myrdal says:

> Not only occasional acts of violence, but most laziness, carelessness, unreliability, petty stealing and lying are undoubtedly to be explained as concealed aggression. . . . The truth is that *Negroes generally do not feel they have unqualified moral obligations to white people.* . . . The voluntary withdrawal which has intensified the isolation between the two castes is also an expression of Negro protest under cover.

It is not at all surprising that a people relegated to second-class citizenship should behave as second-class citizens. This is true, in varying degrees, of all of our minorities. What we have lost in money, production, invention, citizenship, and leadership as the price for damaged, thwarted personalities—these are beyond estimate.

The United States can no longer afford this heavy drain upon its human wealth, its national competence.

The International Reason

Our position in the postwar world is so vital to the future that our smallest actions have far-reaching effects. We have come to know that our own security in a highly interdependent world is inextricably tied to the security and well-being of all people and all countries. Our foreign policy is designed to make the United States an enormous, positive influence for peace and progress throughout the world. We have tried to let nothing, not even extreme political differences between ourselves and foreign nations, stand in the way of this goal. But our domestic civil rights shortcomings are a serious obstacle.

In a letter to the Fair Employment Practice Committee on May 8, 1946, the Honorable Dean Acheson, then Acting Secretary of State, stated that:

> ... the existence of discrimination against minority groups in this country has an adverse effect upon our relations with other countries. We are reminded over and over by some foreign newspapers and spokesmen, that our treatment of various minorities leaves much to be desired. While sometimes these pronouncements are exaggerated and unjustified, they all too frequently point with accuracy to some form of discrimination because of race, creed, color, or national origin. Frequently we find it next to impossible to formulate a satisfactory answer to our critics in other countries; the gap between the things we stand for in principle and the facts of a particular situation may be too wide to be bridged. An atmosphere of suspicion and resentment in a country over the way a minority is being treated in the United States is a formidable obstacle to the development of mutual understanding and trust between the two countries. We will have better international relations when these reasons for suspicion and resentment have been removed.
>
> I think it is quite obvious ... that the existence of discriminations against minority groups in the United States is a handicap in our relations with other countries. The Department of State, therefore, has good reason to hope for the continued and increased effectiveness of public and private efforts to do away with these discriminations.

The people of the United States stem from many lands. Other nations and their citizens are naturally intrigued by what has happened to their American "relatives." Discrimination against, or mistreatment of, any racial, religious or national group in the United States is not only seen as our internal problem. The dignity of a country, a continent, or even a major portion of the world's population, may be outraged by it. A relatively few individuals here may be identified with millions of people elsewhere, and the way in which they are treated may have world-wide repercussions. We have fewer than half a million American Indians; there are 30 million more in the Western Hemisphere. Our Mexican American and Hispano groups are not large; millions in Central and South America consider them kin. We number our citizens of Oriental descent in the hundreds of thousands; their counterparts overseas are numbered in hundreds of millions. Throughout the Pacific,

Latin America, Africa, the Near, Middle, and Far East, the treatment which our Negroes receive is taken as a reflection of our attitudes toward all dark-skinned peoples.

In the recent war, citizens of a dozen European nations were happy to meet Smiths, Cartiers, O'Haras, Schultzes, di Salvos, Cohens, and Sklodowskas and all the others in our armies. Each nation could share in our victories because its "sons" had helped win them. How much of this good feeling was dissipated when they found virulent prejudice among some of our troops is impossible to say.

We cannot escape the fact that our civil rights record has been an issue in world politics. The world's press and radio are full of it. This Committee has seen a multitude of samples. We and our friends have been, and are, stressing our achievements. Those with competing philosophies have stressed—and are shamelessly distorting—our shortcomings. They have not only tried to create hostility toward us among specific nations, races, and religious groups. They have tried to prove our democracy an empty fraud, and our nation a consistent oppressor of underprivileged people. This may seem ludicrous to Americans, but it is sufficiently important to worry our friends. The following United Press dispatch from London proves that (*Washington Post,* May 25, 1947):

> Although the Foreign Office reserved comment on recent lynch activities in the Carolinas, British diplomatic circles said privately today that they have played into the hands of Communist propagandists in Europe. . . .
>
> Diplomatic circles said the two incidents of mob violence would provide excellent propaganda ammunition for Communist agents who have been decrying America's brand of "freedom" and "democracy."
>
> News of the North Carolina kidnaping was prominently displayed by London papers. . . .

The international reason for acting to secure our civil rights now is not to win the approval of our totalitarian critics. We would not expect it if our record were spotless; to them our civil rights record is only a convenient weapon with which to attack us. Certainly we would like to deprive them of that weapon. But we are more concerned with the good opinion of the peoples of the world. Our achievements in building and maintaining a state dedicated to the fundamentals of freedom have already served as a guide for those seeking the best road from chaos to liberty and prosperity. But it is not indelibly written that democracy will encompass the world. We are convinced that our way of life—the free way of life—holds a promise of hope for all people.

We have what is perhaps the greatest responsibility ever placed upon a people to keep this promise alive. Only still greater achievements will do it.

The United States is not so strong, the final triumph of the democratic ideal is not so inevitable that we can ignore what the world thinks of us or our record.

Mr. President:
Your Committee has reviewed the American heritage and we have found in it again the great goals of human freedom and equality under just laws. We have surveyed the flaws in the nation's record and have found them to be serious. We have considered what government's appropriate role should be in the securing of our rights, and have concluded that it must assume greater leadership.
We believe that the time for action is now. Our recommendations for bringing the United States closer to its historic goal follow.

THE COMMITTEE'S RECOMMENDATIONS

I. To Strengthen the Machinery for the Protection of Civil Rights, the President's Committee Recommends:

1. **The reorganization of the Civil Rights Section of the Department of Justice to provide for:**

   The establishment of regional offices;

   A substantial increase in its appropriation and staff to enable it to engage in more extensive research and to act more effectively to prevent civil rights violations;

   An increase in investigative action in the absence of complaints;

   The greater use of civil sanctions;

   Its elevation to the status of a full division in the Department of Justice.

   The creation of regional offices would enable the Civil Rights Section to provide more complete protection of civil rights in all sections of the country. It would lessen its present complete dependence upon United States Attorneys and local FBI agents for its work in the field. Such regional offices should be established in eight or nine key cities throughout the country, and be staffed with skilled personnel drawn from the local areas. These offices should serve as receiving points for complaints arising in the areas, and as local centers of research, investigation, and preventive action. Close cooperation should be maintained between these offices, local FBI agents, and the United States Attorneys.

The Department of Justice has suggested that heads of these regional offices should have the status of Assistant United States Attorneys, thereby preserving the centralization of federal criminal law enforcement. The President's Committee is fearful that under this plan the goal of effective, courageous, and nonpolitical civil rights protection in the field will not be reached unless satisfactory measures are taken to prevent these assistants from becoming mere political subordinates within the offices of the United States Attorneys.

Additional funds and personnel for research and preventive work would free the Civil Rights Section from its present narrow status as a prosecutive agency. Through the use of properly developed techniques and by the maintenance of continuous checks on racial and other group tensions, much could be done by the Section to reduce the number of lynchings, race riots, election irregularities, and other civil rights violations. Troublesome areas, and the activities of organizations and individuals who foment race tensions could be kept under constant scrutiny.

A larger staff and field-office facilities would also make it possible for the Section to undertake investigations of suspected civil rights violations, without waiting for the receipt of complaints. There are many problems, such as the possible infringement of civil rights resulting from practices used in committing persons to mental institutions, which might be so studied. These investigations in the absence of complaints could also be combined with educational and mediation efforts to check chronic incidents of police brutality or persistent interferences with the right to vote.

The difficulty of winning convictions in many types of criminal civil rights cases is often great. The Committee believes that the Civil Rights Section should be granted increased authority, by Congress if necessary, to make appropriate use of civil sanctions, such as suits for damages or injunctive relief, suits under the Declaratory Judgment Act, and the right of intervention by means of briefs amicus curiae in private litigation where important issues of civil rights law are being determined.

Finally, the Committee urges congressional action raising the Civil Rights Section to full divisional status in the Department of Justice under the supervision of an Assistant Attorney General. We believe this step would give the federal civil rights enforcement program prestige, power, and efficiency that it now lacks. Moreover, acceptance of the above recommendations looking toward increased activity by the Civil Rights Section and the passage by Congress of additional civil rights legislation would give this change added meaning and necessity.

2. The establishment within the FBI of a special unit of investigators trained in civil rights work.

The creation of such a unit of skilled investigators would enable the FBI to render more effective service in the civil rights field than is now possible. At the present time, its investigators are concerned with enforcement of all federal criminal statutes. In some instances, its agents have seemingly lacked the special skills and knowledge necessary to effective handling of civil rights cases, or have not been readily available for work in this area.

These special agents should work in close harmony with the Civil Rights Section and its regional offices.

3. The establishment by the state governments of law enforcement agencies comparable to the federal Civil Rights Section.

There are large areas where, because of constitutional restrictions, the jurisdiction of the federal government as a protector of civil rights is either limited or denied. There are civil rights problems, unique to certain regions and localities, that can best be treated and solved by the individual states. Furthermore, our review of the work of the Civil Rights Section has persuaded us of the cardinal importance of developing specialized units for the enforcement of civil rights laws. We believe that this is true at the state level too. States which have, or will have, civil rights laws of their own, should buttress them with specially designed enforcement units. These would have the further effect of bringing the whole program closer to the people. They would also facilitate systematic local cooperation with the federal Civil Rights Section, and they would be able to act in the areas where it has no authority.

Here and elsewhere the Committee is making recommendations calling for remedial action by the states. The President's Executive

Order invited us to consider civil rights problems falling within state as well as federal jurisdiction. We respectfully request the President to call these recommendations to the attention of the states and to invite their favorable consideration.

4. **The establishment of a permanent Commission on Civil Rights in the Executive Office of the President, preferably by Act of Congress;**
And the simultaneous creation of a Joint Standing Committee on Civil Rights in Congress.

In a democratic society, the systematic, critical review of social needs and public policy is a fundamental necessity. This is especially true of a field like civil rights, where the problems are enduring, and range widely. From our own effort, we have learned that a temporary, sporadic approach can never finally solve these problems.

Nowhere in the federal government is there an agency charged with the continuous appraisal of the status of civil rights, and the efficiency of the machinery with which we hope to improve that status. A permanent Commission could perform an invaluable function by collecting data. It could also carry on technical research to improve the fact-gathering methods now in use. Ultimately, this would make possible a periodic audit of the extent to which our civil rights are secure. If it did this and served as a clearing house and focus of coordination for the many private, state, and local agencies working in the civil rights field, it would be invaluable to them and to the federal government.

A permanent Commission on Civil Rights should point all of its work towards regular reports which would include recommendations for action in the ensuing periods. It should lay plans for dealing with broad civil rights problems, such as those arising from the technological displacement and probable migration of southern Negroes to cities throughout the land. It should also investigate and make recommendations with respect to special civil rights problems, such as the status of Indians and their relationship to the federal government.

The Commission should have effective authority to call upon any agency of the executive branch for assistance. Its members should be appointed by the President with the approval of the Senate. They should hold a specified number of regular meetings. A full-time director should be provided with an adequate appropriation and staff.

Congress, too, can be aided in its difficult task of providing the legislative ground work for fuller civil rights. A standing committee, established jointly by the House and the Senate, would provide a central place for the consideration of proposed legislation. It would enable Congress to maintain continuous liaison with the permanent Commission. A group of men in each chamber would be able to give prolonged study to this complex area and would become expert in its legislative needs.

5. The establishment by the states of permanent commissions on civil rights to parallel the work of the federal Commission at the state level.

The states should create permanent civil rights commissions to make continuing studies of prejudice, group tensions, and other local civil rights problems; to publish educational material of a civil rights nature; to evaluate existing legislation; and to recommend new laws. Such commissions, with their fingers on their communities' pulses, would complement at the state level the activities of a permanent federal Commission on Civil Rights.

6. The increased professionalization of state and local police forces.

The Committee believes that there is a great need at the state and local level for the improvement of civil rights protection by more aggressive and efficient enforcement techniques. Police training programs, patterned after the FBI agents' school and the Chicago Park District Program, should be instituted. They should be oriented so as to indoctrinate officers with an awareness of civil rights problems. Proper treatment by the police of those who are arrested and incarcerated in local jails should be stressed. Supplemented by salaries that will attract and hold competent personnel, this sort of training should do much to make police forces genuinely professional.

II. To Strengthen the Right to Safety and Security of the Person, the President's Committee Recommends:

1. The enactment by Congress of new legislation to supplement Section 51 of Title 18 of the United States Code which would impose the same liability on one person as is now imposed by that same statute on two or more conspirators.

The Committee believes that Section 51 has in the past been a useful law to protect federal rights against encroachment by both private individuals and public officers. It believes the Act has great potential usefulness today. Greater efforts should be made through court tests to extend and make more complete the list of rights safeguarded by this law.

2. The amendment of Section 51 to remove the penalty provision which disqualifies persons convicted under the Act from holding public office.

There is general agreement that this particular penalty creates an unnecessary obstacle to the obtaining of convictions under the Act and that it should be dropped.

3. The amendment of Section 52 to increase the maximum penalties that may be imposed under it from a $1,000 fine and a one-year prison term to a $5,000 fine and a ten-year prison term, thus bringing its penalty provisions into line with those in Section 51.

At the present time the Act's penalties are so light that it is technically a misdemeanor law. In view of the extremely serious offenses that have been and are being successfully prosecuted under Section 52, it seems clear that the penalties should be increased.

4. The enactment by Congress of a new statute, to supplement Section 52, specifically directed against police brutality and related crimes.

This Act should enumerate such rights as the right not to be deprived of property by a public officer except by due process of law; the right to be free from personal injury inflicted by a public officer; the right to engage in a lawful activity without interference by a public officer; and the right to be free from discriminatory law enforcement resulting from either active or passive conduct by a public officer.

This statute would meet in part the handicap in the use of Section 52 imposed by the Supreme Court in *Screws v. United States*. This was the case in which the Court required prosecutors to establish that defendants had willfully deprived victims of a "specific constitutional right." In later prosecutions, the Civil Rights Section has found it very difficult to prove that the accused acted in a "willful" manner. By spelling out some of the federal rights which run against public officers, the supplementary statute would relieve the Civil Rights Section of this extraordinary requirement.

The Committee considered and rejected a proposal to recommend the enactment of a supplementary statute in which an attempt would be made to include a specific enumeration of all federal rights running against public officers. Such an enumeration would inevitably prove incomplete with the passage of time and might prejudice the protection of omitted rights. However, the committee believes that a new statute, such as the one here recommended, enumerating the rights for the protection of which Section 52 is now most commonly employed, is desirable.

5. The enactment by Congress of an antilynching act.

The Committee believes that to be effective such a law must contain four essential elements. First, it should define lynching broadly. Second, the federal offense ought to cover participation of public officers in a lynching, or failure by them to use proper measures to protect a person accused of a crime against mob violence. The failure or refusal of public officers to make proper efforts to arrest members of lynch mobs and to bring them to justice should also be specified as an offense.

Action by private persons taking the law into their own hands to mete out summary punishment and private vengeance upon an accused person; action by either public officers or private persons meting out summary punishment and private vengeance upon a person because of his race, color, creed or religion—these too must be made crimes.

Third, the statute should authorize immediate federal investigation in lynching cases to discover whether a federal offense has been committed. Fourth, adequate and flexible penalties ranging up to a $10,000 fine and a 20-year prison term should be provided.

The constitutionality of some parts of such a statute, particularly those providing for the prosecution of private persons, has been questioned. The Committee believes that there are several constitutional bases upon which such a law might be passed and that these are sufficiently strong to justify prompt action by Congress.

6. The enactment by Congress of a new criminal statute on involuntary servitude, supplementing Sections 443 and 444 of Title 18 of the United States Code.

This statute should make full exercise of congressional power under the Thirteenth Amendment by defining slavery and involuntary servitude broadly. This would provide a basis for federal prosecutions in cases where individuals are deliberately deprived of their freedom by public officers without due process of law or are held in bondage by private persons. Prosecution under existing laws is limited to the narrow, technical offense of peonage or must be based upon the archaic "slave kidnaping" law, Section 443.

7. A review of our wartime evacuation and detention experience looking toward the development of a policy which will prevent the abridgment of civil rights of any person or groups because of race or ancestry.

We believe it is fallacious to assume that there is a correlation between loyalty and race or national origin. The military must be allowed considerable discretionary power to protect national security in time of war. But we believe it is possible to establish safeguards against the evacuation and detention of whole groups because of their descent without endangering national security. The proposed permanent Commission on Civil Rights and the Joint Congressional Committee might well study this problem.

8. Enactment by Congress of legislation establishing a procedure by which claims of evacuees for specific property and business losses resulting from the wartime evacuation can be promptly considered and settled.

The government has acknowledged that many Japanese American evacuees suffered considerable losses through its actions and through no fault of their own. We cannot erase all the scars of evacuation; we can reimburse those who present valid claims for material losses.

III. To Strengthen the Right to Citizenship and Its Privileges, the President's Committee Recommends:

1. Action by the states or Congress to end poll taxes as a voting prerequisite.

Considerable debate has arisen as to the constitutionality of a federal statute abolishing the poll tax. In four times passing an anti–poll tax bill, the House of Representatives has indicated that there is a reasonable chance that it will survive a court attack on constitutional grounds. We are convinced that the elimination of this obstacle to the right of suffrage must not be further delayed. It would be appropriate and encouraging for the remaining poll tax states voluntarily to take this step. Failing such prompt state action, we believe that the nation, either by act of Congress, or by constitutional amendment, should remove this final barrier to universal suffrage.

2. The enactment by Congress of a statute protecting the right of qualified persons to participate in federal primaries and elections against interference by public officers and private persons.

This statute would apply only to federal elections. There is no doubt that such a law can be applied to primaries which are an integral part of the federal electoral process or which affect or determine the result of a federal election. It can also protect participation in federal election campaigns and discussions of matters relating to national political issues. This statute should authorize the Department of Justice to use both civil and criminal sanctions. Civil remedies should be used wherever possible to test the legality of threatened interferences with the suffrage before voting rights have been lost.

3. The enactment by Congress of a statute protecting the right to qualify for, or participate in, federal or state primaries or elections against discriminatory action by state officers based on race or color, or depending on any other unreasonable classification of persons for voting purposes.

This statute would apply to both federal and state elections, but it would be limited to the protection of the right to vote against discriminatory interferences based on race, color, or other unreasonable classification. Its constitutionality is clearly indicated by the Fourteenth and Fifteenth Amendments. Like the legislation suggested under (2) it should authorize the use of civil and criminal sanctions by the Department of Justice.

4. The enactment by Congress of legislation establishing local self-government for the District of Columbia; and the amendment of the Constitution to extend suffrage in presidential elections, and representation in Congress to District residents.

The American tradition of democracy requires that the District of Columbia be given the same measure of self-government in local affairs that is possessed by other communities throughout the country. The lack of congressional representation and suffrage in local and national elections in the District deprives a substantial number of permanent Washington residents of a voice in public affairs.

5. The granting of suffrage by the States of New Mexico and Arizona to their Indian citizens.

These states have constitutional provisions which have been used to disfranchise Indians. In New Mexico, the constitution should be amended to remove the bar against voting by "Indians not taxed." This may not be necessary in Arizona where the constitution excludes from the ballot "persons under guardianship." Reinterpretation might hold that this clause no longer applies to Indians. If this is not possible, the Arizona constitution should be amended to remove it.

6. The modification of the federal naturalization laws to permit the granting of citizenship without regard to the race, color, or national origin of applicants.

It is inconsistent with our whole tradition to deny on a basis of ancestry the right to become citizens to people who qualify in every other way.

7. The repeal by the states of laws discriminating against aliens who are ineligible for citizenship because of race, color, or national origin.

These laws include the alien land laws and the prohibition against commercial fishing in California. The removal of race as a qualification for naturalization would remove the structure upon which this discriminatory legislation is based. But if federal action on Recommendation 6 is delayed, state action would be eminently desirable.

8. The enactment by Congress of legislation granting citizenship to the people of Guam and American Samoa.

This legislation should also provide these islands with organic acts containing guarantees of civil rights, and transfer them from naval administration to civilian control. Such legislation for Guam and American Samoa has been introduced in the present Congress.

9. The enactment by Congress of legislation, followed by appropriate administrative action, to end immediately all discrimination and segregation based on race, color, creed, or national origin, in the organization and activities of all branches of the Armed Services.

The injustice of calling men to fight for freedom while subjecting them to humiliating discrimination within the fighting forces is at once apparent. Furthermore, by preventing entire groups from making their maximum contribution to the national defense, we weaken our defense to that extent and impose heavier burdens on the remainder of the population.

Legislation and regulations should expressly ban discrimination and segregation in the recruitment, assignment, and training of all personnel in all types of military duty. Mess halls, quarters, recreational facilities and post exchanges should be nonsegregated. Commissions and promotions should be awarded on considerations of merit only. Selection of students for the Military, Naval, and Coast Guard academies and all other service schools should be governed by standards from which considerations of race, color, creed, or national origin are conspicuously absent. The National Guard, reserve units, and any universal military training program should all be administered in accordance with these same standards.

The Committee believes that the recent unification of the armed forces provides a timely opportunity for the revision of present policy and practice. A strong enunciation of future policy should be made condemning discrimination and segregation within the armed services.

10. **The enactment by Congress of legislation providing that no member of the armed forces shall be subject to discrimination of any kind by any public authority or place of public accommodation, recreation, transportation, or other service or business.**

The government of a nation has an obligation to protect the dignity of the uniform of its armed services. The esteem of the government itself is impaired when affronts to its armed forces are tolerated. The government also has a responsibility for the well-being of those who surrender some of the privileges of citizenship to serve in the defense establishments.

IV. To Strengthen the Right to Freedom of Conscience and Expression the President's Committee Recommends:

1. **The enactment by Congress and the state legislatures of legislation requiring all groups, which attempt to influence public opinion, to disclose the pertinent facts**

about themselves through systematic registration procedures.

Such registration should include a statement of the names of officers, sources of financial contributions, disbursements, and the purposes of the organization. There is no question about the power of the states to do this. Congress may use its taxing and postal powers to require such disclosure. The revenue laws should be changed so that tax returns of organizations claiming tax exemption show the suggested information. These returns should then be made available to the public.

The revenue laws ought also to be amended to require the same information from groups and organizations which claim to operate on a non-profit basis but which do not request tax exemption. The Committee also recommends further study by appropriate governmental agencies looking toward the application of the disclosure principle to profit-making organizations which are active in the market place of public opinion.

Congress ought also to amend the postal laws to require those who use the first-class mail for large-scale mailings to file disclosure statements similar to those now made annually by those who use the second-class mail. The same requirement should be adopted for applicants for metered mail permits. Postal regulations ought also to require that no mail be carried by the Post Office which does not bear the name and address of the sender.

2. Action by Congress and the executive branch clarifying the loyalty obligations of federal employees, and establishing standards and procedures by which the civil rights of public workers may be scrupulously maintained.

The Committee recognizes the authority and the duty of the government to dismiss disloyal workers from the government service. At the same time the Committee is equally concerned with the protection of the civil rights of federal workers. We believe that there should be a public enunciation by responsible federal officials of clear, specific standards by which to measure the loyalty of government workers.

It is also important that the procedure by which the loyalty of an accused federal worker is determined be a fair, consistently applied, stated "due process." Specific rules of evidence should be laid down. Each employee should have the right to a bill of particular accusations, representation by counsel at all examinations or hearings, the right to subpoena witnesses and documents, a stenographic report of proceedings, a written decision, and time to prepare a written brief for an appeal. Competent and judicious people should have the responsibility for administering the program.

The Attorney General has stated to the Committee in a letter, "It is my firm purpose, insofar as my office has control over this program, to require substantial observance of the safeguards recommended by the President's Committee."

V. To Strengthen the Right to Equality of Opportunity, the President's Committee Recommends:

1. In general:

The elimination of segregation, based on race, color, creed, or national origin, from American life.

The separate but equal doctrine has failed in three important respects. First, it is inconsistent with the fundamental equalitarianism of the American way of life in that it marks groups with the brand of inferior status. Secondly, where it has been followed, the results have been separate and unequal facilities for minority peoples. Finally, it has kept people apart despite incontrovertible evidence that an environment favorable to civil rights is fostered whenever groups are permitted to live and work together. There is no adequate defense of segregation.

The conditioning by Congress of all federal grants-in-aid and other forms of federal assistance to public or private agencies for any purpose on the absence of discrimination and segregation based on race, color, creed, or national origin.

We believe that federal funds, supplied by taxpayers all over the nation, must not be used to support or perpetuate the pattern of segregation in education, public housing, public health services, or other public services and facilities generally. We recognize that these services are indispensable to individuals in modern society and to further social progress. It would be regrettable if federal aid, conditioned on nonsegregated services, should be rejected by sections most in need of such aid. The Committee believes that a reasonable interval of time may be allowed for adjustment to such a policy. But in the end it believes that segregation is wrong morally and practically and must not receive financial support by the whole people.

A minority of the Committee favors the elimination of segregation as an ultimate goal but opposes the imposition of a federal sanction. It believes that federal aid to the states for education, health, research and other public benefits should be granted provided that the states do not discriminate in the distribution of the funds. It dissents, however, from the majority's recommendation that the abolition of segregation be made a requirement, until the people of the states involved have themselves abolished the provisions in their state constitutions and laws which now require segregation. Some members are against the nonsegregation requirement in educational grants on the ground that it represents federal control over education. They feel, moreover, that the best way ultimately to end segregation is to raise the educational level of the people in the states affected; and to inculcate both the teachings of religion regarding human brotherhood and the ideals of our democracy regarding freedom and equality as a more solid basis for genuine and lasting acceptance by the peoples of the states.

2. For employment:

The enactment of a federal Fair Employment Practice Act prohibiting all forms of discrimination in private employment, based on race, color, creed, or national origin.

A federal Fair Employment Practice Act prohibiting discrimination in private employment should provide both educational machinery and legal sanctions for enforcement purposes. The administration of the act should be placed in the hands of a commission with power to receive complaints, hold hearings, issue cease-and-desist orders and seek court aid in enforcing these orders. The Act should contain definite fines for the violation of its procedural provisions. In order to allow time for voluntary adjustment of employment practices to the new law, and to permit the establishment of effective enforcement machinery, it is recommended that the sanction provisions of the law not become operative until one year after the enactment of the law.

The federal act should apply to labor unions and trade and professional associations, as well as to employers, insofar as the policies and practices of these organizations affect the employment status of workers.

The enactment by the states of similar laws;

A federal fair employment practice statute will not reach activities which do not affect interstate commerce. To make fair employment a uniform national policy, state action will be needed. The successful experiences of some states warrant similar action by all of the others.

The issuance by the President of a mandate against discrimination in government employment and the creation of adequate machinery to enforce this mandate.

The Civil Service Commission and the personnel offices of all federal agencies should establish on-the-job training programs and other necessary machinery to enforce the nondiscrimination policy in government employment. It may well be desirable to establish a government fair employment practice commission, either as a part of the Civil Service Commission, or on an independent basis with authority to implement and enforce the Presidential mandate.

3. For education:

Enactment by the state legislatures of fair educational practice laws for public and private educational institutions, prohibiting discrimination in the admission and treatment of students based on race, color, creed, or national origin.

These laws should be enforced by independent administrative commissions. These commissions should consider complaints and hold hearings to review them. Where they are found to be valid, direct negotiation with the offending institution should be undertaken to secure compliance with the law. Wide publicity for the commission's findings would influence many schools and colleges sensitive to public opinion to abandon discrimination. The final sanction for such a body would be the cease-and-desist order enforceable by court action. The Committee believes that educational institutions supported by churches and definitely identified as denominational should be exempted.

There is a substantial division within the Committee on this recommendation. A majority favors it.

4. For housing:

The enactment by the states of laws outlawing restrictive covenants;

Renewed court attack, with intervention by the Department of Justice, upon restrictive covenants.

The effectiveness of restrictive covenants depends in the last analysis on court orders enforcing the private agreement. The power of the state is thus utilized to bolster discriminatory practices. The Committee believes that every effort must be made to prevent this abuse. We would hold this belief under any circumstances; under present conditions, when severe housing shortages are already causing hardship for many people of the country, we are especially emphatic in recommending measures to alleviate the situation.

5. For health services:

The enactment by the states of fair health practice statutes forbidding discrimination and segregation based on race, creed, color, or national origin, in the operation of public or private health facilities.

Fair health practice statutes, following the pattern of fair employment practice laws, seem desirable to the Committee. They should cover such matters as the training of doctors and nurses, the admission of patients to clinics, hospitals and other similar institutions, and the right of doctors and nurses to practice in hospitals. The administration of these statutes should be placed in the hands of commissions, with authority to receive complaints, hold hearings, issue cease-and-desist orders and engage in educational efforts to promote the policy of these laws.

6. For public services:

The enactment by Congress of a law stating that discrimination and segregation, based on race, color, creed, or national origin, in the rendering of all public services by the national government is contrary to public policy;

The enactment by the states of similar laws;

The elimination of discrimination and segregation depends largely on the leadership of the federal and state governments. They can make a great contribution toward accomplishing this end by affirming in law the principle of equality for all, and declaring that public funds, which belong to the whole people, will be used for the benefit of the entire population.

The establishment by act of Congress or executive order of a unit in the federal Bureau of the Budget to review the execution of all government programs,

and the expenditures of all government funds, for compliance with the policy of nondiscrimination;

Continual surveillance is necessary to insure the nondiscriminatory execution of federal programs involving use of government funds. The responsibility for this task should be located in the Bureau of the Budget which has the duty of formulating the executive budget and supervising the execution of appropriation acts. The Bureau already checks the various departments and agencies for compliance with announced policy. Administratively, this additional function is consistent with its present duties and commensurate with its present powers.

The enactment of Congress of a law prohibiting discrimination or segregation, based on race, color, creed, or national origin, in interstate transportation and all the facilities thereof, to apply against both public officers and the employees of private transportation companies;

Legislation is needed to implement and supplement the Supreme Court decision in *Morgan v. Virginia*. There is evidence that some state officers are continuing to enforce segregation laws against interstate passengers. Moreover, carriers are still free to segregate such passengers on their own initiative since the *Morgan* decision covered only segregation based on law. Congress has complete power under the Constitution to forbid all forms of segregation in interstate commerce. We believe it should make prompt use of it.

The enactment by the states of laws guaranteeing equal access to places of public accommodation, broadly defined, for persons of all races, colors, creeds, and national origins.

Since the Constitution does not guarantee equal access to places of public accommodation, it is left to the states to secure that right. In the 18 states that have already enacted statutes, we hope that enforcement will make practice more compatible with theory. The civil suit for damages and the misdemeanor penalty have proved to be inadequate sanctions to secure the observance of these laws. Additional means, such as the revocation of licenses, and the issuance of cease-and-desist orders by administrative agencies are needed to bring about wider compliance. We think that all of the states should enact such legislation, using the broadest possible definition of public accommodation.

7. For the District of Columbia:

The enactment by Congress of legislation to accomplish the following purposes in the District;

Prohibition of discrimination and segregation, based on race, color, creed, or national origin, in all public or publicly-supported hospitals, parks, recreational facilities, housing projects, welfare agencies, penal institutions, and concessions on public property;

The prohibition of segregation in the public school system of the District of Columbia;

The establishment of a fair educational practice program directed against discrimination, based on race, color, creed, or national origin, in the admission of students to private educational institutions;

The establishment of a fair health practice program forbidding discrimination and segregation by public or private agencies, based on race, color, creed, or national origin, with respect to the training of doctors and nurses, the admission of patients to hospitals, clinics, and similar institutions, and the right of doctors and nurses to practice in hospitals;

The outlawing of restrictive covenants;

Guaranteeing equal access to places of public accommodation, broadly defined, to persons of all races, colors, creeds, and national origins.

In accordance with the Committee's division on antidiscrimination laws with respect to private education, the proposal for a District fair education program was not unanimous.

Congress has complete power to enact the legislation necessary for progress toward full freedom and equality in the District of Columbia. The great majority of these measures has been recommended in this report to Congress and to the states to benefit the nation at large. But they have particular meaning and increased urgency with respect to the District. Our nation's capital, the city of Washington, should serve as a symbol of democracy to the entire world.

8. The enactment by Congress of legislation ending the system of segregation in the Panama Canal Zone.

The federal government has complete jurisdiction over the government of the Panama Canal Zone, and therefore should take steps to eliminate the segregation which prevails there.

VI: To Rally the American People to the Support of a Continuing Program to Strengthen Civil Rights, the President's Committee Recommends:

A long term campaign of public education to inform the people of the civil rights to which they are entitled and which they owe to one another.

The most important educational task in this field is to give the public living examples of civil rights in operation. This is the purpose of our recommendations which have gone before. But there still remains the job of driving home to the public the nature of our heritage, the justification of civil rights and the need to end prejudice. This is a task which will require the cooperation of the federal, state, and local governments and of private agencies. We believe that the permanent Commission on Civil Rights should take the leadership in serving as the coordinating body. The activities of the permanent Commission in this field should be expressly authorized by Congress and funds specifically appropriated for them.

Aside from the education of the general public, the government has immediate responsibility for an internal civil rights campaign for its more than two million employees. This might well be an indispensable first step in a large campaign. Moreover, in the armed forces, an opportunity exists to educate men while in service. The armed forces should expand efforts, already under way, to develop genuinely democratic attitudes in officers and enlisted men.

As the Committee concludes this Report we would remind ourselves that the future of our nation rests upon the character, the vision, the high principle of our people. Democracy, brotherhood, human rights—these are practical expressions of the eternal worth of every child of God. With His guidance and help we can move forward toward a nobler social order in which there will be equal opportunity for all.

A Chronology of Events concerning
To Secure These Rights
(1938–1968)

1938

Formation of interracial Southern Conference for Human Welfare (SCHW). President Franklin D. Roosevelt's New Deal reforms come to an end. The president backs away from vigorously supporting anti–poll tax and anti-lynching measures, so as not to offend southern Democrats.

1939

Creation of the Civil Liberties Unit in the Justice Department, later re-named the Civil Rights Section (CRS), to prosecute civil rights violations.

1940

War Department establishes a training base for African American pilots at Tuskegee Institute in Alabama.

1941

A. Philip Randolph threatens a march on Washington to protest racial dis-crimination in the defense industry and segregation in the armed forces.

June 25 President Roosevelt issues Executive Order 8802, creating the Fair Employment Practice Committee (FEPC). Randolph calls off the march.

1942

Congress of Racial Equality (CORE) mounts sit-in demonstrations against segregated public accommodations in Chicago.

April Secretary of the Navy reverses policy of assigning blacks only as service workers. Blacks also accepted into the Marines.

October Black leaders meet in Durham, North Carolina, and issue "mani-festo" condemning compulsory segregation.

1943

Female students at Howard University wage a nonviolent sit-in campaign against segregated lunch counters and cafeterias in Washington, D.C.

Some 240 racial disturbances erupt throughout the United States as a result of wartime tensions over jobs, housing, transportation, and recreation.

African American women admitted into the WAVES (Women Accepted for Volunteer Emergency Service) in the navy. Black women are already serving in the Women's Army Corps (WACS).

1944

April 3 The Supreme Court, in *Smith v. Allwright,* rules that the Democratic white primary in Texas is an unconstitutional violation of the Fifteenth Amendment.

A research team headed by Gunnar Myrdal publishes *An American Dilemma,* which argues for racial equality as part of the American creed.

Creation of the interracial Southern Regional Council (SRC).

1945

April 5 Black pilots of the 477th Bombardment Group stage protests against segregated facilities at Freeman Field in Indiana.

April 12 President Roosevelt dies of a stroke. Vice President Harry S Truman succeeds him in office.

Army and navy abolish quotas and open up recruitment to black women in Armed Forces Nurses' Corps.

Conference to organize the United Nations held in San Francisco.

African American soldiers return home to their communities.

Postwar relations with the Soviet Union begin to deteriorate.

1946

Successful voting rights drive in Atlanta, in which black women play a prominent role, adds 18,000 new voters.

February 13 Isaac Woodard is blinded by police in South Carolina.

February 25 Racial dispute in Columbia, Tennessee, sparks a riot resulting in the deaths of two black men.

March 5 Former British prime minister Winston Churchill, accompanied by President Truman, delivers an address in Fulton, Missouri, in which he declares "an Iron Curtain" has been constructed by the Soviet Union across Eastern Europe. Reflects an increase in cold war tensions.

June 3 Supreme Court rules segregated seating in interstate bus travel unconstitutional in *Morgan v. Virginia.*

July 25   Two married black couples are murdered by the Ku Klux Klan in Monroe, Georgia.

August 8   In Linden, Louisiana, two black men are kidnapped by a mob of whites and a deputy sheriff. One man escapes; the other is murdered.

July–September   Protests are launched in Washington, D.C., against mob violence.

September 19   National Emergency Committee Against Mob Violence (NECAMV) meets with President Truman at the White House.

November 5   Republicans win congressional elections and control both houses of the Eightieth Congress.

December 5   Truman appoints the President's Committee on Civil Rights (PCCR).

1947

The President's Committee meets throughout the year.

January 5   Senator Theodore Bilbo of Mississippi is barred from taking his seat until the Senate can investigate charges that he intimidated black voters. Bilbo dies of cancer before the investigation is completed.

March 12   The President issues the "Truman Doctrine," which becomes the basis for the strategy to contain Soviet expansion in the cold war.

March 21   Truman establishes a federal loyalty board to investigate alleged Communists working for the federal government.

April 9–23   Freedom riders test whether states in the upper South are complying with the Supreme Court decision desegregating bus travel. Twelve freedom riders are arrested for violating local segregation laws.

June 29   President Truman addresses the NAACP annual meeting at the Lincoln Memorial.

October   The NAACP files a petition with the United Nations charging human rights violations against African Americans. The UN refuses to interfere.

October 29   President's Committee on Civil Rights delivers *To Secure These Rights* to the president.

November   In Georgia, Rosa Lee Ingram and her two teenage sons are convicted of murdering a white man who assaulted her. Protests waged to commute their death sentences to life in prison.

1948

February 2   Truman delivers a special message to Congress on civil rights. Eightieth Congress blocks president's civil rights proposals.

July 12–15   Democrats nominate Truman and adopt a strong civil rights platform pushed by Hubert H. Humphrey.

July 26   Truman calls special session of Congress to consider civil rights measures without any success. On the same day Congress convenes, Truman issues an executive order calling for desegregation of the military following a threat by A. Philip Randolph to mobilize black men not to cooperate with the draft.

Truman's Justice Department files a brief to the Supreme Court challenging racially restrictive housing covenants. *Shelley v. Kraemer* supports the position of the NAACP and the federal government.

July–November   In his successful bid for the presidency, Truman is the first Democratic candidate to campaign in Harlem.

1949

Truman authorizes the Justice Department to file "friend of the court" briefs in cases concerning desegregation of dining facilities on interstate trains and desegregation of graduate and professional education.

1950

United States enters the Korean War with integrated troops.

The Supreme Court declares segregation unconstitutional in interstate train travel (*Henderson v. United States*), law schools (*Sweatt v. Painter*), and graduate schools (*McLaurin v. Oklahoma State Regents*).

1951

December 3   Truman creates the Committee on Government Contract Compliance to promote compliance with nondiscrimination orders in government contracts awarded to private businesses.

December 24   KKK murders Florida NAACP leader Harry T. Moore.

1953

Truman leaves office. He is succeeded by Dwight D. Eisenhower.

1954

Brown v. Board of Education declares segregated schools unconstitutional.

1957–1968

Congress enacts three major civil rights laws that reflect the proposals recommended by the PCCR, including school desegregation, desegregation of public accommodations, prohibition of employment discrimination, creation of new federal machinery to enforce civil rights statutes and monitor violations, and protection of the right to vote.

Questions for Consideration

1. How did World War II influence the struggle for racial equality? Why were African Americans more successful in pressing their case for equal rights after World War II than after World War I?
2. The civil rights struggle after World War II is often called "The Second Reconstruction." How does it compare with the first Reconstruction, after the Civil War?
3. What were the main goals of the African American freedom movement in the period during and after World War II?
4. Discuss the relative influence of political and moral considerations on President Truman's response to racial crises.
5. How important a role did black veterans play in pressing for racial equality?
6. Explain how women were important to the civil rights movement. Were they motivated by the same considerations as those of men?
7. Women played an important role in the civil rights movement. Why do textbooks focus on men's roles and why do women not get the credit they deserve?
8. How important were white liberals to the black freedom struggle?
9. How does violence affect the prospects of obtaining civil rights?
10. How does the federal system of government, which leaves law enforcement, voting regulations, and public schooling mainly in the hands of state and local government, affect civil rights enforcement by the national government?
11. What assumptions did the President's Committee on Civil Rights hold about the meaning of civil rights? How did it define equality?
12. Do you think that such a carefully balanced committee was helpful or a hindrance in promoting civil rights? What were the strengths and weaknesses of the "Noah's ark" approach?
13. How did the cold war affect the arguments for racial equality? Did it cause more harm than good?

14. What economic arguments did the President's Committee make in support of furthering civil rights? Did the legal right not to be discriminated against in employment guarantee black economic success?

15. What is the difference between civil rights and civil liberties? How are they connected? Is it possible to protect one without protecting the other?

16. Did the report omit any recommendations that you would have included to secure civil rights?

17. What was the impact of *To Secure These Rights?* How did it influence the civil rights movement? How did it influence the federal government?

18. Why did southern white opponents of civil rights have so much influence in Washington, D.C.? How were they able to block the congressional majority's will on civil rights legislation?

19. How far do you think President Truman would have moved on civil rights without pressure from African Americans and their white liberal allies?

20. How important are presidents in creating and sustaining social movements?

21. At the time Truman stepped down from office in 1953, most of the recommendations of his civil rights committee remained unfulfilled. Over the next two decades, what would it take for African Americans to achieve their goals?

Selected Bibliography

Berman, William C. *The Politics of Civil Rights in the Truman Administration.* Columbus: Ohio State University Press, 1970.

Bernstein, Barton J. "The Ambiguous Legacy: The Truman Administration and Civil Rights," in *Politics and Policies of the Truman Administration,* ed. Barton J. Bernstein. Chicago: Quadrangle Books, 1970.

Borstelmann, Thomas. *The Cold War and the Color Line: American Race Relations in the Global Arena.* Cambridge, Mass.: Harvard University Press, 2002.

Capeci, Dominic, Jr. *Race Relations in Wartime Detroit: The Sojourner Truth Housing Controversy of 1942.* Philadelphia: Temple University Press, 1984.

Carr, Robert K. *Federal Protection of Civil Rights: Quest for a Sword.* Ithaca: Cornell University Press, 1947.

Dittmer, John. *Local People: The Struggle for Civil Rights in Mississippi.* Urbana: University of Illinois Press, 1994.

Dudziak, Mary L. *Cold War Civil Rights: Race and the Image of American Democracy.* Princeton: Princeton University Press, 2001.

Egerton, John. *Speak Now Against the Day.* Chapel Hill: University of North Carolina Press, 1994.

Farmer, James. *Lay Bare the Heart.* New York: Arbor House, 1985.

Ferrell, Robert H., ed. *Off the Record: The Private Papers of Harry S. Truman.* New York: Harper and Row, 1980.

Frederickson, Kari. *The Dixiecrat Revolt and the End of the Solid South 1932–1968.* Chapel Hill: University of North Carolina Press, 2001.

Gardner, Michael J. *Harry Truman and Civil Rights: Moral Courage and Political Risks.* Carbondale: Southern Illinois University Press, 2002.

Garfinkel, Herbert. *When Negroes March.* New York: Atheneum, 1969.

Jack Greenberg. *Crusaders in the Courts.* New York: Basic Books, 1964.

Gullan, Harold L. *The Upset That Wasn't: Harry S. Truman and the Crucial Election of 1948.* Chicago: Ivan R. Dee, 1998.

Hall, Jacquelyn Dowd. *Revolt Against Chivalry: Jesse Daniel Ames and the Women's Campaign Against Lynching.* New York: Columbia University Press, 1979.

Hamby, Alonzo. *Man of the People: A Life of Harry S. Truman.* New York: Oxford University Press, 1995.

Hine, Darlene Clark. *Black Victory: The Rise and Fall of the White Primary in Texas.* New York: KTO Press, 1979.

Homan, Lynn, and Thomas Reilly. *Black Knights: The Story of the Tuskegee Airmen.* Gretna, La.: Pelican Publishing, 2001.

Honey, Michael. *Southern Labor and Black Civil Rights: Organizing Memphis Workers.* Urbana: University of Illinois Press, 1993.

Horne, Gerald. *Communist Front? The Civil Rights Congress, 1946–1956.* Rutherford, N.J.: Fairleigh Dickenson University Press, 1988.

Jackson, Walter A. *Gunnar Myrdal and America's Conscience: Social Engineering and Racial Liberalism, 1938–1987.* Chapel Hill: University of North Carolina Press, 1990.

Juhnke, William E. "Creating a New Charter of Freedom: The Organization and Operation of the President's Committee on Civil Rights, 1946–1948." Ph.D. diss., University of Kansas, 1974.

———. "President Truman's Committee on Civil Rights: The Interaction of Politics, Protest, and Presidential Advisory Commissions." *Presidential Studies Quarterly* 19 (1989): 593–610.

Kluger, Richard. *Simple Justice.* New York: Alfred A. Knopf, 1976.

Korstad, Robert, and Nelson Lichtenstein. "Opportunities Lost and Found: Labor Radicals and the Early Civil Rights Movement." *Journal of American History* 75 (Dec. 1988): 786–811.

Lawson, Steven F. *Black Ballots: Voting Rights in the South,* 2nd edition. Lanham, Md.: Lexington Books, 1999.

———. *Running for Freedom: Civil Rights and Black Politics in America Since 1941,* 2nd edition. New York: McGraw-Hill, 1991.

Levine, Daniel. *Bayard Rustin and the Civil Rights Movement.* New Brunswick, N.J.: Rutgers University Press, 2000.

McCoy, Donald R., and Richard T. Reutten. *Quest and Response: Minority Rights and the Truman Administration.* Lawrence: University of Kansas Press, 1973.

McCullough, David G. *Truman.* New York: Simon & Schuster, 1992.

Meier, August, and Elliott Rudwick. *CORE: A Study of the Civil Rights Movement, 1942–1968.* New York: Oxford University Press, 1973.

Murray, Pauli. *The Autobiography of a Black Activist, Feminist, Lawyer, Priest, and Poet.* Knoxville: University of Tennessee Press, 1989.

Myrdal, Gunnar. *An American Dilemma: The Negro Problem and Modern Democracy.* New York: Harper and Brothers, 1944.

O'Brien, Gayle Williams. *The Color of the Law: Race, Violence, and Justice in the Post–World War II South.* Chapel Hill: University of North Carolina Press, 1999.

Pfeffer, Paula E. *A. Philip Randolph, Pioneer of the Civil Rights Movement.* Baton Rouge: Louisiana State University Press, 1990.

Public Papers of the Presidents of the United States, Harry S Truman, 1947. Washington, D.C.: Government Printing Office, 1963.

Reed, Linda. *Simple Decency and Common Sense: The Southern Conference Movement, 1938–1963.* Bloomington: Indiana University Press, 1991.

Reed, Merle E. *Seedtime for the Modern Civil Rights Movement: The President's Committee on Fair Employment Practice, 1941–1946.* Baton Rouge: Louisiana State University Press, 1991.

Savage, Barbara Dianne. *Broadcasting Freedom: Radio, War, and the Politics of Race, 1938–1948.* Chapel Hill: University of North Carolina Press, 1999.

Scott, Lawrence P., and William M. Womack Sr. *Double V: The Civil Rights Struggle of the Tuskegee Airmen.* East Lansing: Michigan State University Press, 1994.

Sitkoff, Harvard. "Years of the Locust: Interpretations of Truman's Presidency Since 1965," in Richard S. Kirkendall, ed., *The Truman Period as a Research Field: A Reappraisal, 1972.* Columbia: University of Missouri Press, 1974.

———. *A New Deal for Blacks: The Emergence of Civil Rights as a National Issue, the Depression Decade.* New York: Oxford University Press, 1978.

Sosna, Morton. *In Search of the Silent South: Southern Liberals and Race Relations.* New York: Columbia University Press, 1977.

Southern, David. *Gunnar Myrdal and Black-White Relations: The Use and Abuse of an American Dilemma, 1944–1969.* Baton Rouge: Louisiana State University Press, 1987.

Sullivan, Patricia. *Days of Hope: Race and Democracy in the New Deal Era.* Chapel Hill: University of North Carolina Press, 1996.

Thurber, Timothy N. *The Politics of Equality: Hubert H. Humphrey and the African American Freedom Struggle.* New York: Columbia University Press, 1999).

Truman, Harry S. *Memoirs: Years of Trial and Hope,* Vol. 2. Garden City, N.Y.: Doubleday & Company, 1956.

Weiss, Nancy J. *Farewell to the Party of Lincoln: Black Politics in the Age of FDR.* Princeton: Princeton University Press, 1983.

Index

195

INDEX